COMPUTER GENEALOGY

A Guide to Research through High Technology

Ex Libris

Joseph R. Muratore

COMPUTER GENEALOGY

A Guide to Research through High Technology

By Paul A. Andereck & Richard A. Pence

Published by
Ancestry Incorporated
P.O. Box 476
Salt Lake City, Utah 84110
1985

Library of Congress Catalog Number 84-72693
ISBN Number 0-916489-02-7

First Printing 1985
10 9 8 7 6 5 4 3 2 1

Printed in the United States of America

Contents

Foreword

With the publication of this book, genealogical computing has come of age. As recently as March 1981, personal computers were first presented to genealogists in Dr. Jack McKay's article in the *National Genealogical Society Quarterly,* and the Society established a clearinghouse for the exchange of information among computerists/genealogists. Then in May 1981 at the Society's Annual Conference in the States at Atlanta, Georgia, there appeared the first sales booth offering a personal computer and genealogy software, and the topic was included among the conference presentations. And, in July 1981, the Anderecks' bimonthly magazine *Genealogical Computing* was initiated.

Who could have foreseen then the rapid succession of developments which occurred? The genealogical marketplace of 1985 is filled with a bewildering array of hardware and software. The products of 1981 are already obsolete. The term "personal computer" is overheard whenever genealogists get together. The ancestor hunter still ignorant of the rules of genealogical evidence may already be processing irrelevant data on a 32-bit computer with 256 K RAM. Beginning genealogists who don't know a Virkus from a Jacobus can expound on the comparative merits of floppies versus hard disk drives.

The sudden burgeoning of information and products must overwhelm the majority of ancestor hunters and genealogists, researchers, and professionals who realize that this new tool can be of help, but who don't know how to proceed. This would-be computerist/genealogist need wait no longer for authoritative guidance. Andereck and Pence, in this book *Computer Genealogy,* have fulfilled our requirement for a plain-language non-technical guide. In the following chapters they lead us gently through the sometimes complex subject of genealogical computing.

This book will be of value to computerists who are considering the upgrading of their system or the broadening of its applications. It will also be of value to beginners contemplating the acquisition of a personal computer and software for genealogical applications.

George Ely Russell, C.G. Fellow, American Society of Genealogists; Fellow, National Genealogical Society; Editor, *National Genealogical Society Quarterly;* Contributing Editor, *The American Genealogist.*

Introduction

This book was written for family researchers who suspect that personal computers might be both affordable and useful in genealogical research and family records management. Their suspicions are correct. Dick and I have clarified for these readers *what* computers do, *how* they do it, and in what ways other family researchers use their computers. The genealogist should find this an economical, quick, and authoritative lesson in "genealogical computing."

The book was also written for nongenealogists. Those who have already bought personal computers (and are looking for nontrivial applications for them) will discover how they and their family members can put the power of their computers to better use. Writing the family's story with a word processing program is both productive and fun. Keeping track of births, deaths, migrations, and other events in a family's history exercises a database management program to its limits. This book tells you how.

Genealogy is the third most popular hobby in America (only coin and stamp collecting appearing to have a larger following). Considering the noise being made about it—TV commercials, magazine and newspaper advertisements, office chatter, and conversations of the young—you would think computing was the hobby everyone shared. Not so. But, personal computing is rising rapidly as an avocation, and for good reason. We've never before had an in-home tool that gives us the power to amplify our minds and labors as we go about performing intellectual tasks and enjoying the pursuit of our hobbies. This book is a guide to combining the power of a computer with the fascination of genealogy.

One of the most important rules in genealogy is "cite your sources." Some go so far as to say that family information is worthless if you can't tell where you learned the facts. The more supporting sources you can bring in, the better. Further, the genealogist is supposed to present the information exactly as it is found in the source, without gratuitous rephrasing.

This seems to be at direct odds with the common practice in nonfiction writing. The researcher is encouraged always to use his or her own words unless a principle simply cannot be stated as briefly, as accurately, or as well as in a given information source. Direct quotations are permissible but should be used sparingly.

As a genealogist, I have some trouble with the practices of the nonfiction-writing world. I am to use my own words—but where did those words come from in the first place? What do I know that I didn't learn from some other person or book? Obviously, it is impossible to trace all the information in this book to its true sources, but where possible we have tried to make appropriate attributions.

This book contains many direct quotations. The authors are not engineers; we are not able to examine our computers directly and know what they are about. We must tell you what we have learned from others. We will use the words of others when they are the most accurate, most brief, and best-said explanations we can find. Software is even harder to observe directly. It's invisible! How else can we explain to you about intangibles of computing, except as we have learned from others about it? We will *quote* those information sources.

If you respect the clarity with which quoted persons explain things, you can buy their books and find considerable expansion on the information we have quoted. Dick Pence and I wish to acknowledge the contributions of experts named in this book's end-notes and give a special thanks to these persons and companies for their significant illustrative materials:

Steve Vorenberg, owner of Quinsept, Inc., has (at our invitation) supplied the genealogy software manual we have used in the walk-through of how a genealogy computer is used. *Genealogical Computing* chose his *Family Roots* as "the genealogy software to beat" in its September 1984 issue. The reason why will be evident to you.

Many—The Church of Jesus Christ of Latter-day Saints; Commsoft, Inc.; Array Systems, Inc.; Karen Cavanaugh, and others—have contributed printout specimens, feature descriptions, and other genealogy software information vital to the exploration of our subject. As each contribution is presented, we will identify the contributor. At this point we wish to tell you that each and all of these organizations and persons are paving the way for genealogical uses of computers; we are merely describing that pathway.

To the entire staff of Ancestry Publishing go thanks as well. Robert Welsh for his editorial supervision, Emily Watts for the very fine copyediting, and Linda Cunningham for her consistently accurate proofreading deserve mention. The publisher would also like to thank Mr. Gerald Wise of Super Group, Inc. for the translation and transfer of the authors' manuscript on floppy disks to their mainframe storage.

I wish to acknowledge that Richard Pence has taken the book I have researched, written, and organized and made it into a *better* book (by far) than I had put together. Following is an outline of the process of authorship and collaboration we used to put together this book. We include it to demonstrate how easily the steps could be executed by you and your family.

1. Andereck took charge of negotiating the scope, content, approach, length, and other overall parameters with the publisher, Ancestry, Inc.

2. All research notes, quotes, and ideas were computerized using *Lazywriter* (a word processing program), a Radio Shack Model 4P computer, and two printers: EPSON RX-80 and Radio Shack's DW II. The former is a fast, inexpensive dot-matrix printer, and the latter is a high-quality final-draft printer.

3. Nothing that was "typed" was ever retyped. Once computerized, the text and notes were arranged, rearranged, and shaped into a book draft. Andereck submitted drafts of his progress to the publisher and coauthor as each was readied.

4. A copy of the computerized files was mailed to the publisher as each draft was produced. The publisher used them to practice file transfer from a similar computer (using identical computer software) to be ready for a final-draft transfer from the Andereck files to Ancestry, Inc.'s own word processor computer and program control. These disk copies were mailed, along with draft printouts.

5. When the book was formed, cut to size, and roughly shaped to its final form, Pence began the rewrites that used his journalistic skills, computer experience, and genealogist views to make a book into a good book. He used his *Electric Pencil* word processing program and a SOL computer (an antique by microcomputer-market standards) to computerize his version of the book. (We might note here that the publisher was in Utah and the authors were about five miles apart in Virginia.)

6. Andereck and Pence received feedback from the publisher and shaped the final draft accordingly—each complying with changes in his own fashion and via his own computer and software.

7. Andereck and Pence established a phone link between their computers using *Omniterm* and a 300 baud Radio Shack acoustically coupled modem and, LMODEM and a PMMI modem board, respectively. Despite Andereck using TRSDOS 6.1.2 and Pence using CP/M as disk operating systems, they moved the Pence version from his computer to the Andereck computer disks—file by file.

8. Andereck called up the Pence files from his own computer and edited them to conform to his own file style (getting rid of special codes and extra linefeeds the Pence computer had put in the files).

9. Finally (almost), the "final draft" files, Andereck-change files, and Pence-version files were integrated into a single final-final draft

in the Andereck computer and under *Lazywriter's* program control. Another printed draft was produced, the computer files were copied (again), and the product was mailed to the publisher.

10. Although the authors were finished with their book, the publisher still had to move the files from a computer compatible with Andereck's to his own word-processor computer. Then, when the book was ready for publishing, the control codes for the typesetter's computer were inserted in the files and they were moved to the printing firm's typesetter, where camera-ready book-copy was produced and reproduced on the pages you are reading.

The whole thing is, admittedly, a bit sticky; it is like a four-cushion shot in billiards, I think. But it worked, and the authors and publisher are now experienced in what had been a theoretical capability before. With "garden variety" computers and the software they use as genealogists, the authors became phone-linked collaborators who are very sure that you can do it, too!

Paul Andereck, 1984

CHAPTER 1

Computers and Genealogy— Converging Fields

THE RISE OF THE COMPUTER

The United States census—that vital source of much family information—was also a major force affecting the growth of computing. By the time of the eleventh census in 1880, the task of counting the population had become nightmarish. Data was still being processed in 1887 and the next census was right around the corner. The Census Office decided that the solution was to hold a competition among various counting devices and settled on three systems for a final test.

The test "featured Mr. William C. Hunt and his colored cards, Mr. Charles F. Pidgen and his color-coded tokens and Mr. Herman Hollerith and his amazing tabulating machine." Hollerith's system won hands down and was selected for the 1890 census. The system worked so well that six weeks after the census it was announced that the population of the country was 62,622,250.

Hollerith set up his own company in Washington, D.C., and when he died in 1929 at the age of sixty-nine, he was still a consultant to his company, which by then was called the International Business Machine Corporation—today known as IBM.[1]

Hollerith's marvelous invention was the punch card (for which he devised processing machinery), which survived as a basic sorting and counting method for nearly a hundred years. It wasn't until 1984 that IBM announced it was closing its last punch-card production facility.

The demise of the punch card was brought about by an even more marvelous invention: the digital computer. Its rise as a business—and now a personal—tool has been spectacular:

> 1939—Aiken is credited with the MARK I, which was the first electro-mechanical digital computer.
>
> 1946—Eckert and Mauchey breathed life into the ENIAC, the first all-electronic computer. It weighed thirty tons, occupied three thousand cubic feet, went only hours between failures, and had far less memory capability than any of today's "home computers."
>
> 1954—Remington Rand brought out the first commercial computer, the UNIVAC.

1965 – Kemeny, Kurtz, and others developed "time-sharing," allowing shared cost and shared use of still-too-expensive computers.

1975 – DEC and Hewlett-Packard created the first "minicomputer." It cost $5,000 for each keyboard and viewing screen, which could only be used by time-sharers.

1975 – Altair brought out a microcomputer kit for hobbyists (born with soldering tips instead of fingernails on their index fingers). It could be programmed and operated only by turning a series of switches on and off.

1976 – Processor Technology combined the Altair 8800 with a keyboard and a video display monitor to create the first "easy-to-use" microcomputer, and began marketing it as the Sol Terminal Computer the next year.

1977 – Commodore introduced the PET, then the first complete home computer sold.

1977 – Apple and Radio Shack introduced their Apple II and TRS-80 Model I computers, respectively.

From then on the benchmarks came too fast and plentiful to mention. Today, hardly a week goes by without some new and spectacular breakthrough in the world of computing.

Why only now, after such a history of computing, is a computer a genealogist's tool? A quick glance over the technological progress outlined above makes the answer clear. Over the years the twenty tons of business machinery have been condensed into a few tiny microprocessor chips. The price of computers has shrunk in a comparable manner, so that they are now available to groups and individuals who could never have afforded them before. These new computer users have worked out applications of the computer to fit their specific needs, such as performing genealogical tasks. With the ever-increasing availability of computers and appropriate software, the hour of the computer genealogist has at last arrived.

Someone (a lot of someones, really) has been at work for us without knowing that the genealogist is the beneficiary of all his work:

Personal and business microcomputers are remarkable machines when you consider that all the odds say they really shouldn't work. For one thing, the performance of a modern micro depends on the precision with which millions of fleeting electrical pulses interact each second, never missing a beat as the seconds build into minutes, hours, or even days. Further, these pulses must mirror the logic of some of the most sophisticated algorithms ever developed by the human mind. . . . And yet we know that microcomputers do work – reliably and at imaginative levels that can be a joy to experience. The reason seems to be that we've learned to harness the complexities of micro systems by continually re-packaging their evolving structures as new entities, as deceptively simple building blocks that let newcomers tackle the best computing has to offer right from the start.[2]

For those interested, there is an excellent book by Paul Frieberger and Michael Swaine called *Fire in the Valley: The Making of the Personal Computer* (Berkeley, Calif.: Osborne/McGraw-Hill, 1984), which carries its readers from the very beginning to the takeover of microcomputing by big business.

Computers are hardware. We should acknowledge the birth of "software," too. You'll see how important computer software is once we explain *what* it is. *Time* magazine tells us:

> Primitive forms of software first appeared 150 years ago. Charles Babbage, a mathematics professor at Cambridge University who also invented the speedometer and the locomotive cowcatcher, in 1834 designed a machine called the analytical engine to solve mathematical equations; it is generally considered the forerunner of today's computer. Augusta Ada, the Countess of Lovelace, daughter of the poet Lord Byron, helped finance the project. Credited with being the world's first programmer, she used punched cards to tell the machine what to do. The idea was inspired by the cards used on Jacquard looms to determine the designs in cloth. She said: "The analytical engine weaves algebraic patterns just as the Jacquard loom weaves flowers and leaves." The analytical engine was hopelessly complicated for its time and was never completed. But 117 years later, punch cards that were not to be folded, spindled or mutilated became the heart of software technology. In 1951 the U.S. Census Bureau used punched cards for UNIVAC I, the first commercial computer.[3]

Thus we have the folding over of the history of the census, the history of microcomputers, and the history of software into the history of a new field: genealogical records management and family research with the aid of personal computers. We'll call it "genealogical computing" for short.

COMPUTERS AROUND US

Computers are so commonplace today that we often don't even realize their presence. The controls of your microwave oven or new sewing machine no doubt contain small, special-purpose computers. Your wristwatch probably contains computer circuitry instead of a mainspring. Your children or grandchildren likely have some computer-operated toys.

Even with so many computers around us, many of us—especially those of us over forty—shy away from trying to understand or use them. But for today's genealogist, they are tools too valuable to ignore.

Let's suppose we are similar in many regards: You are a person long involved in genealogical research. You have boxes, notebooks, and file drawers full of information on your family. You developed your own system of keeping notes, maps, photos, letters, charts, forms, and other family records as you acquired them. Card files or typed lists may index or cross-index spouses and family members, but the only real master index exists in your own mind. The ceaseless task of organizing, reorganizing, typing, and retyping has become more of a burden than the joy it once was. And if something were to happen to you, chances are that much of what you have gathered would be meaningless to those who would inherit your genealogy files.

If that situation describes you, you are a candidate for owning your own genealogy computer.

GENEALOGY MEETS THE COMPUTER

The purpose of this book is not to tell you how to go about being a family researcher or a genealogist. There are many excellent books on that topic. What we hope to do is to tell you how a computer can help you in your genealogy work. We will try to provide you with enough information about this high technology to help you make intelligent decisions if and when you buy a computer.

Those of us who are old enough to remember the precomputer days are conditioned to be fearful of them. One reason is our belief that computers are too expensive—we remember that a few years ago, only the government, universities with government grants, or the largest corporations could afford them. Another is our belief that only the brainiest of men and women could program and operate computers. Besides, we "know" that computers are gigantic number-crunchers into which you feed cards that shouldn't be folded, spindled, or mutilated. And any over-forty genealogist is sure that the only place you can keep a real computer is behind glass walls in a dust-free, humidity controlled environment requiring heavy-duty electrical and air-conditioning facilities. No computer capable of real jobs can exist in the corner of a den or in the clutter of a family room.

And those computers we see advertised today as "user friendly," "home," or "personal" computers surely are nothing but glorified game machines that do trivial "real jobs" like keeping track of kitchen recipes or holiday card mailing lists, and balancing checkbooks. At best, they are worth having only so that the children in the house can grow up knowing how to use them because their jobs may someday require it.

In short, we think computers are for the very rich, the very smart, and the very young—and are probably fad items that no amount of media blitzing can make relevant to our lives and genealogies.

But a few people interested in genealogy recognized early that computers could help them. No doubt, the first genealogical use of computers was on the sly. After work or on weekends, those who were both genealogists and computer workers began slipping punched cards into the big machines to get printed alphabetical or chronological lists of family members. These exploratory uses of computers for assistance in genealogy were clandestine, experimental, peripheral experiences. And even genealogists who had access to computers were still keeping records by hand and publishing family histories on typewriters. They merely got computer aid in generating lists.

This venturesome group was the vanguard, though. And each time computer costs dropped or complexities decreased or power improved, the number venturing into computer ownership and genealogical computing increased.

From the time of the introduction of microcomputers (about 1975) to the burst of interest in computers by genealogists (about 1983?), only the venturesome among us were computer-using genealogists. No doubt these are the same people who were among the first to accept other new technologies, like microwave ovens or video recorders. Not only that, but they were willing to put up with high prices, frequent breakdowns, inadequate user manuals, maddening arrays of choices, and the necessity to learn a lot about computing in order to use a personal computer. And in the beginning, many genealogical uses of a personal computer were trivial: perhaps a Soundex translator or a date calculator.

The good news is that today's genealogist will not have to put up with the mystique, the high cost, the unreliability, and the long hours of learning that these first-wave computing genealogists abided. And there are now a wide variety of significant genealogy jobs the computer will do.

At first, the personal computer was a by-product of high technology. Now it is a new high technology unto itself.

FOOTNOTES

1. Christopher Evans, *The Micro Millennium* (New York: Washington Square Press, 1981), pp. 21,23.

2. Thomas A. Dwyer and Margot Critchfield, *CP/M and the Personal Computer* (Reading, Mass.: Addison-Wesley, 1983), P. vii.

3. Alexander L. Taylor III (reported by Michael Moritz and Peter Stoler), "The Wizards Inside the Machines," *Time* 123, no. 16 (April 16, 1984): 57.

CHAPTER 2

Adjusting to the Computer Age

M ost of us are ill-equipped to cope with computers. We who are older may even be downright afraid of them. We are afraid we could never learn how to use one, or might even damage it beyond repair if we tried.

You may have to undergo a certain amount of reconditioning if you are a genealogist over forty. You grew up in a world without computers and know that you have so far managed to survive without them. Even if you concede that new tools are worth considering, you might wonder if it isn't a little late in life for you to start learning about such a complicated thing as a computer.

You already mastered the art of threading microfilms in a film reader because you found census records and other documents available only in microfilm form. You found that photocopying documents and book pages was not so complicated, and it helped you save valuable research time. Even tape recorders became easy for you to use. Those were really the only "new" technologies you had to master to carry on your family research. Beyond that, you realized that many of those helpful indexes were being computer generated. But you didn't have to learn to operate a computer to get them. You simply bought them or read them at the library.

Now, however, each passing day brings you new evidence that owning a computer might be worth the complexities and the costs. Word of other family researchers' satisfaction with computers for genealogy is reaching you and you wonder if the subject of genealogical computing is worth probing.

Young or old, many genealogists are seeing the use of microcomputers growing in the offices where they work, the libraries where they research, the schools their children attend, and the homes of their friends. Suddenly, their lives are being saturated by computers, and there's a growing suspicion that a family file might be something like the "databases" and "word processing" everywhere at work.

ARE YOU SMART ENOUGH TO USE A COMPUTER?

"Technophobia and computer mania are strong forces in modern society. There are workers who fear that robots and computers will claim their jobs – to these people technology is an enemy. Computer maniacs speak a language that excludes novices – to the maniacs, technology is a god of sorts. Most people, especially those discovering the increasing ease and excitement of computer communications, probably fall somewhere between those extremes."[1]

Young or old, we suspect that people who "understand computers" must be somehow different than we are. They must be smarter than we are because they can do marvelous and mysterious things with computers.

If you feel you might not be up to the task of learning how to use a computer, consider whether you can understand the following instructions:

> Before turning on the power, you need to insert the DOS diskette into Drive A of your system. Find the disk in its pocket in the back cover of the DOS manual and remove it from its paper sleeve, being careful not to bend the disk or touch its shiny surface where its permanent protective jacket leaves it exposed. Install the DOS disk in Drive A, the left-hand drive. . . . First open the door on Drive A. Hold the disk between your thumb and forefinger and gently slide the disk into the drive until it clicks softly into place. When inserted correctly, the disk will slide easily, without catching. When the disk is in all the way, close the drive door gently until it clicks shut. If the door does not close easily, remove the disk and try putting it in again. Never force a disk into a drive. If it does not slide in easily, check for obstructions. Check once more to make sure that everything in your system is connected and plugged into the wall socket.[2]

This excerpt is from a book published to help you learn to use a computer. The instructions are for starting up an IBM Personal Computer, but they would be similar for almost any computer you might buy today.

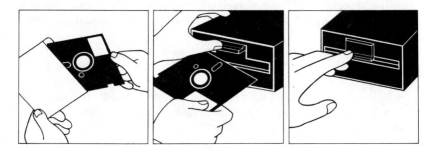

Was that so tough? Ask yourself if you could have started the computer if, while reading, you were looking at the computer and the illustrations in the book.

Understanding that instruction – or any of the many others you will need to understand and perform – doesn't take a different kind or amount of intelligence than you possess. Computing is full of exacting and exact procedures, but all of them are accompanied by the necessary build-up of user knowledge that makes them clear. Believe in yourself. With the help of manuals, illustrations, examples, and instructions, the how and why of operating a computer will be clear to you.

True, the first computers needed the genius-types to design, program, and operate them. Early computers had rows of switches that were used to enter data and programs in binary form, one digit at a time. There was no keyboard. Instead of typing in a word like "CHICAGO," the programmer had to communicate to the computer in terms of "1" or "0" (binary numbers) by flipping switches on and off. "CHICAGO" might have been expressed as something like: 10110011 00111001 11010110 00010110 11101101 10101011 10000101. Each letter was broken into eight binary (two-number) components whose one-zero patterns added up to the whole characters "C," "H," "I," "C," "A," "G," "O."

If it didn't take genius, it took exactness and tremendous patience to program a computer in the "old days." No wonder programming was the the domain of bright people! Today, however, computers "understand" words, numbers, and instructions that almost anyone can feed them – even though they still operate internally only with binary numbers. Computers now understand people, and the evidence is all around us. Secretaries and other skilled and semiskilled employees – even managers – use them every day.

We believe that because you are interested in genealogy, you have a head start on many people. For it is precisely the tools you have as a genealogist that make you a likely candidate to use a computer. You have an inquisitive mind, you like solving puzzles, you have the determination to "see the job through." These are the attributes that make computing right up your alley! All you have to do is follow the rules that the programmer and the computer designer invented and installed in the machine.

ARE YOU TOO OLD TO LEARN TO USE A COMPUTER?

Most genealogists aren't concerned about the condition of their gray matter, but some may believe that their gray hair makes them ineligible to own and operate a computer. Take a word of advice: The older you are, the more helpful a computer can be!

Suppose, for instance, you have to copy all of your family records with a typewriter, and in the process organize them into a family book. Think about this: If you're going to type it all anyway, why not "type" it with a computer? Among a computer's best functions is to act as a "smart typewriter." Even though computers first gained notice as "number crunchers," their most widely used application today is as word processors.

Being able to massage a good thought into a better one, put a lot of paragraphs into a more logical arrangement, or create second and third drafts of your writing–without having to retype everything each time–is a blessing that is almost beyond the ardent genealogist's favorite dream. (Only finding that long-lost fourth or fifth great grandfather can exceed it!)

There is a simple formula: The longer you have lived, the more genealogical records you have accumulated and the greater the task of putting them into that family history you want to leave behind. A computer can be the biggest aid you have in accomplishing that job. It's almost axiomatic that the young defer publishing their findings while they continue searching; it is the older people who want to record what they have found.

Unfortunately, the computer hasn't been around long enough to have managed your records from the beginning. If it had, you could at any time be only a few days away from being ready to publish them. But the computer is here now, and it can make it a whole lot easier for you to have your research in usable shape for any eventuality.

Even if publishing your records is not your goal, we'll wager that you would like them to have "carry-on capability." You hope that someone in your family, a son or daughter or niece or nephew, will pick up where you left off. It is far more likely that he or she will do so if you have computerized your records instead of leaving a couple of dozen boxes of notes on your research. If they are already organized with a computer, chances are that the next generation will be able to pick up quickly where you left off.

Your fingers may not be as nimble as they once were, but so long as your mind is active you are a candidate for genealogical computing. You may even be able to enlist the fast fingers and sharp eyes of younger family members during the process of transferring your notes and files into a computerized record-keeping system. Remember: Accumulating those records is a genealogical skill you have developed; entering them into a computer is *not* a genealogical skill. With your assistance, almost anyone can do it. And once entered into the computer, those records are yours to correct, add to, sort, search, or print out–the possibilities are almost limitless.

Creating a "database" (your file of usable information) is boring and seemingly endless. Developing information from that computerized database is easy and fun.

Our experience tells us that it will be the older genealogists who will turn to computers to aid them. Why? First of all, they have the time–and the inclination–to devote to genealogy. Second, they have–if ever they are going to–the disposable income to afford the equipment. Third, they have the need to organize their bulging boxes and drawers full of information. And fourth, they have the desire to leave what they have accumulated to posterity.

The bottom line is that being "mature" may help, rather than hurt.

CAN YOU AFFORD A COMPUTER THAT CAN HANDLE GENEALOGY?

You will want a computer that is approximately like the ones used by other genealogists, and that will do things other genealogists are doing with their computers. The experience of these others provides a base for determining what you will need and how much it will cost.

In the early months of 1982, 125 genealogists described the typical "genealogy computer system" as a Radio Shack TRS-80 Model I or an Apple II computer. It had two 5 1/4-inch minifloppy disk drives and an Epson MX-80 dot-matrix printer. It cost an average of $4,171.[3] A year later, 635 genealogists reported owning computers. The Apple II was by far the most popular and the IBM PC was rising in popularity. The average investment had dropped to $3,503.[4]

Although these samples, from surveys taken by *Genealogical Computing*, show shifting popularity between models the figures revealed that, generally, computers that were considered "genealogically adequate" and "affordable" cost between $2,000 and $5,000.

Table I gives statistics on the computers owned by 223 genealogists in the winter of 1982-83.

If you are familiar with the microcomputer marketplace, you might smile at the list of models on the table. Many are no longer being sold; others have weaknesses that you might not tolerate. Nevertheless, in that "time gone by" these were what genealogists bought, and what they spent.

Something in the table worth noting: $2,000 was the least expensive of the forty-eight Apple II computers, yet at least one user spent $8,000 for an Apple II. Bare-bones versions and greatly expanded versions of the same computer can vary widely in costs and capabilities.

If these figures come as a shock (because you were thinking about a computer advertised for $200 in the mail-order catalog) consider these cost-related ideas:

    1. You may want to consider pooling your money and your needs with other genealogists. "Shared time" was the manner by which the early-era expensive computers were used by many business owners who could not afford computers of their own. Genealogists can also gather into owner groups.

    2. A genealogy system can be built (bought) in stages, with each stage adding a capability as you need it and can afford it. A letter-quality printer,

Number Cases	Average Cost	Investment Range Lowest – Highest	Computer Type
2	$ 160	$ 100 – $ 220	SINCLAIR Z81
3	200	150 – 250	TIMEX 1000
3	867	300 – 2,000	TI 99/4A
3	970	150 – 2,360	CBM 8032 COMMODORE
8	1,239	400 – 2,000	TRS-80 CC
2	1,950	1,500 – 2,400	COMMODORE PET
16	2,292	1,790 – 3,370	OSBORNE 1
8	2,418	1,250 – 4,300	ATARI 800
6	2,455	1,790 – 3,370	KAYPRO II
30	2,753	430 – 7,000	TRS-80 MODEL I
2	2,800	2,500 – 3,100	HEATH H8
2	3,100	3,000 – 3,200	IMSAI 8080
27	3,477	1,000 – 5,200	TRS-80 MODEL III
8	3,513	2,000 – 5,000	HEATH/ZENITH H89
48	3,558	2,000 – 8,000	APPLE II
33	4,576	3,000 – 9,000	IBM PC
2	5,500	5,000 – 6,000	Z-80 CUSTOM-MADE
6	5,763	4,600 – 10,000	APPLE III
8	6,375	1,900 – 10,000	TRS-80 MODEL II
4	7,125	5,000 – 8,000	TRS-80 MODEL 16
2	7,150	6,300 – 8,000	XEROX 820

Table 1. Genealogy Computer Costs. (From Paul Andereck, "Sampling of 1983 Survey Responses," *Genealogical Computing* 2, no. 5 (March 1983): 6.

---

the second of two disk drives, memory expansion, and a modem are among the components you can add later.

3. You can divide the computer cost among the various other uses your family makes of your "genealogy computer." Why charge to genealogy the whole expense of a tool that will be used in education, entertainment, business, and/or other family enterprises?

A "GENEALOGICALLY ADEQUATE" COMPUTER

Since a genealogist's needs will affect the configuration (and, therefore, the cost) of a computer, we need to see what genealogy hardware needs are. Based on our own experiences and the experiences of those who responded to the *Genealogical Computing* surveys, we believe that you should have at least the following for your computer system:

•A computer that has a minimum internal memory capacity of 64,000 characters. Today, this is hardly a problem, for 64K ("K" for kilo or thousand) memory machines are generally the minimum size on the market.

•A screen (or monitor) that will display 80 characters per line and 24 lines. Again, this is not a problem in today's market, for 80 by 24 screens are almost the standard.

•A typewriter-like keyboard. Both "membrane" and "chiclet" keyboards can be found on inexpensive calculators. If you find those on a computer, it is not worth buying for *any* purpose.

•Two disk drives, either built-in or external to the computer's case. Get disk drives that use disks that are 5 1/4 inches in diameter and "double-density." Smaller disks may prove to be a future standard, but for now stick with what most genealogists use. (With only one disk drive, you have to go through complicated procedures to copy your information to another disk as a backup in case your original disk is damaged. Get two drives.)

•A printer. We will discuss printers—and other computer system needs and characteristics—in later chapters. Without a printer, however, your computer can only absorb data and can never put it on paper for publication or sharing with others.

The above are key features of a computer that a genealogist would want. Many brands and models of computers can supply those features. As mentioned earlier, they are likely to cost somewhere between $2,000 and $5,000 today.

Computers are expensive compared with other "appliances" in your home. Fortunately, a computer you can use for managing your genealogy records is likely to be the same computer you would buy for other serious use—or even for entertainment.

PRICE VS. PERFORMANCE

Toy stores, department stores, mail-order firms, and other sources today offer computers that sell for less than $1,000. And there are genealogists who proudly (or defensively) insist they do just fine with them.

Bluntly, *any* computer and any genealogy program looks good if you have been handling growing files and research notes for years. But the sole virtue of low-cost computers is their low cost. If you are looking to this book to discover a way to get into genealogical computing inexpensively, we can't ratify your hope. We ask you to keep in mind that an "adequate" genealogical computer is something more than a game computer and something less than a business computer. If you want the right kind of equipment to do the job you'll probably end up spending about $3,000.

The number of microcomputers owned by individuals, organizations, companies, universities and other schools, and governments has grown from zero in 1974 to nearly ten million. Mass production and stiff competition have made computers more affordable and more attractive for genealogists. There is, however, a countering force at work. Competition is forcing computer makers to create *better* computers than others are making. They add free software, more memory capacity, or other features to make their machines more attractive – instead of lowering prices.

There is a price point for everything you buy (television sets, automobiles, freezers – and computer systems), below which the performance drops off faster than the item cost does, and above which the price rises faster than the item's performance does. Seeming bargains throw out too much performance in order to cut the price; high-priced items throw in gold-plated doodads of no relevant use to you. By the time you add up the bill for computer, memory, screen, two disk drives, dot matrix printer, letter-quality printer, modem, cables, computer table, and useful programs you will find the bottom line will fall in the $2500 to $3000 range. A significantly lower ($1500?) bottom line means you are shopping in marginally adequate equipment models and will enjoy immediate savings but suffer ongoing frustrations. If the bottom line is near $5000, we think you are looking at equipment models with features you will seldom use (such as "faster CPU speed," "multi-tasking," "multi-user," and other capabilities the genealogist has no real need for).

We could give you a list of computer and printer models we think are representative of the optimum price and performance point, but it would be rendered obsolete by next week's or next month's marketplace offerings. Instead, our chapter on computer hardware will explain a computer's parts and what they do for you. Use that information for shopping and see what you can buy for $2000 to $3000 while including the components we have described for you.

HOW LONG WILL A COMPUTER LAST?

As far as microcomputers are concerned, the answer to the question of how long they will last isn't known yet. There are many machines that are six, seven, or eight years old that are still working fine. The critical period for a computer is during the first few days of operation – this is when the "chips" are most likely to fail. Most manufacturers "burn in" their machines for a couple of days to detect these failures. Chances are that if your computer works fine the first few days after you bring it home it will keep working for years. It no doubt will be obsolete before it wears out.

A word about obsolescence: In a strictly technical sense, most microcomputers today are "obsolete" almost before you get them home.

Every day some new innovation comes forward to make a Model T out of your shiny new creature. A common dilemma for prospective computer purchasers is when to buy. Many say they are just waiting until the technology levels out and the prices stabilize.

If you are postponing your purchase for those reasons, you may never get around to buying! The important thing to remember about computer obsolescence is this: In a practical sense, your computer is never obsolete so long as it will efficiently and effectively perform the work you want done.

Your microprocessor will likely run for many years, but its peripherals— the monitor, the disk drives, or the printer—are prone to more failures. A disk drive, for instance, is a piece of machinery with many mechanical parts. These wear and occasionally need adjusting. Printers in a home environment should last several years because the demands put on their mechanical parts seldom reach those of an office environment.

Manufacturers usually come out with "better" machines about every three years, and each model is "fully supported" (maintaining service, parts, and software upgrades) for about six years. How long your computer will last depends largely on how long you can get necessary parts and repair support.

Longevity of computers brings us to another way to look at a genealogy computer's cost: Would you be willing to pay fifty dollars a month for five years to have someone come in and be your genealogy records manager and research assistant? A computer system costing $3000 and lasting five years would equate to that proposition (using a pro rata cost of fifty dollars per month for a five-year computer life.) Paying too much for a computer ($5000 and up?) may make the proposition very unattractive; paying too little will buy you a bumbling records manager and lousy research assistant (the computer system being, functionally, that genealogical aide). It is all a matter of worth, price, and performance.

MUST YOU LEARN A LOT ABOUT COMPUTERS TO USE ONE?

How much do you really have to know about computers in order to be able to operate one yourself? Several analogies come to mind in answer to this question.

You can buy a microwave oven, read the instructions for using the time and heat buttons, then live a stereotypic bachelor's life as a "cook"— following the instructions on packages of frozen foods.

You can buy an electronic organ and read the book—and produce chords and drumbeats while one-fingering tunes that please your ear. You are a "musician."

And, you can buy a computer and a program or two, read the manuals, turn it on, and be a "computer-using genealogist."

In each of these cases you would be making a minimal investment of self, and the payoff could be very satisfying. You are cook, musician, and computer-using genealogist at the entry level.

You don't have to learn the art and science of cooking if you don't want to; ovens are smart and foods are packaged in goof-proof ways. If you don't care to learn to read music and hate to practice, you can rely on many-buttoned organs to "make songs."

It follows that plug-in-and-run computers and programs are available if that is all you want. You do not ever need to know what a byte is, what RAM or ROM are, or anything else about your computer.

But we're betting you'll want to learn more about your computer and want to get more from it than slight performance. This is relevant to the last topic—cost. At *any* price, a genealogy computer is too expensive if it is used only minimally. Each time you use the computer, it is paying you back for its keep; whenever it is closeted, it is costing you without giving any benefit.

It may occur to you that taking a class in computing is a useful strategy for becoming ready to purchase and use a genealogy computer wisely. Community colleges, adult education agencies, computer stores, and commercial computer schools offer a variety of introductory, elementary, and advanced computer courses. These classes, necessarily, are aimed at pupils with diverse interests and skill levels. The result is that what you usually end up with after such a course is "computer appreciation." And it will be a rarity for any instructor to have a knowlege of the demands of genealogy as they relate to using a computer.

A more successful method of learning about computing and computers is the "coach-pupil" method. Driving a car, riding a bicycle, running a sewing machine, flying a plane, sailing a boat or operating a shop tool are skills best learned this way.

You can learn about computers best and fastest by sitting in front of one and using it. Most of us have a friend or neighbor who already is "into computing" and is willing to serve as coach. If you are lucky, you even have a friend who is into computers *and* genealogy.

See if you can't spend a few evenings actually working your way through the manuals that came with your friend's computer. As you read what the book says, *do* what it says, and then consider what you have learned. If something you do doesn't teach you what it should, consult your "coach."

This method will also work if you decide to go ahead and buy a computer. Many computerists forged ahead, bought a computer—then sat at home interacting with the manual and computer until they learned how to operate it. We'll bet that most of them had a friendly "coach" who didn't mind answering an evening or Saturday phone call or two. We learned that way, and you can, too.

Remember this as you learn: Nothing is dangerous and few things are catastrophic when a "know-nothing" handles a computer. Microcomputers and their electrical circuits are safe. About the worst thing that can happen is that you will cause a "computer crash." This means that the computer aborts the operation at hand. A restart will bring it back to life. Although physical damage can be done by abuse (mishandling disks or banging equipment around), most of the errors made by entering the wrong keys or commands are easily corrected.

Probably the easiest way for most people to learn about computing is with a word processing program. As you write merrily away, you'll learn about computer commands, computer files, and computer capabilities — lessons you can apply to learning about other software.

WHAT PERSONAL ATTRIBUTES DO YOU NEED?

Do you think being male is a requirement for computer using? Charlotte Beyers, writing in *Family Computing* magazine, tells us there was little difference in achievement between boys and girls who took a required computer course. She writes that researchers at Stanford University also have found that adults are reluctant to purchase computers for their daughters. Further, in MIT's graduate computer-science department, the ratio of men to women is seven to one and at the University of California at Berkeley, less than a quarter of the computer-science majors are women.[5]

Beyers says:

"As computers become more and more common in the job market, many people predict that young women who shun computers will shut themselves out of a wide range of careers . . . Like other male-dominated endeavors women suffer from a lack of experience, not a lack of talent. 'There is no evidence that girls have any less ability,' says Irene Miura, one of the Stanford researchers. 'The problem may be that they lack confidence or interest. Or that their parents do not provide the same encouragement they do for boys.'"[6]

We need to realize the problems of inequity in this field, and to present a positive picture to that overlooked half of the population that needs extra encouragement. Genealogy should not create computer widows; it *could* create widowers instead. That's both ironic and a step toward equity, we think.

Although almost anyone can operate a computer and eventually get it to do what he or she wants, it appears that people with certain personal qualifications more quickly adapt to the tasks at hand. Fortunately, most of the attributes of a "natural" computer user can be developed with practice.

NIMBLE FINGERS (AND GOOD EYESIGHT)

Fingers and eyes create the connection of the human to the computer. It follows that good eyesight and nimble fingers are two attributes of considerable importance to computing.

Nimble fingers permit quick and sure key stroking. If you don't type at all, you will be greatly disadvantaged in using a computer. However, even if you are only a "two-finger" or "hunt-and-peck" typist, the computer is easier to operate than a typewriter because errors can be so easily corrected.

In the future, there will be scanning devices that will allow passing a wand over lines of typewritten (or perhaps even handwritten) material to enter the data into a computer. Devices such as these already exist, but it's doubtful they will be a part of the genealogist's computer system within the next several years, at least.

If you aren't able to touch-type, consider these alternatives: Find a volunteer family member who can and will enter your data. Or buy one of the many inexpensive computer programs that tutor you in touch-typing. The time you spend learning to touch-type will pay great dividends later on.

PATIENCE

Another attribute that is helpful in computing is one you probably already possess: patience. If you have enough patience to pursue genealogy, you no doubt have enough to work through the use of a computer. Entering all of your genealogical data into a computer is a time-consuming – even boring – job.

AND, AN ENVIRONMENT

You'll be spending a great many hours at your machine, so before you buy a computer, make sure that you have a good work area for your computer. A typewriter-height table will keep your arms from tiring during work sessions. Proper screen height will ease strain on neck muscles. A good office-type chair is a must. Today, many offices are buying "computer furniture" as they charge headlong into automation. The "typewriter furniture" they get rid of could be just the thing for you. Used office equipment forms the basis for many a home computer center.

One nice thing about computers is that they don't make a lot of noise – but the printers do. Therefore, your "computer center" can be located almost anywhere in the house without disturbing the rest of the family if it's in an area with some privacy (away from the TV) and with room for expansion. You'll need space for manuals and supplies – and add-on computer peripherals.

Try to reserve an entire electrical circuit of your home for your computer equipment; don't plug in a coffeepot or other power-surge-causing equipment in that circuit while you are using the computer! And forbid (if you can enforce it) eating, drinking, and smoking in your computer area. You are now adjusted to the computer age!

FOOTNOTES

1. David Meyer II, "The Complete Communicator, An Interview With Alfred Glossbrenner," *Link-Up* 1, no. 5 (February 1984): 46.
2. Lyle J. Graham and Tim Field, *Your IBM PC – A Guide to The IBM PC (DOS 2.0) and XT* (Berkeley, Calif.: Osborne/McGraw-Hill, 1984), p. 17.
3. Paul Andereck, "Personal Computing in Genealogy: An Evaluation," *Genealogical Computing* 1, no. 6 (May 1982): 2.
4. Paul Andereck, "State of Genealogical Computing: A Report of Reader Survey Results," *Genealogical Computing* 2, no. 6 (May 1983): 8-18.
5. Charlotte Beyers, "Bridging the Gender Gap," *Family Computing* 2, no. 8 (August 1984): 38-39.

CHAPTER 3

Reasons for Using a Computer

O ne good way of learning about using computers for genealogical work is to listen to people who have already used them for that purpose. Here's what some of them say:

Joanna Posey:

Novice family researchers, as well as professional genealogists, have discovered that personal computers and genealogical software can be extremely valuable tools. Professionals find that computers can help them in five major areas of genealogical studies: records management, telecommunications, graphics, word processing and business. Of these, however, you'll probably find records management software to be of the greatest value to you.[1]

Posey adds in another instance that "the real blessing of a personal computer system comes . . . with the retrieving of family data . . . . Family group sheets, pedigree charts, . . . the 1850 census, odds and ends of data which really don't fit anywhere . . . indices, marriage records. . . . Information can be accessed by keywords, names, dates, places, family members, record groups . . . in a variety of combinations . . . . What a fantastic finder's tool, in seconds!"[2]

Wade Starks:

The computer has altered our recordkeeping and access methods drastically. Though the future will doubtless bring marvelous advances in computer architecture and technology, we need wait no longer to acquaint ourselves with these new tools. Today, microcomputers are available in a wide variety of packages, capabilities and prices. Many are affordable and suitable for the genealogist.[3]

Diane Dieterle:

The fun part of genealogy is the detective work. The un-fun part is the paperwork. A computer can be used for all the repetitious clerical work that a genealogist does: keeping current pedigree charts and family group sheets; keeping a record of correspondence; keeping a research calendar; keeping updated documentation for your

research; writing form letters to record offices; writing letters to relatives to bring your genealogy up to date; making research time reports
for clients; printing alphabetical lists of records . . . ; indexing
genealogies.[4]

John J. Armstrong:

An elderly aunt provoked my interest in genealogy. She spoke
of various family members as having done notable things in their lives
or having been the father, mother, spouse or child of another person.
These facts were quite confusing to me, particularly since I had never
known most of these individuals. I had recently bought
a . . . microcomputer and set about designing a system to store and
recall information on family members that my aunt had spoken about
or had shown me their genealogy charts. I had a lengthy learning
experience . . . . That experience and the onslaught of additional
family tree information would require a computer with a larger data
storage capacity.[5]

Langston J. Goree:

In developing the automated family records file system it is recognized that there are those who will prefer to continue using manual
records with which they are comfortable, and that are familiar and
time tested . . . . Personal computers are proliferating, and many
are now being used by amateur and professional genealogists and
family historians. In future years it will be the computer-automated
family records file system that will become comfortable, and their utility and efficiency will become familiar and time tested.[6]

Let's take a look at some good examples of computerized genealogy. These
illustrations are from *Roots II,* provided by Commsoft, Inc., of Palo Alto,
California. The *Roots II* program was released in September 1984.
    Note: Fifty genealogy-software publishers responded to the authors'
request for specimens of their software printouts. To display them all would
have required at least two hundred pages. Therefore, we regrettably had
to select only a few representative samples. A directory of genealogy software appears elsewhere in this book; with it you can solicit printout copies
of any software in which you are interested.

    Plate 1: Alistair BRIGHT is the subject of pedigree Chart 2. His line
continues with Marlin BRIGHT's ancestors on Chart 17. Another chart
(Chart 1) has as its subject Albert Morehouse BRIGHT and has Alistair
as person no. 16. This chart is typical of good computer handling of ancestry display and is automatically generated from information stored on disk.

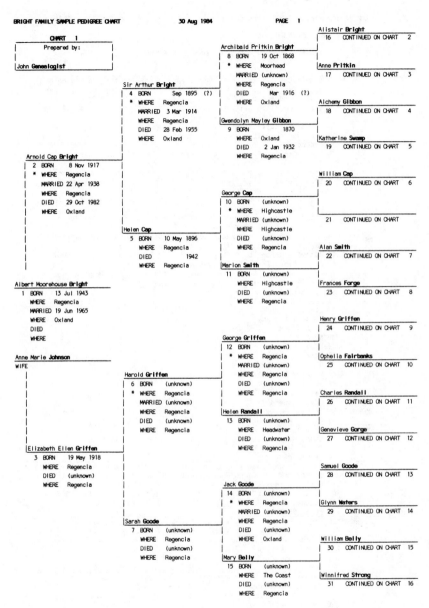

BRIGHT FAMILY SAMPLE PEDIGREE CHART   30 Aug 1984   PAGE 1

```
CHART  1
|   Prepared by:   |
|                  |
| John Genealogist |

                                    Sir Arthur Bright
                                    |  4  BORN       Sep 1895  (?)
                                    | *  WHERE   Regencia
                                    |    MARRIED  3 Mar 1914
                                    |    WHERE    Regencia
                                    |    DIED     28 Feb 1955
                                    |    WHERE    Oxland
     Arnold Cap Bright
     |  2  BORN      8 Nov 1917
     | *  WHERE   Regencia
     |    MARRIED 22 Apr 1938
     |    WHERE   Regencia
     |    DIED    29 Oct 1982
     |    WHERE   Oxland
     |                              Helen Cap
     |                              |  5  BORN   10 May 1896
     |                              |    WHERE   Regencia
     |                              |    DIED       1942
     |                              |    WHERE   Regencia
 Albert Moorehouse Bright
 1  BORN    13 Jul 1943
    WHERE   Regencia
    MARRIED 19 Jun 1965
    WHERE   Oxland
    DIED
    WHERE

Anne Marie Johnson
WIFE
     |                              Harold Griffen
     |                              |  6  BORN   (unknown)
     |                              | *  WHERE   Regencia
     |                              |    MARRIED (unknown)
     |                              |    WHERE   Regencia
     |                              |    DIED    (unknown)
     |                              |    WHERE   Regencia
     Elizabeth Ellen Griffen
     |  3  BORN    19 May 1918
     |    WHERE   Regencia
     |    DIED    (unknown)
     |    WHERE   Regencia
     |                              Sarah Goode
     |                              |  7  BORN   (unknown)
     |                              |    WHERE   Regencia
     |                              |    DIED    (unknown)
     |                              |    WHERE   Regencia
```

```
                                              Alistair Bright
                                              | 16   CONTINUED ON CHART  2
Archibald Pritkin Bright
|  8  BORN    19 Oct 1868
| *  WHERE   Moorhead                         Anne Pritkin
|    MARRIED (unknown)                         | 17   CONTINUED ON CHART  3
|    WHERE   Regencia
|    DIED       Mar 1916  (?)
|    WHERE   Oxland                            Alchemy Gibbon
Gwendolyn Mayley Gibbon                        | 18   CONTINUED ON CHART  4
|  9  BORN       1870
|    WHERE   Oxland                            Katherine Swamp
|    DIED     2 Jan 1932                        | 19   CONTINUED ON CHART  5
|    WHERE   Regencia

                                              William Cap
                                               | 20   CONTINUED ON CHART  6
George Cap
| 10  BORN    (unknown)
| *  WHERE   Highcastle                         21   CONTINUED ON CHART
|    MARRIED (unknown)
|    WHERE   Highcastle
|    DIED    (unknown)                         Alan Smith
|    WHERE   Regencia                           | 22   CONTINUED ON CHART  7
Marion Smith
| 11  BORN    (unknown)                        Frances Forge
|    WHERE   Highcastle                         | 23   CONTINUED ON CHART  8
|    DIED    (unknown)
|    WHERE   Regencia

                                              Henry Griffen
                                               | 24   CONTINUED ON CHART  9
George Griffen
| 12  BORN    (unknown)
| *  WHERE   Regencia                          Ophelia Fairbanks
|    MARRIED (unknown)                          | 25   CONTINUED ON CHART 10
|    WHERE   Regencia
|    DIED    (unknown)
|    WHERE   Regencia                          Charles Randall
|                                               | 26   CONTINUED ON CHART 11
Helen Randall
| 13  BORN    (unknown)
|    WHERE   Headwater                         Genevieve Gorge
|    DIED    (unknown)                          | 27   CONTINUED ON CHART 12
|    WHERE   Regencia

                                              Samuel Goode
                                               | 28   CONTINUED ON CHART 13
Jack Goode
| 14  BORN    (unknown)
| *  WHERE   Regencia                          Glynn Waters
|    MARRIED (unknown)                          | 29   CONTINUED ON CHART 14
|    WHERE   Regencia
|    DIED    (unknown)
|    WHERE   Oxland                            William Belly
|                                               | 30   CONTINUED ON CHART 15
Mary Belly
| 15  BORN    (unknown)
|    WHERE   The Coast                         Winnifred Strong
|    DIED    (unknown)                          | 31   CONTINUED ON CHART 16
|    WHERE   Regencia
```

***Plate 1**.* Commsoft, Inc. *Roots II* Pedigree Chart

Prepared by: John **Genealogist**

1 Albert Moorehouse **Bright**, occ. Librarian, b. 13 Jul 1943 in
  Regencia, ch. 14 Jul 1943 in Regencia, m. 19 Jun 1965 in Oxland,
  ref: AMBRIG43
2 Arnold Cap **Bright**, occ. Shop Keeper, b. 8 Nov 1917 in Regencia,
  d. 29 Oct 1982 in Oxland, m. 22 Apr 1938 in Regencia, en. 1 Jan
  1938 in Regencia
3 Elizabeth Ellen **Griffen**, b. 19 May 1918 in Regencia, ch. 27 Jun
  1918 in Regencia, d. in Regencia
4 Sir Arthur **Bright**, occ. Writer, b. Sep 1895(?) in Regencia, d. 28
  Feb 1955 in Oxland, bu. 4 Mar 1955 in Regencia, m. 3 Mar 1914 in
  Regencia
5 Helen **Cap**, b. 10 May 1896 in Regencia, d. 1942 in Regencia, bu.
  18 Apr 1942 in Regencia
6 Harold **Griffen**, b. in Regencia, d. in Regencia, m. in Regencia
7 Sarah **Goode**, b. in Regencia, d. in Regencia
8 Archibald Pritkin **Bright**, occ. Farmer, b. 19 Oct 1868 in
  Moorhead, ch. 1868, d. Mar 1916(?) in Oxland, bu. Mar 1916 in
  Oxland, m. in Regencia
9 Gwendolyn Mayley **Gibbon**, b. 1870 in Oxland, d. 2 Jan 1932 in
  Regencia, bu. in Regencia
10 George **Cap**, b. in Highcastle, d. in Regencia, m. in Highcastle
11 Marion **Smith**, b. in Highcastle, d. in Regencia
12 George **Griffen**, b. in Regencia, d. in Regencia, m. in Regencia
13 Helen **Randall**, b. in Headwater, d. in Regencia
14 Jack **Goode**, b. in Regencia, d. in Oxland, m. in Regencia
15 Mary **Belly**, b. in The Coast, d. in Regencia
16 Alistair **Bright**
17 Anne **Pritkin**
18 Alchemy **Gibbon**
19 Katherine **Swamp**
20 William **Cap**
22 Alan **Smith**
23 Frances **Forge**
24 Henry **Griffen**
25 Ophelia **Fairbanks**
26 Charles **Randall**
27 Genevieve **Gorge**
28 Samuel **Goode**
29 Glynn **Waters**
30 William **Belly**
31 Winnifred **Strong**
32 Michael **Bright**
40 Henry **Cap**
41 Melody **Smithe**
56 James **Goode**
64 James **Bright**, occ. Carpenter, b. Jul 1791(?) in Oxland, Nexis, d.
  30 Nov 1856 in North Fork, Temberold, bu. 1 Dec 1856 in Oxland,
  Nexis, m. Nov 1821 in Nexis
65 Samantha **Wenderford**, b. 27 Oct 1793 in Nexis, d. 25 Dec 1853
80 Elkhorn **Cap**
112 Peter **Goode**
128 Morton **Bright**, occ. Sea Captain, b. 5 Jan 1773 in New Sumpter,
  Nexis, d. 9 May 1803 in Oxland, Nexis, bu. 10 May 1803 in Oxland,
  Nexis
129 Jennifer **Lockley**
160 Elijah **Cap**
224 George **Goode**
256 Merlin **Bright**, occ. Merchant, b. 7 Aug 1748 in New Sumpter,
  Nexis, ch. 8 Aug 1748 in New Sumpter, Nexis, d. 15 Feb 1798(?) in
  New Sumpter, Nexis, bu. 17 Feb 1798 in Oxland, Nexis
320 Henry **Cap**
512 John **Bright**, occ. Merchant, b. 18 Mar 1725/6 in Oxland, Nexis,
  ch. 13 Apr 1726, d. 22 Dec 1796 in New Sumpter, Nexis
1,024 Thomas **Bright**, occ. Farmer, b. 18 Sep 1706 in Oxland, Nexis, ch.
  25 Sep 1706 in Oxland, Nexis, d. 12 Jul 1768 in Oxland, Nexis,
  bu. 14 Jul 1768 in Oxland, Nexis

Plate 2. Commsoft, Inc. *Roots II* Ahnentafel

BRIGHT FAMILY SAMPLE DESCENDANT CHART

Prepared by: John Genealogist

```
0   1   2   3   4   5   6   7   8   9   10  11  12  13  14  15
Thomas Bright  .   .   .   .   .   .   .   .   .   .   .   .   .   .
 .  John Bright  .   .   .   .   .   .   .   .   .   .   .   .   .
 .   .  Merlin Bright  .   .   .   .   .   .   .   .   .   .   .
 .   .   .  Morton Bright  .   .   .   .   .   .   .   .   .   .
 .   .   .   .  James Bright  .   .   .   .   .   .   .   .   .
 .   .   .   .   .  Michael Bright  .   .   .   .   .   .   .
 .   .   .   .   .   .  Alistair Bright  .   .   .   .   .   .
 .   .   .   .   .   .   .  Gloria Smith Bright  .   .   .   .
 .   .   .   .   .   .   .   .  Kenneth Johnson Endel   .   .
 .   .   .   .   .   .   .  Archibald Pritkin Bright*   .   .
 .   .   .   .   .   .   .  Meredith Holmes Bright   .   .
 .   .   .   .   .   .   .   .  Sir Arthur Bright*   .   .   .
 .   .   .   .   .   .   .   .  Henry Bright   .   .   .
 .   .   .   .   .   .   .   .  Florence Bright  .   .   .
 .   .   .   .   .   .   .   .  Arnold Cap Bright*   .   .
 .   .   .   .   .   .   .   .   .  Albert Moorehouse Bright
 .   .   .   .   .   .   .   .   .   .  John Arnold Bright
 .   .   .   .   .   .   .   .   .   .  Jennifer Bacon Bright
 .   .   .   .   .   .   .   .   .   .  Michael Moorehouse Bright
 .   .   .   .   .   .   .   .   .   .  John Bright  .   .   .
```

Plate 3. Commsoft, Inc. *Roots II* Descendant Chart

Plate 2: An ahnentafel (or ancestor list) provides the ancestors of any specified individual. In this type of list, the subject is designated as no. 1, his or her father as no. 2, paternal grandfather as no. 4, and so on. Note that this program provides for skipping those numbers for which no information is known about the individual. Good genealogy software allows this and other options for displaying ancestry or descendancy.

Plate 3: Descendancy is assymetrical (no visual balance in the display). Thomas BRIGHT descendants are shown on the *Roots II* display which has a capability of showing fifteen generations of descendants. Good software will allow a computer to pick out family members from data files and report *either* his ancestors or descendants. Descendancy charts are the most difficult to produce by computer because of their lack of symmetry.

```
BRIGHT FAMILY SAMPLE FAMILY GROUP SHEET            30 Aug 1984    PAGE   6
HUSBAND: Albert Moorehouse Bright*
Birth:           13 Jul 1943      WHERE: Regencia, Ober CTY, Nexis
Christened:      14 Jul 1943      WHERE: Regencia, Ober CTY, Nexis
Resides:                          WHERE: Oxland, North CTY, Nexis
Buried:                           WHERE:
Probate:                          WHERE:
Immigration:                      WHERE:
Occupation:      Librarian        REF:   AMBRIG43
Married:         19 Jun 1965      WHERE: Oxland
Divorced:                         WHERE:
Engagement:      20 May 1964      WHERE: Merrinews, Brgn CTY, Nexis
HUSBAND'S FATHER:   Arnold Cap Bright
HUSBAND'S MOTHER:   Elizabeth Ellen Griffen
WIFE:      Anne Marie Johnson
Birth:           15 Aug 1944      WHERE: Oxland, North CTY, Nexis
Christened:      22 May 1975      WHERE: Oxland, North CTY, Nexis
Resides:                          WHERE: Oxland, North CTY, Nexis
Buried:                           WHERE:
Probate:         (unknown)        WHERE:
Immigration:     (unknown)        WHERE:
Occupation:      Registered Nurse REF:   AMJOHN44
WIFE'S FATHER:      Richard Everton Johnson
WIFE'S MOTHER:      Carolyn Kendleton Kesey
CHILDREN (X = ancestor of preparer)
 1│John Arnold Bright
M│Birth:         25 Dec 1969      WHERE: Oxland, North CTY, Nexis
 │Christened:    11 Jan 1977      WHERE: Oxland, North CTY, Nexis
 │Married:                        WHERE:
 │To:
 │Resides:                        WHERE: Oxland, North CTY, Nexis
 │Buried:                         WHERE:
 │Probate:       (unknown)        WHERE:
 │Immigration:   (unknown)        WHERE:
 2│Jennifer Bacon Bright
F│Birth:         29 Sep 1971      WHERE: Oxland, North CTY, Nexis
 │Christened:    22 May 1976      WHERE: Oxland, North CTY, Nexis
 │Married:                        WHERE:
 │To:
 │Resides:                        WHERE: Oxland, North CTY, Nexis
 │Buried:                         WHERE:
 │Probate:       (unknown)        WHERE:
 │Immigration:   (unknown)        WHERE:
 3│Michael Moorehouse Bright
M│Birth:          1 Nov 1974      WHERE: Oxland, North CTY, Nexis
 │Christened:    (unknown)        WHERE:
 │Married:                        WHERE:
 │To:
 │Resides:                        WHERE: Oxland, North CTY, Nexis
 │Buried:                         WHERE:
 │Probate:       (unknown)        WHERE:
 │Immigration:   (unknown)        WHERE:

Prepared by: John Genealogist

Rel to husband:                          Rel to wife:
```

Plate 4. Commsoft, Inc. *Roots II* Family Group Sheet

```
BRIGHT FAMILY SAMPLE FAMILY GROUP SHEET                30 Aug 1984    PAGE    8
```

Albert Bright story and persons living or dead is completely coincidental.

Albert Bright's birth certificate entered 14 July 1943 Regencia courthouse.

Christened at Regencia Unified Unorthodox Church on 14 July 1943, Reverend Smith officiated.   See RUUC record book for 1943 found in RUUC library.

AMBRIG43.USR:

Albert Bright's current mailing address:

Albert M. Bright
Post Office Box 123B
Regencia, Nexis   90123

Telephone: (415) 555-1212

He is currently employed at the Regencia library in the reference section.

AMJOHN44.TXT:

Anne Marie Johnson was born in Oxland in the Oxland General Hospital at 8:23 AM.   She weighed 7 pounds 4 ounces at birth.

Anne attended public schools in Oxland, and graduated from Oxland High School with honors.   She went on to study economics at Oxland State, where she met her husband, Albert.

Plate 5. Commsoft, Inc. *Roots II* Footnote

Plate 4: A computer can use the same data files that generated the information in the previous charts to easily generate a family group sheet for any selected individual.

Plate 5. Page 8 of the BRIGHT Family sample group sheet shows the footnoting capability of *Roots II*. Narratives, source citations, and research comments are part of a good genealogy program's reporting capability.

Plate 6: Index preparation is an essential part of genealogy and genealogy software capabilities. An alphabetical list of BRIGHT family members (Mary Belly through Samuel Goode) shows one variation of computer indexing. Other variants will be discussed later.

These illustrations show why genealogists use computers. Computers do what genealogists have always done: prepare pedigree charts, create group or individual sheets, keep track of information sources and research notes, and prepare indexes. And once family data are entered and saved, the computer makes many of these processes automatic—and quick and painless, compared with manually managing family files.

BRIGHT FAMILY SAMPLE INDEX   28 Aug 1984   PAGE   9

Mary Belly, 1, 3	Janet Carter
William Belly, 3, 1	Alice Corn
Albert Moorehouse Bright, 1, 3, 6, 5, 7	Jonathan Springfield Endel
Alistair Bright, 2, 3, 1, 5	Kenneth Johnson Endel, 5
Archibald Pritkin Bright, 1, 3, 5	Ophelia Fairbanks, 3, 1
Arnold Cap Bright, 1, 3, 5, 6	Myra Fieldstone
Florence Bright, 5	Darrell Foot
Gloria Smith Bright, 5	Everett Foot
Henry Bright, 5	Mary Foot
James Bright, 2, 3, 5	Walter Foot
Jennifer Bacon Bright, 6, 5	Frances Forge, 3, 1
John Bright, 4, 5	John Genealogist
John Bright, 5	Alchemy Gibbon, 3, 1
John Arnold Bright, 6, 5	Alwin Gibbon
Meredith Holmes Bright, 5	Dudley Gibbon
Merlin Bright, 4, 2, 5	Ellen Gibbon
Michael Bright, 2, 3, 5	George Gibbon
Michael Moorehouse Bright, 6, 5	Gwendolyn Mayley Gibbon, 1, 3
Morton Bright, 2, 3, 5	Harry Gibbon
Sir Arthur Bright, 1, 3, 5	Hazel Gibbon
Thomas Bright, 5, 4	Horace Gibbon
Elijah Cap, 3	Merlin Gibbon
Elkhorn Cap, 3	George Goode, 4
George Cap, 1, 3	Jack Goode, 1, 3
Helen Cap, 1, 3	James Goode, 3
Henry Cap, 4	Peter Goode, 3
Henry Cap, 3	Samuel Goode, 3, 1
William Cap, 3, 1	

Plate 6. Commsoft, Inc. *Roots II* Alphabetical Index

PREPARING FAMILY HISTORY PUBLICATIONS

The computer brings us a technology that can help us organize, index, and publish our holdings, as well as do research.

Donald R. Barnes and Richard S. Lackey have given sound advice that sets the stage for computer publishing:

> This intervening step [writing] between research and publishing has been a stumbling-block for many genealogists who have seen writing as an impossible task. As a result these genealogists have at their deaths left a mass of unorganized papers which often have been thrown away by heirs who could not understand their contents or, when preserved in an archival institution, have been of minimal value to others because there was no order to the collection. At some stage, every genealogist should stop doing research, compile his notes and write, and should by all means – WRITE IT RIGHT! . . . Writing your genealogy or family history is an excellent end result of all those countless hours you have spent on research. To share is the greatest gift

we have! We agree with the well-known genealogist, Dr. Neil Thompson, C.G., F.A.S.G., who often says, "One of the best ways to see where you stand with your research is to write." A real pleasure comes to those who write. The pleasure is not just seeing your finished work but in doing the writing. Most genealogists have experienced the personal satisfaction of doing research. If you have not been writing, you are in for an additional treat.[7]

You are the one who should (must!) write the book. Either get it done while you can, or get its components in shape so someone else can!

A computer's version of data storing is similar to making voice tape recordings on a cassette recorder. However, the preferred form is "diskette" rather than "cassette," and the information is stored as typed characters rather than as spoken words. In either case, words are changed from voice or typed words into magnetized spots on the coating of plastic material. Whereas a cassette is a ribbon of tape, a computer diskette is a circular version of the same flexible plastic base. Diskettes are encased in square heavy paper jackets; cassettes are wound on little shafts inside plastic cases. The computer condenses the stored data so much that a few diskettes can hold all of your family group sheets. Several more diskettes may hold all the documentation and text of documents or letters. Collectively, a fully computerized version of your family files would probably fit in a shoebox.

Once you have your family information on diskettes, identical copies of each diskette can be quickly made – at a rate of about one every two minutes. Once computerized, you can make safety copies, you can create identical computer copies for anyone who is interested in your holdings, and you can be assured that your files require little space in someone's attic.

Using a computer as a smart typewriter, you can be writing your "book" from the moment you begin computerizing. Once you have begun managing family files by computer, you are ready to create interim versions of a book; you will be able to revise any and all of the computerized records without having to retype anything already typed, and you are able to make safety copies of your files at any moment. That's a comfortable feeling!

Using a computer necessarily causes you to "format" your records in a consistent way. This is equivalent to filling out blank family group sheet forms or pedigree charts. Because there is a recognizable consistency in the format of your records, they can easily be read by anyone. Computerized research notes and biographical sketches remove the illegibility that grows as your ink fades or handwriting gets shaky; all characters are as well formed as a typewriter might make them.

The direct translation of manually kept files into computerized files seldom occurs. Things that were informal and variable (even sloppy) in your data files must be "shaped up" during the data-entry process when you keyboard the facts into a computer. This shaping-up process is important – in order for the computer to handle additions, corrections, manipulations, or printouts, it must know precisely where the records are and in what form. The discipline is worth the effort. You will be guided by the computer to enter your facts, narratives, and source documentation in a uniform way.

Using a computer for genealogical records management is easier than using a typewriter. You can erase mistakes by backspacing and typing over them. When one record is entered, the computer repeats the prompts for entering the next. Genealogists usually find using a computer more fun than work, once they get used to it.

The big payoff is immediate. Neat printouts are ready to photocopy, mail, send to the printer, or be proofread. If your proofreading reveals mistakes you made in entering data, you can mark the copy and make corrections during your next session of keyboarding.

Although procedures vary from one computer to another and from one program to another, the functions are all basically the same. You add, change, or print records individually or print the whole file, at your choice.

Your records are readily copied and compactly stored in case you don't finish your book; the next generation (a computer-literate generation!) will more readily understand and carry on your research work and will publish that book.

Making interim editions is quick and easy. A good book can later become a better book as you continue the accumulation and modification of the interim edition. The computer is an excellent self-publishing device. You can make one copy of your book and have it photocopied and bound relatively inexpensively.

You might consider serially publishing your family's history. In this way you can be sure findings are disseminated (whether or not you eventually publish a family book). A family newsletter is a natural by-product of computerized files. By using a word processing program you can create an inexpensive periodical, and you can manage the mailing list for it with another program.

ORGANIZING RESEARCH FINDINGS

Genealogy programs will be bought by people who are not genealogists. Unfortunately, the programs do not come with this reminder: "*Warning*: Gathering names, dates, and places without recording the sources is bad genealogy!"

A computer is wonderful for organizing family research, but it also may be the vehicle for enhancing the appearance of garbage genealogy.

Therefore, we want to emphasize clearly the importance of documenting facts.

Noel Stevenson is especially authoritative on the subject: "The superior genealogical compilation is not limited to names, dates and places, but includes in addition to such statistical data, family history, biography, interpretation and explanation of the facts presented whenever it is necessary. The inclusion of references to the source of the facts discovered during the research process is extremely important."[8]

Genealogical research does not consist solely of locating information — this is only the first step. The genealogist must interpret the facts or source material and also determine their reliability. He or she may have to reject information for lack of sufficient documenting information. Stevenson quotes Neal F. Mears, a professional genealogist, on this subject:

> There are nearly 10,000 family histories and compilations in print and probably not more than 10 percent of them are worth the paper on which they are written. This is due solely to the fact that the worthless ones were compiled by persons who had no knowledge of the science of genealogy and particularly no comprehension of what constitutes proof. Anything they heard or saw from any source whatsoever, was good enough.[9]

Stevenson's concern for improving genealogy practice is reinforced by Elizabeth and Gary Mills:

> Among archivists and professional historians alike, genealogists have suffered a reputation for shallow research, amateurish methodology and poor standards. This general charge is no longer just; countless genealogists are doing superb work. They have fought an uphill battle for several decades to introduce rigid standards into the study of genealogy and to convince the millions of genealogical newcomers of the crucial importance of these standards. Then came *Roots,* a book advertised as an authentic family history, as the ultimate expression of the black experience in America, despite the caveats of some leading black historians . . . . The question of *Roots'* validity as a black family history is an important one to genealogists of all races.[10]

The Millses do not discount oral history altogether, but point out its rightful role in genealogies:

> Family tradition is invaluable as a beginning point in the research process. It holds the clues to ancestral identities, to the places and time frames in which those ancestors might be found and to the special circumstances in which they may have been involved. Utilized

in this manner, tradition is a powerful tool, but it can also be the proverbial millstone around one's neck if one exalts tradition to a state of sacredness that it does not possess.[11]

SHARING AND FINDING FAMILY INFORMATION

More than a few serious researchers fight dead-ends by placing a "query ad" in a genealogical periodical. The wording of such ads amounts to: "I give up. Does anyone out there know Person X who lived in Place Y during Time Z and married Martha Jane Doe, daughter of John Doe?" Whether by ad placing or other strategies, genealogists get around dead-end searches with the help of others who may be "coming the other way" along a family search line. As they meet in the search tunnels through which they burrow, there is often a happy and mutual exchange of findings between researchers. They can copy records and notes for mutual benefit in an information exchange. Until now, the medium of exchange was paper copies sent by mail.

Computerization of records provides a new exchange medium: computer-readable data that can be sent from one computer to another by telephone or exchange of diskettes by mail. If both genealogists have computerized records, this is the new and marvelously simple tool for finding and assimilating other searchers' data.

The assumption that many genealogists have computerized records systems is premature. Perhaps in a few years this will be the new-wave way by which much more information will be swapped. For now, you are likely to be the one with the computer and the other party will be without one. Nevertheless, your computer can help you "cut out of the herd" those ancestors and collateral relatives of interest to the other genealogist. You can use your computer to search for the individuals the other person is interested in, then make customized reports of your findings. A press of another key and a printout is quickly made, ready for mailing.

SHORING WHILE TUNNELING IN SAND

Few family researchers are continuously climbing the branches of their family trees. Lack of time, energy, or fertile information sources cause lapses between sessions of "doing genealogy."

When you finally do get back to genealogy, often it takes a lot of wasted time to rediscover where you were in your research. Computer organization of family data provides the "shoring up" of the walls and ceiling of the tunnel which otherwise caves in behind you as you progress. The facts fade from your memory. You look at your own "cold" research notes and wonder if you will ever be able to produce a family history, which will depend so much on the memory of how bits and pieces fit together. Computer users find themselves looking at where they left off; nothing has eroded and the computer has forgotten nothing it has been "told" to remember. A new enthusiasm for family research returns quickly.

PERFORMANCE CONSISTENCY

The computer program always runs the same way each time it is "booted up," and the genealogist soon becomes comfortable with the routine even after weeks away from it.

Of the several good reasons for automating offices, performance consistency is one of the best. Different employees using the same computer and software will produce data files or perform information processing in exactly the same format. And, over a period of time, each employee's performance will be on a par with what it was in the beginning, as far as computer-generated information is concerned. It is comforting to think that, with a computer, long interludes of inactivity will not tax your memory cells each time you begin anew, and that your genealogy "products" will maintain consistency.

SPEEDING UP REPETITIOUS TASKS

In manually kept records, you have to type or write a surname in each of the many places it appears. If you have five thousand Smith family records, you will write "Smith" no fewer than five thousand times—and you are likely to write it many more times than that. If your family's migrations and dispersals cause you to write place names over and over, you will find recording the city-county-state names a monotonous, repetitious drudgery. The fascination of family research is in the finding rather than the recording of information. Speeding up repetitious word or phrase entry is a quite ordinary computer capability.

Some personal computers have "user-defined function keys." If you see "F1," "F2," "F3," and other such "F" keys on a keyboard, they are function keys. They can usually be "programmed" to serve many purposes. One of these purposes is to create multicharacter strings of letters to be computer entered by just a single press of a key. You might, for instance, assign to these keys the following values:

F1 = Smith   F3 = Chicago, Cook County, Illinois
F2 = Blanton   F4 = Warsaw, Kosciusko County, Indiana

You can guess how popular such a feature can be in genealogical computing!

Some word processing programs invite users to define each of the ten number keys (1, 2, 3, . . . 0) as words or "strings" (a combination of letters or numbers). If you tap the 1 key, you will get a "1." However, if you hold down some special key (on some computers this is called a "control" key; others are different and are indicated in the user's guide) while tapping the "1" key, the stored word or phrase of your choice is automatically entered. Imagine holding down the "control" key and pressing the number "4" and getting "Warsaw, Kosciusko County, Indiana!" And, through the magic of the computer, you will never make a mistake if you enter it this way.

Even with word processors that don't support function keys, you can accomplish the same thing with the "global search and replace" feature available on most of them. Instead of typing "Warsaw, Kosciusko County, Indiana," each time, type an abbreviation such as "WKI." At the end of your data-entering session, use the search and replace feature to change all occurences of "WKI" to "Warsaw, Kosciusko County, Indiana."

Still another kind of procedure will create the same kind of hit-one-get-many keystroking speed. You may build "vocabularies" and store them as computer files usable with almost any program you are running. You could select your "genealogy vocabulary" file and have it reside in the computer's memory along with whatever program and files you are working with. Call on it when you need to enter repetitious data.

The availability of at least one of several of these data-entry helps is one of the characteristics of a good "genealogy computer." Look for them when you shop. There are other similar considerations we will be discussing later.

Multiplying your keystrokes as described above and using cut-and-paste techniques for reusing already prepared text or forms are but two of the speed-ups that help to trim down to manageable size the monumental task of family data entry or correspondence handling. Speeding up things is one of the famous attributes of computers. If you ask the blunt question, "What can I do with a computer that I can't do without one?" an honest answer would be, "Nothing." But many tasks take so much time to do by computerless methods that they simply wouldn't get done. There is far too much labor involved in manual processes when repetition of like tasks is involved. Without a computer, many people simply don't do what they *might* do.

MINIMIZING LABORS

While speed-up of repetitive tasks is the result of computer use, labor saving is its cause. Computers extend the capacity of individual human beings by taking over menial tasks that must be done over and over or complex tasks that can be reduced to programmed instructions to the computer.

Programmers of genealogy software deliberately search for ways to have the computer take over genealogy labor burdens. "User friendly" is a catchy term that applies to simplifying complicated computer operations for the user. People who experience computer help in tasks they must perform are impressed with the division of labor. Humans do what they do best, the machine does what it does best, and the joining of a person and a computer in the accomplishment of tasks is a most delightful collaboration. (Presumably, the computer doesn't mind getting the dull work to do.)

One example of labors a genealogy computer can minimize is in family group sheet preparation. Ordinarily, the uncomputerized family records file will contain forms on which immediate families are recorded. There is a subject (usually the male family head). While this form contains information about the birth and death of the subject, there is also information about a spouse, parents of both the subject and spouse, and children from this marriage. Such a record system has annotations concerning information sources, dates, places, relationships, and sometimes church-related, occupational, or military data.

If computerized, the same kind of record keeping is treated (by the computer programmer) in a way that minimizes redundancy and saves a lot of labor in data entries. Current genealogy programs require that you enter the names, places, and dates of critical events in the life of each person. The computer (or user) supplies an identification number that is exclusively assigned to the person whose record is being computerized. Thereafter, the computer operator can refer to that person by a few keystrokes (perhaps as few as four strokes expressing the ID number of that person).

After many family members are individually entered into the computer and identified by number, you can print out lists in alphabetical or ID number order. Or you can run a "program module" to ascertain the blood and marriage links among specific individuals. (Genealogy programs are set up so that separate modules handle different kinds of operations; these options can be selected from a "menu" that appears on your computer screen.)

Usually you have to enter only an ID number. The computer is programmed to find the full name of that individual and can also locate the spouse of that individual and his or her parents and children. Each person's vital data is entered into the computer only once, as opposed to, for instance, entering it manually three times in group sheet preparation (as parent in a child's group sheet, as a principal on his or her group sheet, and as a child on the parent's group sheet).

Once a record is entered, the saving of your labor comes not only in accessing that record but in creating reports from it. You save labor in correcting information, too. Only the information that needs correcting has to be changed – not the whole record or page as would be true for manual or typewritten records.

Pedigree chart printing (either descendants or ancestors or a family member) is an ordinary capability of genealogy programs. You can let the computer create multipage, multigeneration charts for any person in your records. Call this module from the menu, enter the desired individual's ID number, and sit back and relax while the computer does the work.

Having a computer is like having a large, unpaid staff working for you at any time you wish to work on your genealogy and in exactly the way you want it to work. It is consistent in performance and quickly handles repetitive tasks – and saves you a lot of labor in the process.

In the following chapters, we'll discuss just how all these "miracles" are performed by the computer.

FOOTNOTES

1. Joanna W. Posey, "Tracing Your Roots by Computer," *Software Supermarket* 1, no. 1 (January 1984): 11-12.

2. Joanna W. Posey, "The Use of Personal Computing Systems in Genealogical Family Organizations," *Genealogical Computer Pioneer* 1, no. 1 (November 1982): 29.

3. Wade C. Starks, "The Computer and the Genealogist," in Arlene Eakle and Johni Cerny, eds., *The Source: A Guidebook of American Genealogy* (Salt Lake City: Ancestry Publishing, 1984), p. 651.

4. Diane Dieterle, *Basic Programming for Genealogists* (Atlanta, Ga.: Genealogical Center Library, 1982), p. 1.

5. John J. Armstrong, *Genealogy – Compiling Roots and Branches, a Computerized System Description* (Mobile, Ala.: 1981), pp. 1-2.

6. L. J. Goree, *Family Records File System* (College Station, Tex.: L. J. Goree Company, 1980), p. 1 (software manual).

7. Donald R. Barnes and Richard S. Lackey, *Write It Right, A Manual for Writing Family Histories and Genealogies* (Ocala, Fla.: Lyon Press, 1983), pp. vii, 1, 7, 9.

8. Noel C. Stevenson, *Genealogical Evidence, A Guide to The Standard of Proof Relating to Pedigrees, Ancestry, Heirship, and Family History* (Laguna Hills, Calif.: Aegean Park Press, 1979). p. 146.

9. Ibid., p. 147.

10. Elizabeth Shown Mills and Gary B. Mills, "The Genealogist's Assessment of Alex Haley's Roots," *National Genealogical Society Quarterly* 72, no. 1 (March 1984): 35.

11. Ibid., p. 37.

CHAPTER 4

What Computer Hardware Does for You–and How

E sther Anderson, the first chairperson of the National Genealogical Society's Computer Interest Group, was one of the earliest to use a computer for genealogy tasks. She discussed her experiences in an article in the Society's quarterly:

> Questions about what computers can do and how they can be used by the genealogist cannot be answered briefly. This is not something you learn in a hurry. It is best learned through practical experience by getting involved with computers . . . . The computer has a tenacious memory and can store large amounts of information in this memory . . . . [It] is a faithful scribe and can retrieve information from memory . . . . [It] is a tireless worker, who does exactly what it is told to do, and is especially good at repetitive tasks . . . . The computer works at speeds such that some of the operations can only be measured in nanoseconds (a nanosecond being one billionth of a second) . . . . To a certain extent we will have to adapt to the computer's ways, and it may take some study on our part to learn to make the best of the computer's unusual attributes.[1]

In order to help us understand what some of the computer's unusual attributes are, let's take a look, first, at the computer itself and then some of its add-on devices.

THE COMPUTER

If you take the lid off a personal computer (which voids the warranty of some of them), you will see arrangements of little dominoes standing with silvery legs stuck in plastic boards. Between and around and among these dominoes are trails of silvery solder or wires that connect all the members of this little squadron of multilegged, chocolate-looking pieces.

In the corner may be a tiny loudspeaker for producing sounds, and there could be a few transformers and tiny switches – perhaps the only familiar-looking gadgets you will find. Largely, the microcomputer is a collection of new kinds of electronics. Looking "under the hood" doesn't tell you much at a glance. You won't even see one of those legendary chips!

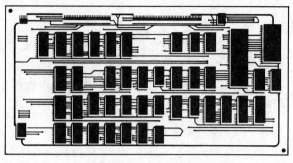

ELECTRONIC CIRCUIT BOARD

The chips that do things so quickly and cheaply and with mind-boggling versatility are actually inside those solid little blocks of dominoes. Those metal legs are the only visible evidence that there are chip circuitries inside the blocks. They are connectors to the pathways your family data will follow as they are processed, stored, or displayed for you.

Leave your computer's "box" unopened and consider its innards from an intellectual view rather than a strictly physical one. The magic of electronics is largely microscopic, anyway. You have to take on faith the mechanics of how a computer works. A computer is demonstrable only in its performance and not by its visible parts. Half of the computer (said by many to be the important half) is not visible at all. That's the software half, which we'll discuss in the next chapter. All you can see of this is the package that stores it. The hardware half is visible, even though much is microscopic.

THE CENTRAL PROCESSING UNIT

The heart (or is it the brain?) of any computer is the central processing unit or CPU. The CPU is extremely small, which is why it is called a microprocessor. It's one of those domino-like things with the metal legs.

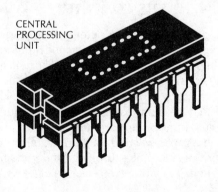

CENTRAL PROCESSING UNIT

Every computer has a central processing unit that controls the operation of the computer and its external equipment, such as disk drives or printers.

Microcomputer is the name given to a computer that uses an "integrated-circuit" processor, consisting of several different types of electronic circuits. A microprocessor is a processor that is contained on one IC (integrated-circuit) chip.

The turning point in the electronics world was the arrival of the transistor. Replacing the cumbersome vacuum tube, the transistor vastly improved computer design, allowing for smaller, faster machines that didn't get so hot. A few years later, a solid-state device was developed that could contain several components on one unit, or "chip." The computer's large amount of switching circuits, formerly built from separate components, could now be constructed into a few "integrated circuits." This combining of computer circuits into one IC chip produced the first of the so-called microprocessors.

Steve Gibson, president of Gibson Laboratories, has reduced the most exotic part of the computer to understandable terms:

We talk so easily and glibly about these chips, the hearts and brains of our computers. But what, really, are chips? Where do they come from? . . . These integrated circuits (ICs) begin as thin, round and flat sheets (called wafers) of ultrapure silicon (pronounced *sili-con*) . . . . Silicon is one of a very few natural elements which can be made to function in a "semiconducting" way. When silicon is ultrapure, it is a very good insulator and will not conduct electricity. But when tiny amounts of special impurities are added, . . . it becomes a semiconductor. A semiconductor does what its name suggests: It is a material that sort of (semi) conducts electricity. At times it's a good conductor and electricity flows through it easily; at other times you couldn't force an electron through it using all the power of Hoover Dam! The process of adding the impurities (which are either positive or negative in nature) is called doping. Wherever positively doped silicon touches negatively doped silicon a "junction" is formed. This junction functions like an off/on switch—electricity is able to flow across the junction or it's not; it's either on or off. You've probably heard that there are "tens of thousands of transistors on a single integrated circuit chip." So the big question is: How do you get them all on there? . . . It turns out to be just a matter of stencils and spray paint . . . . A stencil is a "mask," which keeps paint off the areas where it should not go and lets it pass through where it should . . . . [A] transistor is really just regions of positive and negative impurities in silicon that are next to each other. It happens that an ultrapure silicon wafer is able to absorb these impurities when they are present in the surrounding air. To create an integrated circuit with thousands of these impure regions and thus thousands of tiny transistors, a mask (or stencil) is placed on the silicon wafer while positive impurities are circulated in the surrounding air, then the same process is repeated with a different mask for the negative impurities . . .

The masks are generated by computer-driven photoplotters . . . . directly onto photographic film . . . [which is] reduced 200 times from the original size (about the size of a bedspread) to about one-eighth inch on a side! This pattern is then repeated in a grid that covers the entire wafer. The resulting masks create the patterns of impurities that form the basis of our modern "integrated" circuitry.[2]

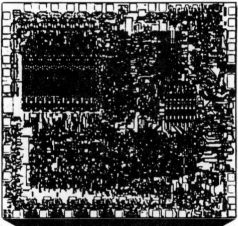

COMPUTER CHIP

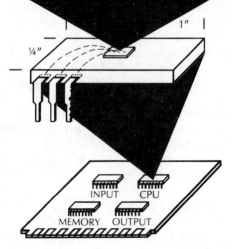

COMPUTER "BIT" SIZES

There's no doubt that a computer's CPU has a number of complexities. Among those is the "bit size" of a given microprocessor. The following discussion may tell what you really want to know—skimming over it won't put you at a disadvantage as a computer-using genealogist. However, there are computer-*buying* considerations relating to bit size of which you should be aware.

Evolutions in microprocessor chip design have brought dramatic changes in bit size. The key steps in this progression were: 4-bit computers (those of the computer-kit days), 8-bit computers (now the major kind of affordable computer), 16-bit computers (the IBM PC started the movement to this bit size and it will likely be the major size for several years to come), 32-bit computers, (only now dawning and represented by Apple's Macintosh and Lisa models), and 64-bit computers (predictably coming in a few more years of computer evolution).

Think of bit size as you might think of the number of cylinders in your automobile's engine (that is, don't think about it at all). Simplistically, a larger bit size provides faster operation and more "computer power"—just as more cylinders in your auto engine give you subtle, but certain, improved performance.

A single computer circuit contains a BInary digIT or "bit" of information. This bit can be either "on" ("1") or "off" ("0"). With one bit, then, we can represent only one of two situations. To represent more than two conditions with binary logic, several bits are connected to provide a usable logical unit called the "word." Each word can be used to represent a different condition by choosing various combinations of bit patterns. With 8 bits we can represent 256 different conditions. With 16 bits, however, more than 65,000 different conditions can be represented! (These things grow, you will note, in the same progression as do ancestors on a family tree from generation to generation.)

The more recent computers are of the 16-bit type. Among their advantages are that they can process twice as much information in the same amount of time, and they can use larger memories.

Many of these new computers also avert the problem of having to convert software from 8-bit to 16-bit computer models by providing "dual processor capability" that allows the use of either 8-bit or 16-bit software. Programs written for the 8-bit microprocessor operate with that processor, but the user can switch to the 16-bit processor. This capability takes advantage of the increased performance and allows access to future software released for the 16-bit microprocessor. The 8-bit capability, particularly if it works with a common operating system such as CP/M (see next chapter), allows access to thousands of programs presently available.

Consider, however, this advice if you think that 16-bit technology is the way to go: "There is little doubt that the 16-bit processor can improve the throughput of a low-cost business computer system, but considering some of the tasks that the computer is used for, it is doubtful whether the increased capability is justified in all applications . . . . Since a word processing task typically handles a single 8-bit word for each character represented, it would be difficult to demonstrate an increase in performance for a word processor based solely on the fact that a 16-bit computer has taken the place of an 8-bit computer."[3]

In choosing between an 8-bit and a 16-bit processor, you will want to consider that the increased performance of the latter may not warrant the corresponding increase in price for your situation. The 8-bit product is by no means obsolete, and for genealogical applications it is likely to be completely satisfactory. The potential computer buyer should evaluate both cost and performance in selecting a system for his or her needs.

INTERNAL MEMORY

The "memory" of a computer generally consists of two major types: internal and external. The internal memory is that which is actually a part of the computer itself, rather than a device (such as a disk) used to store information on. We'll discuss internal memory first, then look at peripheral storage devices later.

The most important thing to know about internal computer memory is that you need plenty of it—or at least "enough."

Internal memory is used to hold the instructions of the currently executing program, plus part or all of the required data which is being processed. Each memory word has a distinct location, called a "memory address," and the information is stored as a set of voltages that represent binary ones and zeros. The amount of main memory available is an indication of the power of the system. A system with a main memory of 32,000 "byte" locations is obviously not as powerful as one with 256,000 bytes.

Names, dates, and places are the staple of the genealogist. And each character of each of those staples requires one byte of information. The name "John Doe," for instance, requires 8 bytes of memory—one for each letter and one for the space between the first name and surname. (We have already noted that it may take 8 bits to "create" the letter "J," for instance, so it can be seen that bytes—characters—are made up of bits—the elements that distinguish one character from another.)

Inside your computer, "John Doe" is remembered by memory chips while the computer program chases down his father, his spouse, his birthdate, or whatever. If a name was all the computer had to remember, the size of its memory wouldn't be so important. But the computer also must remember the program's instructions, where it keeps "John Doe" and other parts of his record, as well as many other things.

The internal memory of most computers consists of two types, called ROM and RAM.

ROM stands for *read-only memory.* A computer's ROM holds permanent information or programs. When you turn on your computer, the ROM and its instructions are automatically available. These instructions or programs cannot be altered by the user. They also are "nonvolatile"—that is, they don't require power to keep them in existence. Every time you turn your computer on, they come back in their original, permanent form.

The amount of ROM varies from machine to machine. Some, for instance, have just enough memory to hold operating instructions for the computer. Others might also include a BASIC language interpreter or other programs.

RAM stands for *random-access memory.* This is the internal memory of the computer into which the programs you want to run and the data you want to manipulate are placed. When computers are said to be "64K" or "128K" machines, it is the RAM which is being described.

A "K" is computerist shorthand to describe a "kilobyte" or 1,000 bytes. Actually, a K is equal to 1,024 bytes. So a machine with 64K of RAM would actually have a storage capacity of 65,536 bytes. The amount of K described is generally rounded down this way.

RAM memory is "volatile." Turn your computer off and—poof!—your RAM-held data and program are gone. RAM has been described as "the blackboard of your computer system. You can put information (write) on the blackboard, take information (read) from the blackboard, erase all or part of the blackboard, and start over again. Your computer needs this blackboard-type memory to process your programs and information."[4]

How does a computer keep track of the information you are processing?

As soon as you run a program, the computer sets up a series of pigeonholes in memory, one for every variable, and stores the current value for each variable in its own special slot. *Variable* is the name given to a piece of information that has a value that can change; the birthdate of an ancestor is a variable that could be first entered as "about 1886" and later be changed to "12 December 1885." Every time you change the value of a variable, the computer goes back to the pigeonhole to change its contents to the new value.

The computer starts setting up these memory locations for your variables as soon as you tell it to run, and it creates one storage space for each variable in the order it actually encounters them during program execution.[5]

We started out by saying that the important thing about internal memory is that you need plenty of it. By now you should be able to see why. The amount of memory determines the kind, size, and degree of sophistication of the programs you run, the amount of information you can work with, and the ways in which you can manipulate that information.

You also likely have noted that the RAM is not only the place you store the information you are working on, but also the place where at least portions of the instructions from the operating system and the current applications program must reside before you can work with that information. Thus, the amount of memory available for storing data depends on the complexity and length of the software you are using (see Chapter 5).

To a degree, lack of internal memory can be overcome by "external memory" or peripheral devices which store your data to be used when the computer needs it.

PERIPHERAL DEVICES

If it isn't a central processing unit, internal memory, power supply or interfacing device, it must be a peripheral! Things you hang on your computer—or things that were hung on your computer before you got it—are peripherals. We'll cover the vital peripherals and skip over those which have little relevance to genealogy.

Peripheral devices for computers are used for either "input" or "output" of data. Nothing comes into a computer or goes out of it except by way of the interface between the central processing unit and peripheral devices.

Interface is the name for the connection and electronic circuits between a computer and its peripherals. Interfaces are classified as parallel or serial, according to how peripheral devices are linked to the computer. In a *parallel* interface all 8 bits of the byte are transmitted simultaneously. At least eight separate wires are used; one for each bit in the byte. Parallel cable connections have between twenty and fifty wires, and the additional wires carry information used to coordinate the moving of bytes of information between the peripheral device and the CPU. In *serial* connection, the byte's 8 bits are broken up and sent one at a time. A serial connection cable uses a maximum of twenty-five wires. Two handle the actual data, with one sending data and the second receiving it. The signals passing through the other lines coordinate the movement of information between the CPU and the peripheral device. Additional bits of information are sent with the information bytes to help the receiving device find the beginning and end of the byte. It really does not matter which type of device you use on a computer, but it matters that you have the right interface for your device: A parallel device cannot use a serial interface, nor will a serial device work with a parallel interface.[6]

EXTERNAL MEMORY

External memory is, as implied, a device for storing information outside of the computer. The term *mass storage* is usually applied to external memory devices because they can store massive amounts of data (compared with the finite capacity of internal memory). Your genealogy programs, family-record data files, and computerized research notes will be kept in external memory.

We've already noted that internal memory is "volatile": "Amnesia strikes a computer without data-storage capacity when the computer's power is turned off. If you want to save information that you have entered into a computer's memory, you need a means of storing data. Storage devices record data by transforming the electronic signals held in RAM into magnetic form. Then the devices read the recorded information back into memory when you want to reuse it. Storage devices include cassette tape drives, floppy disk drives, hard disk drives, backup devices, bubble memory and optical disks."[7]

These several kinds of external memory devices are worth considering individually. We'll discuss them from the least expensive (and least satisfactory) to the most expensive (and newest technology).

CASSETTE TAPE

Computer data can be stored on most better-quality audio cassette tape recorders. While this method of storing programs and data is inexpensive, most genealogists will want a faster, more efficient way of doing the job. You can survive with only cassette tape storage, but chances are you'll want to move to disk storage, even though it may cost you $500 for the storage device instead of $50.

The basic drawback of recording information on a tape is that you must first wind the tape to the place where that information is stored, then "play" that tape into the computer. Disk devices, on the other hand, almost instantly locate and read into memory particular pieces of information. If you depend on cassette tape as your medium for mass storage, you'll spend a lot of frustrating hours transferring data from tape to memory and back.

FLOPPY DISKS

The floppy disk drive is the storage device most commonly used by genealogists and other computer users. Actually, two disk drives are par for genealogical computers, according to surveys of users. This is because one drive usually is needed for the program currently in use and the other to store the data being created or altered.

The "floppy" (because it is somewhat pliable as opposed to "hard") disk, or diskette, looks somewhat like a 45 rpm record. It comes in two

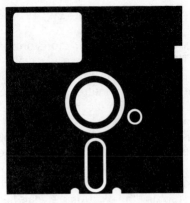

FLOPPY DISK

sizes: an 8-inch diameter, or a 5 1/4-inch diameter (sometimes called a minifloppy). The disk has a vinyl recording surface; this passes over a magnetic head in the drive which reads data from the disk or writes it onto the disk. Even smaller sizes are beginning to appear on the market, and they may become more popular in the future.

The disk drive consists of a rotating magnetic recording medium (the disk) and a read/write head that can move across the complete recording area. Magnetic disk drives are often referred to as "random-access" devices since the read/write head can move directly to any portion of the disk to read or record data. This means that any desired piece of information can be located in a fraction of a second and loaded into memory in just a few seconds more.

DISK DRIVE UNIT

Storage capacities of floppy disks range from several thousand to hundreds of thousands and even millions of characters, depending on the type of computer being used and its formatting capabilities, and whether the disk is "single density" (SD) or "double density" (DD). Some drives can record information on both sides of a diskette, thus doubling its capacity. In computer terms, these are referred to as double-sided or DS. A designation such as DSDD means the disk drive will record information on both sides and uses a double-density disk; SSSD means single-sided, single density.

If you decide on a system with double-sided read-and-write capability, you should make certain you purchase disks designed for recording on both sides. Although you sometimes (with a little manipulation of the disk protective cover) can copy on the reverse side of a disk designed for single-sided use, most manufacturers do not maintain quality control of the second side. If you save information on a double-sided disk, you may not be able to retrieve it with a single-sided disk drive. Any given block of copy in a sequence may have been written on the reverse side of the disk.

Word processing is a major genealogical use of the computer, and a two-disk system is certainly desirable – if not necessary – to carry out this task efficiently or to use other genealogy programs. A sophisticated program might occupy a major portion of the available space on a single disk, leaving scant room for the data files you will be working with. It is often possible to swap disks in a single-drive system after loading the program, but this is inconvenient and can leave the way open for errors which could result in a major loss of data.

Remember: Just because a fellow genealogist uses minifloppy disks on his or her computer just like you do, just because you and your friend buy disks by the ten-pack and split the cost to share the savings of bulk buying, just because you both use the same genealogy software, this doesn't mean you can mail a diskette to your friend and have your family files run on your friend's computer. This likely won't be possible unless you have nearly identical computers and controlling software. Different computers and different software usually format data on the disk in different ways.

While this incompatibility between systems may be decreasing, it likely will be a serious problem for years to come. Even newer versions of the same machine sometimes can't use data disks created by an older version. Technological advances often dictate that new ways of putting more information on a disk be adopted, or various manufacturers may cling to their method either because they believe it to be better or because they want to maintain an "exclusive territory."

There are methods of transferring information between incompatible systems, however. Computers can be "backed" (connected by cables through various input or output devices), or information can be transferred over phone lines. Tasks such as these are usually the domain of experienced users who are quite familiar with their machines, and probably require special software. (See the Introduction for a description of how the authors and publisher moved this book's text among several com-

puters which were incompatible in regard to disk format and other factors.)
   One final thought: Treat your floppy disks as if they were a valuable
collection of high-fidelity recordings. Their surfaces are so sensitive that
even touching an exposed disk area can create problems. And *always* make
backup copies of data after–even during–work sessions. There is nothing more discouraging than having spent hours updating records only to
discover later that your disk has somehow become damaged and you can't
access all that great information. Backup copies can minimize your losses.

HARD DISKS
   If you are working with large amounts of information–more than can
be stored on a half-dozen or a dozen data disks–you may want to consider a hard disk drive for your system.
   These drives will

> provide fast and economic storage for large amounts of information.
> A hard disk is made up of a motor that rotates an aluminum platter
> coated with a magnetic medium. Read and write heads can be moved
> to any location on the platter. The heads float on a cushion of air
> to prevent disruption of the magnetic surface. Hard disks are sealed
> to protect their components, which are easily damaged by dirt and
> dust. Hard disks find and transfer information up to ten times faster
> than floppy disk drives and store much more information. A typical
> hard disk stores 5 to 10 megabytes [millions of characters] of data,
> compared to the 360 kilobytes [thousands of characters] stored on
> the [IBM] PC's floppy disks . . . . Hard disks, however, don't elimi-
> nate the need for a floppy disk drive in the PC [or any computer]
> because you must have a way to load programs to the hard disk."[8]

   Until recently, hard disks were very expensive and not very reliable.
But if you compare the cost-per-byte of a hard disk to the cost-per-byte
of a floppy disk drive today, you'll find that now the hard disk may even
be more economical.
   The hard disk is something you probably won't need when you first
begin doing genealogy with a computer–but it's something you might
want to consider adding to your system later on. Family databases always
exceed the storage capacity of a single diskette. Swapping disks to access
family records distributed over many diskettes will end when you graduate to a hard disk operation.
   Our advice to genealogists is: Buying a less expensive computer and
spending your money on hard disk storage is preferable to buying a more
expensive computer. You will gain more utility from a hard disk than you
will from theoretical capabilities (such as color, graphics, multi-tasking,
multi-user functions, or faster CPU speed) of expensive business
computers.

Hard disks come in several physical sizes, with the 5 1/4-inch disk the one usually interfaced with microcomputers. Both surfaces of a platter are used to record data and there is a read/write head for each surface. Also, multiple platters may reside in one drive housing.

BUBBLE MEMORY STORAGE

This is a "coming technology" that is not, as yet, practical for genealogy. To learn more about bubble memory, see an article by Ken Freeze "Bubble Memory Gradually Becoming a Micro Reality," on page 124 of the July 1984 *Infoworld*.

OPTICAL MEMORY

Like bubble memory, optical disk memory is still on the horizon. If you want to know more about it, see page 300 of *Datamation*, June 1, 1984: "Optical Disks Foreseen," by Edith Myers.

KEYBOARDS AND DISPLAY SCREENS

The keyboard of a computer and the display screen (on which you see what you have typed or what the computer program has brought from memory) would seem to be integral rather than peripheral computer parts. They are essential components. But sometimes (though infrequently) you must buy a keyboard as a separate purchase; video display screens are quite often chosen and bought separately. A genealogist can't get along without either one of them.

COMPUTER KEYBOARDS

The keyboard is like a pair of shoes—to be picked for comfort and with all due care. IBM had to replace the keyboard sold with its PCjr computer, and it also redesigned the keyboard for its PC model. That's how critical a good keyboard is to users and to computer sales. Don't take less than the best-feeling keyboard! You are going to spend a lot of time with it while entering data, so reject anything but the best. Nothing about the A through Z keys should be unlike a fine electric typewriter keyboard (an IBM Selectric keyboard is a good measuring stick).

Aside from the normal alphabet letter keys, you'll run across some new keys on any computer. They will vary in kind or placement from one computer to another.

Chris DeVoney explores a typical computer keyboard for us:

The ESCAPE KEY is unique to computers. It is normally used to prefix a command to the printer, video screen or modem.

The CONTROL KEY is also unique to computers. It acts like a supershift key. When you hold the control key down and tap a letter

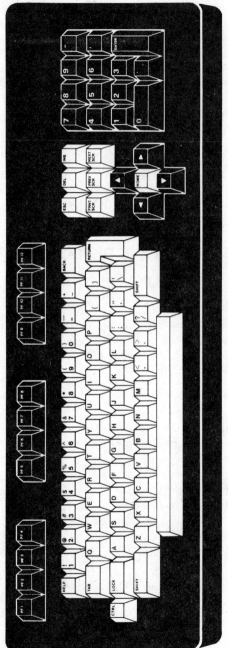

COMPUTER KEYBOARD

key, you can produce 26 unique computer characters.

ALT is another unique computer key, used to type an "alternate" set of characters or words. Because computer manufacturers have not agreed on what ALT should do, its use may vary among computers.

The four keys with arrows pointing up, down, left and right are the cursor-control keys. The CURSOR is the flashing underline or box on the terminal or video screen. The cursor shows you where the next character will be placed on the screen.

Your computer may have several keys that perform different editing functions . . . . The keys marked F1, F2, etc., are special-function keys you or your programs can use to answer questions, select items from a menu, or type a line of characters into the computer. All of these things can be accomplished by pressing one particular key. As with the Alt key, the use of special-function keys can vary from computer to computer and from program to program."[9]

COMPUTER VIDEO DISPLAYS

Your eyes are going to spend a lot of time looking at the computer's screen. Try the contrast and brightness controls (the only controls you'll usually find on a video-display screen). If you still don't like the looks of the text on the screen, remember this: It isn't going to get any better.

Aside from the keyboard feel, the screen is the most "personal" thing about a personal computer. You are *not* going to like using regular television sets for family data work – get a video monitor. Further, you can spend money on a color monitor if you want to play computer games or see vivid business charts, but for genealogy work you really want a monochrome (one-color) screen. Amber and green screens are alleged to be easier on the eyes than black and white (usually white on black). Look around at several computer monitors and see which will be the kind your eyes like best.

VIDEO DISPLAY SCREEN

The simplest and least expensive display is a standard television set, but the limitation of a TV-set display lies with the number of characters it can display: 25 lines with about 40 characters per line or a total of about 1,000 characters. Another type of display is a dedicated monochrome monitor. If you don't need color, a monchrome monitor is adequate (color isn't needed for word processing, database management, and other non-graphics applications). Most monitors provide 25 lines per screen and 80 characters per line. A third kind of display is called a composite video color monitor. This monitor is a color TV with direct video input and provides a cleaner image than a color TV. Of the best, an RGB (red-green-blue) display is more expensive than a composite video monitor but can (with the three colors) create any visible color. All four monitor groups use picture tubes called cathode ray tubes (CRTs) and high-voltage power supplies.

In case you were wondering how bits and bytes can become letters and numbers on a screen, here is an explanation: The video display monitor is built around a character generator ROM memory chip, which generates a character font. This integrated circuit creates 35 dots in a five by seven dot matrix (sometimes more or less) and, according to the letter typed, creates a single character on the display screen.[10]

The latest thing in microcomputers is the portable or notebook-size computer. These little computers do not have TV-tube displays. Jim Bartimo explains why and how:

> The desire of computer manufacturers to miniaturize computers has necessitated the creation of alternatives to the bulky cathode-ray tubes used to provide the display in most computers. Companies that are making . . . notebook-and brief-case-size computers . . . are turning to technologies like liquid crystal displays (LCDs) . . . to cut down drastically on the weight, size and power consumption on small machines by CRTs . . .

MINICOMPUTER

The problem of creating small displays was almost insurmountable when manufacturers were limited to CRTs, invented in the 1930s for use in military applications (such as radar) and in measuring devices. Even though a CRT's screen can be made to measure only a few inches across and still be read comfortably, the inherent nature of the CRT requires a greater depth. The image shown on a CRT is created by electron beams fired from a cathode ray gun striking small particles of materials called phosphors, causing them to glow. The tube is bulky because the gun must be behind the screen's face and far enough from the phosphors to work correctly.

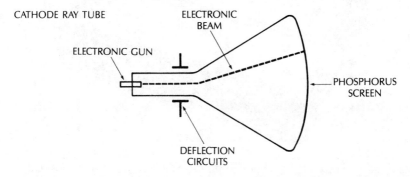

Besides being bulky, CRTs need high voltages to fire electron beams. Thus, they require large power supplies and a source of current stronger than that provided by most batteries. Those power supplies, and the glass and magnetic parts of the CRT, are quite heavy . . . . The LCD, which started as a one-line display for calculators and watches, uses little power, mostly because it relies on reflected ambient light to make it readable. In contrast, a CRT produces its own light, making it useful in a dark room but requiring much more electricity.

The LCD is no panacea. It has many drawbacks, including poor resolution, a limited viewing angle and a smaller character display than that of typical CRT displays . . . [but] there is little doubt that flat panels of some type will soon become standard issue on microcomputers.[11]

COMPUTER PRINTERS

Not long ago, a "letter-quality" printer for any computer was as expensive as the computer itself. A price range of $2500 to $3500 was not uncommon. With such a cost associated with high-quality printers, computerists tended to buy cheaper dot-matrix printers. The savings were considerable. But the printouts from the cheaper printers "looked like a computer made them." Computer printing got a bad name because it looked cold and mass-produced. Legibility was okay, but the aesthetics of dot-made characters was something less than pleasing. Most people do not realize that it was the *cost* of printers which made many resort to dot-matrix printing.

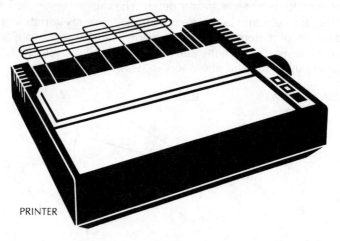

PRINTER

Today, you can buy *both* a letter-quality printer and a dot-matrix printer for less than $1000. It's a good idea to buy both. The speed of dot-matrix printers is useful when preparing drafts (and nine out of ten pages printed from a computer are drafts or "in-house" lists). Reduce wear and tear on the letter-quality printer by plugging it in only when final drafts are needed (or "when you care enough to send the very best").

The following summary is based on an article explaining the many essentials of printer knowledge by Bernard Horn, vice president of Diablo Systems, Inc., a major maker of computer printers.[12]

Printers enable you to take computerized information and print it faster than you can type. Several types of printers are available. The two most common types of printers are letter-quality and dot-matrix. In the future we'll probably see more thermal printers, ink jet printers, and laser printers.

Letter-quality printers work by positioning characters molded on tips of a circulating wheel or thimble. After a character is positioned, a small hammer pushes it against a ribbon, making an impression on paper. Letter-quality printers typically print at speeds of between 18 and 80 characters per second (cps), much more slowly than dot-matrix printers.

Dot-matrix printers are faster; some are capable of 400 cps. However, they do not produce the refined characters that letter-quality printers do. Dot-matrix characters are formed by the impact of a group of "needles" on a ribbon. The printer selects the specific needles within the matrix to imprint a pattern of dots corresponding to a desired character's shape. Besides having the advantage of speed, dot-matrix printers are usually less expensive than letter-quality printers.

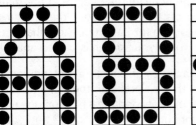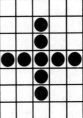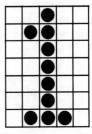

DOT-MATRIX PRINT PATTERN

Thermal printers use heat to form characters on paper. The print quality is similar to that of dot-matrix printers. Thermal printers are quite fast. Their biggest drawback has been their need for expensive, specially coated paper. Also, any heat applied to the paper can turn it blue (or brown or black – according to its printing color) anytime after you have made a printout. Do *not* use a thermal printer for your genealogy.

Ink-jet printers print colored (but not very sharp) graphics and images to produce multicolored maps, charts, and three-dimensional pictures. These printers form characters and images by separating and controlling ink drops with an electric charge or by routing drops through several ink channels. Ink-jet printers are quieter than letter-quality or dot-matrix printers, and some of them print up to 270 cps. They are, however, much more expensive than letter-quality or dot-matrix printers, and have little genealogical usefulness.

Laser printers are quiet and extremely fast, capable of printing twelve pages per minute. They create type by exposing paper to a laser beam. Because laser printers are expensive they are best suited for businesses that generate large volumes of printed material. The genealogist should avoid this kind of printer until the technology and price improve.

In addition to those printers mentioned in Horn's summary, there is a breed of dot-matrix printer which gives you the choice of "quick-and-dirty" or "slow-and-pretty" printing. *High-density dot matrix* printers have two modes: a normal, high-speed dot-matrix mode and a slower, "correspondence-quality" mode. In the slower mode, the printer prints each character several times. The additional printings are usually one dot higher and to the right of the first printing. The shift fills in the gaps between the dots and improves the quality of the type, but the character quality of high-density dot-matrix printers still is not as good as that of a daisy-wheel printer.

The dot-matrix printing process is probably new to most genealogists. To help you understand how it works, we add that the print needles mentioned above are contained in a print head that moves along a bar, generating a line of print, character by character. Computer-programmed instructions move the print head and activate the needles in the matrix. The matrix can vary from 5 by 7 dots to 8 by 16 dots; the greater the number of dots, the better looking is the formation of each character.[13] The *Writer's Digest Guide to Word Processing* has a nice analogy:

> A dot-matrix printer uses a series of pins in a rectangular box. Think of a fist full of pencils with their points in the same direction. If you hold them against a sheet of paper and press hard on one eraser, you get a dot. Press on the right combination of erasers and you get a series of dots that form a letter. You might have to play mental connect-the-dots to see the letter, and that's the fatal flaw of the dot-matrix printer. Even the best of them, using 24 pins instead of the usual nine, can't match the crisp edges of letters formed on the cheapest full-character printer.[14]

An electric typewriter uses a "print ball." Most letter-quality printers use a similar device, called a *daisy wheel*. This is another new element that is worth explaining. Daisy wheel printers have a changeable metal or plastic wheel that revolves. Each wheel has petals that contain one or two characters. An appropriate petal moves into place, a hammer strikes the petal (which strikes the ribbon) and the action prints the character on paper. These printers are usually the type called letter-quality printers because their print is the same quality as a typewriter's.

DAISY WHEEL

It may occur to you that a computer can be hooked to an electric (or electronic) typewriter you already own. Or, you might buy an electric typewriter so it can be used with or without the computer controlling it. Experience has taught us this is not a good idea. Ignore ads that suggest this route to letter-quality computer printing. Some low-cost typewriter/printer ads are appealing but we concur with this opinion: "Don't be fooled by the opportunistic retreading of small typewriters . . . . Some of them are just cheap electric typewriters with a computer port tacked on. They didn't produce good copy when they were typewriters, and they don't produce it now that they are printers."[15]

Even a good quality typewriter remade to work with a computer probably won't be satisfactory. They are almost unbearably slow (compared with any computer printer) and often require special software, computer boards, and an unusual amount of "fiddling" to get them turned on or off.

In addition to printing, a printer also "transports" the paper on which it is printing. The most common way of moving paper is "friction feed," the method used with most typewriters. The paper is pinched between two rollers, one of which provides the motion. The advantage of this system is its ability to use all types of paper (including letterhead paper or forms), and the disadvantage is its inability to move the paper precisely and evenly. Thus, continuous forms cannot be used, for they soon get out of line. Tractor feeds rely on the sprocket holes punched in continuous-form paper for both alignment and paper transport. This is the most accurate method of moving long print jobs through the printer. Most printers come with a friction feed and offer a tractor as an option.[16] You can usually remove the tractor-feed mechanism and use the friction-feed mode. This kind of transport system is what a genealogist needs!

PRINTER WITH TRACTOR-FEED
AND FAN FOLDING DEVICE

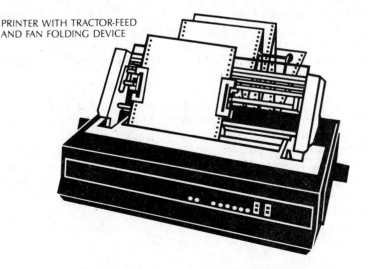

The tractor feed is so important in printing genealogical reports that you should consider it a necessity rather than an option. Once you tear away the sprocket-hole edges and separate each sheet, the standard tractor-fed paper looks just like ordinary 8 ½ by 11 inch paper. You buy this kind of paper by the case and it lays "fan folded" in the box. The printer gathers in the supply of continuous-form paper line by line as it prints. The printouts are stacked neatly by the printer. You can be reading the family history charts and reports that come pouring out and the printer takes care of feeding itself with paper from the box.

In some instances, the amount of information to be put on a page exceeds the page width capability of a letter-quality printer. For example, a five-generation pedigree chart may require using more characters per line than a letter-quality computer printer can produce. Ten-pitch typing produces 80 characters per line and twelve-pitch typing produces 96 characters per line (on standard 8 ½ by 11 inch paper). If your pedigree chart requires longer lines than 80 or 96 characters, you have three practical choices:

1. Turn the paper sideways (perhaps using legal-size paper to get 14-inch width rather than 11-inch width) and computer-print your chart. This assumes you can do that with your printer's carriage.

2. Print the left half of the chart on one sheet of paper and print the right half on the next sheet; then tape the two halves together to get the wide chart you need for expressing the information. This may require some special programming and your program vendor may not be too accommodating (unless convinced that many customers would like to see wide charts in letter-quality).

3. Use a dot-matrix printer and send it the signal which causes it to go into "compressed type" mode. In this mode, there are the same number of lines on your page but the number of characters per line can be increased to 132. Thus, you can get as many as 132 characters on a line even if you are using 8 ½ by 11 inch paper in its usual vertical position (taller than wide).

Genealogy program manuals often specify that you must use 132 characters per line printing; the programmer has planned for more characters per line than can be printed by the usual 80 or 96 characters per line of the letter-quality printer. Throughout this book you will find specimens of genealogy program printouts. Many of them are in dot-matrix print style. If they have no more than 96 characters per line, they could be printed with a letter-quality printer (using the twelve-pitch setting). You can have a copier reduce the size of overly wide pages to obtain standard size if a genealogy is being published. You might make fold-out pages if you use the legal-size paper for oversized pages.

ILLUSTRATIONS OF GENEALOGY PRINTOUTS

Armstrong Genealogical Systems sells *Genealogy: Compiling Roots and Branches*. We have selected John Armstrong's Birthdates (Plate 7), Descendants of Charles Leo Armstrong (Plate 8), and Predecessors of John Yarger Armstrong (Plate 9) to illustrate the use of letter-quality printing.

From *Arbor-Aide* by Software Solutions, we borrow a family group sheet for Daniel Geroge Ritzinger (Plate 10) to show compressed-type dot-matrix printing as it is used to squeeze more information in a standard page width than letter-quality printers allow. Already smallish (because it is in compressed type) this illustration suffers from the size reduction necessary for publishing in this book.

To illustrate dot-matrix printing in the normal mode (not compressed to maximize the characters per line), we show John Doe's family group sheet from *Byteware*, (Plate 11).

For an illustration of economy of space, we show Personal Software's *Family Reunion* which puts six generations of a pedigree chart in dot-matrix compressed type, (Plate 12).

While these plates are also illustrations of the variety in genealogy software capabilities, they are placed here to underscore the point at hand: How computer printouts look is a function of the printer you have chosen to use!

(We should remind you that all printouts in this book were originally on 8 ½ by 11 inch paper, and the reduction in size necessary for inclusion in the book has impaired the legibility of some information-packed pages. Any "fuzzy" specimen you find can be blamed on reproduction quality—some were photocopied and fuzzy when submitted for use in the book.)

MODEMS

The modem is something you will want to add *after* you have your family records computerized. For now, learn a bit about this future add-on. You *will* want to "modem" with other genealogists as a strategy to overcome

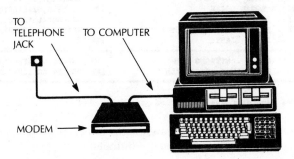

TO TELEPHONE JACK   TO COMPUTER

MODEM ⟶

ARMSTRONG—CORANSON GENEALOGY

Page 1	BIRTHDATES by Month, Day, & Year		11 Feb 1981
Date	**Person**	**ID #**	**Birthplace**
1 Jan 1945	MARY LOU SEIBERT (RUSCO)	473	?
2 Jan 1924	HARDY LYNN HULSEY	244	LADONIA,TEXAS
6 Jan 1930	CLARENCE ALFRED JR. LUCAS	356	WICHITA,KANSAS
7 Jan 1881	WILL FLETCHER	543	?
7 Jan 1944	GLEN LAVERNE WILSON	720	LARNED,KANSAS
9 Jan 1970	JONATHAN CLARK WINGER	101	WICHITA,KANSAS
9 Jan 1974	JAMIE NOELLE SKINNER	254	DENVER,COLORADO
9 Jan 1981	SARA ELIZABETH ARMSTRONG	861	PORTSMOUTH, VIRGINIA
11 Jan 1973	DAVID R. WILSON	749	HUTCHINSON,KANSAS
12 Jan 1914	LEONARD ERIC HOFFMAN	192	PARKSTON,SOUTH DAKOTA
13 Jan 1871	JOHN EHLERS	273	?
15 Jan 1951	CAROL GUNN (ARMSTRONG)	14	DALLAS,TEXAS
15 Jan 1966	SHERRY LYNN WILSON	738	HUTCHINSON,KANSAS
16 Jan 1976	JOHN MATTHEW ARMSTRONG	13	MIDWAY ISLAND
17 Jan 1934	FRANKLIN WAYNE WILSON	706	?
18 Jan 1940	KAREN EDITH RUSCO (BALDWIN)	455	?
22 Jan 1942	HAROLD AMOS WILSON	708	LARNED,KANSAS
24 Jan 1978	JOSEPH DAVID ARMSTRONG	10	PLANO,TEXAS
27 Jan 1860	JOHN ZIMMERMAN	317	?
27 Jan 1870	MARY ELIZABETH ARMSTRONG (BURCHFIE*	126	IDA,MICHIGAN
27 Jan 1961	DAVID GLENN RADENBERG	448	?
30 Jan 1952	KENNETH LEE ARMSTRONG	2	AMARILLO,TEXAS
30 Jan 1952	CAROLEE JOYCE RUSCO (DENNING)	482	GREAT BEND,KANSAS
30 Jan 1973	BRYAN MARCUS ARMSTRONG	12	EUREKA,CALIFORNIA
31 Jan 1980	RYAN LUCAS MCPHAIL	620	HAYS,KANSAS
2 Feb 1968	DOUGLAS DEAN RUSCO	474	HAYS,KANSAS
4 Feb 1941	JUDITH ANN CHUMLEY (RUSCO)	451	?
5 Feb 1845	CHRISTIAN KOOPMAN	664	BADEN,GERMANY
5 Feb 1845	CARL JOHAN CORANSSON	257	ESKILSKUNA,SWEDEN
5 Feb 1880	JOHN DAVID RUSCO	342	?
7 Feb 1913	MATILDA MACCAUGHEY (ARMSTRONG)	108	HONOLULU,HAWAII
8 Feb 1845	REBECCA SMITH (LUCAS)	223	?,VIRGINIA
8 Feb 1877	GEORGE ALLEN LUCAS	343	ASHLAND,ILLINOIS
8 Feb 1904	WAYNE MANLEY ARMSTRONG	21	MENO,OKLAHOMA
9 Feb 1854	SABRA ELIZA ARMSTRONG (DANIELS)	123	UNIONTOWN,PENNSYLVANIA
9 Feb 1948	LYNNA BETH HULSEY (ARMSTRONG)	11	?
9 Feb 1974	BLAKE EDWARD ARMSTRONG	106	VUNG TAU, SOUTH VIETNAM
10 Feb 1942	MARY LYNN WALKER (ARMSTRONG)	104	FREDRICK,OKLAHOMA
14 Feb 1863	BENJAMIN FRANKLIN WILSON	150	BROWN CO.,ILLINOIS
17 Feb 1898	FORREST CHARLES BURCHFIELD	132	NEWKIRK,OKLAHOMA
18 Feb 1959	MONTE JOSEPH MILLER	731	HUTCHINSON,KANSAS
18 Feb 2192	GLENN CARL RADENBERG	446	?
19 Feb 1949	JOHN JAMES ARMSTRONG	3	AMARILLO,TEXAS
23 Feb 1948	BRIAN LOGAN LOCKE	109	SEATTLE,WASHINGTON
26 Feb 1822	LEVI ZIMMERMAN	228	WESTMORELAND CO.,PENNSYL
26 Feb 1960	JEAN MARIE ARMSTRONG (MOORHEAD)	68	FRESNO,CALIFORNIA
28 Feb 1969	ERIC BRIAN LINDER	776	?
1 Mar 1975	HOPE MARIE ARMSTRONG	70	TULARE,CALIFORNIA
3 Mar 1868	CHARLES SHERMAN BURCHFIELD	142	HOWARD CO.,INDIANA

continued...
Asterisk denotes name shortened to fit on page.

Plate 7. Armstrong Genealogical Systems *Genealogy: Compiling Roots and Branches* Birthdates

```
=======================================================================
             DESCENDENTS OF CHARLES LEO ARMSTRONG
=======================================================================
                                            GREAT
                                    GREAT   GREAT
                            GREAT   GREAT   GREAT
                    GRAND   GRAND   GRAND   GRAND
PERSON    CHILDREN  CHILDREN CHILDREN CHILDREN CHILDREN
    *SPOUSE   *SPOUSE  *SPOUSE  *SPOUSE  *SPOUSE
|         |        |        |        |        |
|CHARLES LEO ARMSTRONG
|     b. 14 Jun 1897 at GREAT BEND,KANSAS
|     CHIROPRACTOR
|     4 children
|     m. 12 Oct 1925 to IRENE TIDENBERG (ARMSTRONG) at AMARILLO,TEXAS
|     WIDOWED
|     rm. 24 Mar 1932 to GRACE VERA WELLS (ARMSTRONG) at SANTA MONICA,CALIFORNIA
|
|     MARRIED
|     LIVING  at COTTONWOOD,ARIZONA
|     *IRENE TIDENBERG (ARMSTRONG)
|     b. 4 May 1897 at JONESBORO,PENNSYLVANIA
|     1 child
|     m. 12 Oct 1925 to CHARLES LEO ARMSTRONG at AMARILLO,TEXAS
|     MARRIED
|     d. 10 Oct 1929 at FRESNO,CALIFORNIA
|      |VERN IRL ARMSTRONG
|      |    b. 8 Nov 1928 at FRESNO,CALIFORNIA
|      |    4 children
|      |    m. 29 Dec 1953 to TAMAR HOWARD (ARMSTRONG) at MODESTO,CALIFORNIA
|      |    MARRIED
|      |    d. 21 May 1962 at NORTH FORK,CALIFORNIA
|      |    *TAMAR HOWARD (ARMSTRONG)
|      |    b. 2 Oct 1931 at KELSEYVILLE,CALIF
|      |    4 children
|      |    m. 29 Dec 1953 to VERN IRL ARMSTRONG at MODESTO,CALIFORNIA
|      |    WIDOWED
|      |    LIVING at PIXLEY,CALIFORNIA
|      |     |CHARLES CEDRIC ARMSTRONG
|      |     |    b. 29 Sep 1954 at FRESNO,CALIFORNIA
|      |     |    1 child
|      |     |    m. ?? ?? 1974 to ESPERANZA MARIE CASTILLA (ARMSTRONG)
|      |     |    at ?
|      |     |    DIVORCED
|      |     |    LIVING at VISALIA,CALIFORNIA
|      |     |    *ESPERANZA MARIE CASTILLA (ARMSTRONG)
|      |     |    b. 31 Jul 1954 at RODNEY,NEW MEXICO
|      |     |    1 child
|      |     |    m. ?? ?? 1974 to CHARLES CEDRIC ARMSTRONG at ?
|      |     |    DIVORCED
|      |     |    LIVING at ?
|      |     |     |HOPE MARIE ARMSTRONG
|      |     |     |    b. 1 Mar 1975 at TULARE,CALIFORNIA
|      |     |     |    SINGLE
|      |     |     |    LIVING at ?
|      |     |GALE LOUISE ARMSTRONG
|      |     |    b. 27 Mar 1956 at FRESNO,CALIFORNIA
=======================================================================
Page 1              continued                  19 Feb 1981
=======================================================================
* spouse
```

Plate 8. Armstrong Genealogical Systems *Genealogy: Compiling Roots and Branches* Descendants

```
==========================================================================
           PREDECESSORS OF JOHN YARGER ARMSTRONG
==========================================================================
                                              GREAT
                                      GREAT   GREAT
                              GREAT   GREAT   GREAT
                      GRAND   GRAND   GRAND   GRAND
PERSON    PARENTS   PARENTS  PARENTS  PARENTS  PARENTS
|         |         |        |        |      |
|         |         |        |        |      |ROBERT ARMSTRONG (ID=119)
|         |         |        |        |      |    b. ?? ?? ???? at ?
|         |         |        |        |      |    8 children
|         |         |        |        |      |    m. ?? ?? ???? to ANN ???????? at
|         |         |        |        |      |    ?
|         |         |        |        |      |    MARRIED
|         |         |        |        |      |    d. circa  1771 at ?
|         |         |        |        |JAMES ARMSTRONG (ID=117)
|         |         |        |        |    b. ?? ?? 1754 at ?
|         |         |        |        |    1 child
|         |         |        |        |    m. ?? ?? ???? to SABRA SAMPSON at ?
|         |         |        |        |    MARRIED
|         |         |        |        |    d. ?? ?? 1841 at ?,NEW JERSEY
|         |         |        |        |ANN ???????? (ID=120)
|         |         |        |        |    b. ?? ?? ???? at ?
|         |         |        |        |    8 children
|         |         |        |        |    m. ?? ?? ???? to ROBERT ARMSTRONG
|         |         |        |        |     at ?
|         |         |        |        |    MARRIED
|         |         |        |        |    d. ?? ?? ???? at ?
|         |         |        |ROBERT ARMSTRONG (ID=115)
|         |         |        |    b. 10 Oct 1778 at ?,PENNSYLVANIA
|         |         |        |    SHOEMAKER
|         |         |        |    11 children
|         |         |        |    m. ?? ?? ???? to MARY ELIZABETH MCCLAIN at ?
|         |         |        |    MARRIED
|         |         |        |    d. 21 Jun 1845 at ?
|         |         |        |SABRA SAMPSON (ID=118)
|         |         |        |    b. 25 Jul 1759 at ?
|         |         |        |    1 child
|         |         |        |    m. ?? ?? ???? to JAMES ARMSTRONG at ?
|         |         |        |    MARRIED
|         |         |        |    d. 25 Aug 1841 at JACOB'S CREEK,PENNSYLVAN
|         |DAVID SAMPSON ARMSTRONG (ID=113)
|         |    b. 23 May 1814 at WESTMORELAND CO.,PA
|         |    6 children
|         |    m. 30 May 1844 to MARY JANE YARGER at ?
|         |    MARRIED
|         |    d. 1 Jun 1901 at GREAT BEND,KANSAS
|         |MARY ELIZABETH MCCLAIN (ID=116)
|         |    b. 9 Sep 1776 at ?
|         |    11 children
|         |    m. ?? ?? ???? to ROBERT ARMSTRONG at ?
|         |    MARRIED
|         |    d. 21 Dec 1848 at ?
|JOHN YARGER ARMSTRONG (ID=44)
|    b. 12 Mar 1845 at UNIONTOWN,PENNSYLVANIA
|    KANSAS STATE LEGISLATOR, 1890'S
==========================================================================
Page 1                    continued              11 Feb 1981
==========================================================================
```

Plate 9. Armstrong Genealogical Systems *Genealogy: Compiling Roots and Branches* Predecessors

```
Family Group No. 1
                              Husband:  Ritzinger              Daniel     George
---------- Sources / Notes ----------
                                                  City, Town, Or Place  County or Province  State/Country
                              Birth:     11 Jan 1950  Chippewa Falls    Chippewa            WI  USA
_____ Chr'nd:    00 Jan 1950  Chippewa Falls    Chippewa            WI  USA
                              Marriage:  20 Jun 1970  Chippewa Falls    Chippewa            WI  USA
                              Death:
                              Burial:
_____ Residence: 7378 Zurawski Court   Custer                WI  USA
                              Occupation: Prgrar/Analyst    Rel: Catholic   Military: No
_____ Father:
                              Mother:


_____

                              Wife:   DeLisle                 Sandra     Lee
_____
                                                  City, Town, Or Place  County or Province  State/Country
                              Birth:     21 May 1951  Chippewa Falls    Chippewa            WI  USA
_____ Chr'nd:    00 Jun 1951  Chippewa Falls    Chippewa            WI  USA
Compiled by:                  Death:
  Sandra Lee Ritzinger        Burial:
  7378 Zurawski Court         Residence: 7378 Zurawski Court   Custer                WI  USA
  Custer, WI  54423           Occupation: Housewife       Rel: Catholic   Military:
  06/02/84                    Father:    DeLisle                 Eugene     Daniel
                              Mother:    Trimbell                Mary       Jane


------------------------------------------------------- Children -----------------------------------------------------
      Child/Spouse            ---------Dates---------  City, Town, Or Place  County or Province  State/Country

 1  Scott     Daniel          Birth:     06 Jan 1975  Chippewa Falls    Chippewa            WI  USA
                              Marriage:
                              Death:
                              Burial:

 2  Craig     Matthew         Birth:     21 Jan 1977  Chippewa Falls    Chippewa            WI  USA
                              Marriage:
                              Death:
                              Burial:
```

Plate 10. Software Solutions *Arbor-Aide* Family Group Sheet

disk-format compatibility problems in file swaps, and you *will* want to add to and take from genealogy databases. Put that notion in the back of your mind for now.

Modem is the abbreviation for MOdulator-DEModulator. What it does is take your computer's bits (remember those ones and zeroes?) and change them into audible frequencies (modulation), and vice versa (demodulation).

Dennis Hayes, the president of D.C. Hayes, a major modem manufacturer, says a modem can be thought of as your computer's telephone. With a modem, your computer can hook up to information in the next office, in another city, or even in another country. A modem can be a printed circuit board that fits directly into one of the computer's expansion board slots, or it can be a separate, free-standing unit that connects through a serial port. Your specific needs should determine the speed of the modem you select. People who use data communications only for short exchanges

```
          FAMILY  GROUP  SHEET

                  ByteWare

Compiled by   (Your Name)
```

HUSBAND:JOHN DOE   OCCUPATION:FARMER
  BORN:1 JAN 1900   WHERE:ROSEVILLE IL
  BAP.:3 FEB '00   WHERE:WALNUT GROVE IL
  MARR.:22 APR '23   WHERE:ROSEVILLE IL
  DIED:3 AUG '75   WHERE:AMES IA
  CHURCH AFFIL.:PRESBY.   BUR.:WALNUT GROVE IL
  MILITARY SERV.:US ARMY - AUG 1918 TO MAR 1921
  FATHER:JACK C. DOE   MOTHER:JANE SMITH
  OTHER WIVES:NONE

WIFE:_____
  BORN:_____
  BAP.:_____   WHERE:_____
  DIED:_____   WHERE:_____
  CHURCH AFFIL.:_____ WHERE:_____
  FATHER:_____   BUR.:_____
  OTHER HUSBANDS:_____ MOTHER:_____

                  CHILDREN

1 :JOE DOE   BORN:1 JAN 1925   MARR.:6 AUG '50 DIED:3 AUG '82
                  ROSEVILLE IL   CHICAGO IL   TOPEKA KA
                  SEX:M SPOUSE:HAZEL NUTT   BUR.:TOPEKA

2 :_____   BORN:_____   MARR.:_____ DIED:_____

                  SEX:_ SPOUSE:_____   BUR.:_____

ADDITIONAL REMARKS:
THIS FAMILY GROUP SHEET WAS PREPARED USING FGS 2.5 TO SHOW BOTH A COMPLETED AND
A BLANK WORK SHEET APPEAR. PREPARED 3 AUG 1984

Plate 11. Byteware Family Group Sheet

of text with a remote computer will probably find 300 bps (about 30 characters per second) adequate. Modems limited to 300 bps usually cost less than those which transmit at higher speeds. People who transfer large amounts of text will find communicating at 1200 bps (about 120 cps) faster and therefore less costly, especially if a long-distance call is involved.[17]

This is all we will say about the hardware for telecommunications. Software for computer linking will come up later.

PRICE MAY NOT TELL THE STORY

As we end our computer hardware chapter, we want to make another comment concerning computer costs (which can now be appreciated because you know more about computer hardware):

Some personal computers are advertised at bargain prices, while others are priced much higher. Upon closer investigation, the price differ-

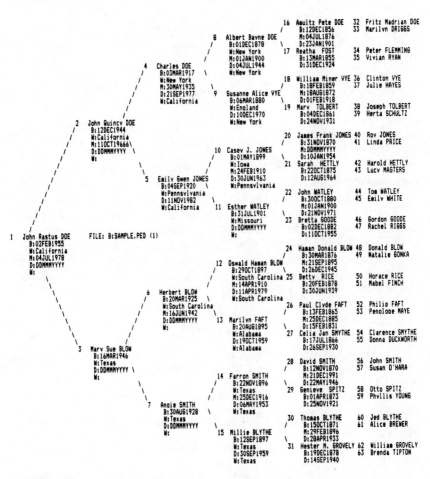

Plate 12. Personal Software *Family Reunion* Pedigree Chart

ence is often revealed to be based on the degree of completeness of the advertised computer. Typically, you can find two competing computer companies advertising in the same magazine; Computer A is priced at $1000 and Computer B sells for $2500. The differential might be this:

	Computer A	Computer B
Keyboard	included	included
Video display screen	extra	included
Memory	64K	128K
Disk drive #1	extra	included
Disk drive #2	extra	included
Printer (dot-matrix)	extra	included
Miscellaneous cables	extra	included

If both computers were sold with comparable components (including amount of computer memory—expressed in "K" or kilobytes), the price difference would not be $1500.

Computer B is reasonably configured and able to do many practical genealogy jobs. Computer A, as listed, would not work at all until and unless you bought most of the additional parts to bring it up to the component-equal of Computer B.

You may be buying a partial computer if you let prices blind you to the reasons behind the prices.

FOOTNOTES

1. Esther A. Anderson, "On Getting Involved with Computers, Some Guidelines for Genealogists," *National Genealogical Society Quarterly* 70, no. 3 (September 1982): 197.
2. Steve Gibson, "Stencils and Spray Paint," *Infoworld* 6, no. 30 (July 23, 1984): 43.
3. Terry Benson, "Micros: The 16-Bit Generation," *Interface Age* 7, no. 11 (November 1982): 86.
4. Chris DeVoney, *MS-DOS User's Guide* (Indianapolis: Que Corporation, 1984), p. 13.
5. Philip I. Nelson, "Journey to the Center of Your C-64," *Run* 1, no. 5 (May 1984): 64.
6. Chris DeVoney, *MS-DOS User's Guide* p. 17.
7. Al Shugart, "Storage," *PC World* (Special Edition, 1984), p. 82.
8. Ibid.
9. Chris DeVoney, *MS-DOS User's Guide*, p. 19.
10. Mitchell Waite and Michael Pardee, *Microcomputer Primer* (Indianapolis: Howard W. Sams & Co., 1976), p. 132.
11. Jim Bartimo, "The Incredible Shrinking Display," *Inforworld* 6, no. 28 (July 9, 1984): 42-43.
12. Bernard Horn, "Printers," *PC World* (Special Edition, 1984), p. 172.

13. Arthur Godman, *The Color-Coded Guide to Micro-Computers* (New York: Barnes & Noble Books Division of Harper & Row, 1983), p. 11.

14. Ronald John Donovan, "The Hard Facts, Part I," *The Writer's Guide to Word Processing* (Cincinnati, Ohio: Writer's Digest, 1984), p. 16.

15. Ronald John Donovan, "The Hard Facts, Part II," *The Writer's Guide to Word Processing* (Cincinnati, Ohio: Writer's Digest, 1984), p. 20.

16. Ibid., p. 19.

17. Dennis Hayes, "Modems," *PC World* (Special Edition, 1984), p. 134.

CHAPTER 5

What Computer Software Does for You—and How

H ardware is what you see. It's the machinery. When you get your computer home and turn it on, what happens? Without software, very little. As a number of writers have noted, computers without software make excellent doorstops.

Software can be divided into three general types: system software, applications software, and programming languages. We'll discuss all three briefly.

PROGRAMMING LANGUAGES

Our discussion of programming languages will be the briefest. It is enough to say that there are any number of languages available for you to program with if you eventually decide you want to. And, there are countless books that explain these languages to you and teach you how to use them. These languages are important because they allow a program writer to "talk" to the computer's central processing unit in language it understands. Some commonly used languages include BASIC (for Beginners All-Purpose Symbolic Instruction Code), FORTRAN, Pascal, and COBOL. Most computers have a BASIC language adapted for use with the system, and often—but not always—it is included as a part of the system you purchase (along with an "operating system"). The other languages mentioned are for specialized tasks and usually are more difficult to learn. Chances are good that if you "get into" computing, you'll end up learning to program in some variation of BASIC. A sound reason for doing so is that it allows you to modify some simple "off-the-shelf" programs to make them more suitable for genealogy uses. Learning to program is not all that difficult, but it does take some time to master—especially if you want programs to interact with disk files. Consider this (but not too deeply): Most schoolchildren today have at least a passing knowledge of BASIC; many are quite proficient with it.

SYSTEM SOFTWARE

No matter what type of computer you choose, you will need system software to make it run. This is the tool that tells your computer how to operate. In fact, it is usually called the "operating system" or "disk operating system" because that's what it does—it tells your computer how to operate its disk drives, its memory, its video display, or its printer. When you turn your computer on, the system software "boots" into memory—either automatically or after the operator types in a predesignated code (depending on the computer). Once that operation is complete, your computer is ready to go to work for you.

SYSTEM SOFTWARE

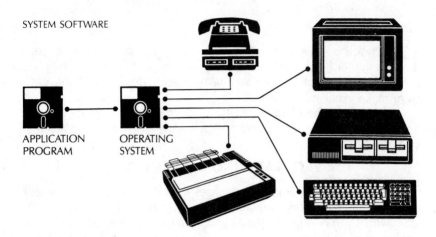

APPLICATION   OPERATING
PROGRAM   SYSTEM

System software is extremely important to you, because it largely determines what applications programs will run on your particular computer. An operating system that is limited to a few computers isn't apt to attract software writers or publishers to the extent that more popular ones do. Software producers usually aim their products at the larger markets. Since applications programs must be written to be compatible with a specific operating system, you will be limited in the choices available to you if you use a less popular system.

Also, operating systems are a key to whether or not you can swap the programs you create with others. In other words, they determine the "transportability" of other software.

DISK OPERATING SYSTEMS

In today's computer world, a few operating systems stand out because of their acceptance by a large number of computer manufacturers and ultimate consumers. Some of these are: CP/M, MS-DOS, TRS-DOS, and Apple DOS. We'll discuss each, not necessarily to evaluate their pros and cons, but to give you a working knowledge of them.

Rick Cook's "Special Report—Operating Systems," *Popular Computing* 3, no. 10 (August 1984) provides the basis for the following discussion of several disk operating systems. His excellent overview of operating systems is worth your examination of the full article from which we draw the following:

CP/M (Control Program/Microprocessors), developed by Digital Research, became the standard for most 8-bit computers other than the Apple or the TRS-80. It was the first operating system not designed specifically for one brand of computer and is the most widely used. Versions were licensed by Digital for most 8080/8085 or Z80 computers, and programs can be relatively easily changed to meet the specific requirements of various computers. The key to this is what is called the "BIOS"– the "basic input-output system." One of the operating system's creators isolated all of those elements which related specifically to a particular computer into one module. Everything else was the same, regardless of which computer was being used. This meant that changing the system from one machine to another involved modifying only one part of the operating system. Even machines that have long been off the market remain useful because of the great quantity and range of applications programs available for CP/M computers. CP/M, however, is not the most "user friendly" of the operating systems. Its commands and utilities – and its documentation – are complex and require more-than-passing study. Many people have been using CP/M for years, in fact, and still are learning its intricacies. (The good news is that most of us have little need for many of the commands and utilities.) Also, with some commands, CP/M can be "unforgiving." Type in the wrong thing and hours of work can go down the drain – a problem not necessarily unique to CP/M.

MS-DOS was developed by MicroSoft for the IBM PC and is becoming for 16-bit computers what CP/M is for 8-bit computers. Many of the MS-DOS commands and utilities are an outgrowth of CP/M, and the systems operate in much the same way. IBM also has its own DOS, which is similar to MS-DOS, and there is a version of CP/M (CP/M-86) for the PC and compatible machines. Generally speaking, most MS-DOS applications programs written for the IBM PC will run on most "IBM compatibles." But this is not always true. Before buying costly programs, make certain they will run on your compatible. And, while IBM originally deliberately made it easy for software writers to develop programs for its PC so as to give users a wider choice (and expand its market), industry magazines have been speculating that IBM may be pulling away from that philosophy. In the long run, as the industry giant increases its share of the computer market, it may elect to develop its own software and make it harder for others to do so, and harder for the compatibles to run it.

Apple DOS is the system used in the Apple II and compatible machines. The Apple uses the 6502 microprocessor, and CP/M is based on the 8080/8085 or Z80 chip, so the Apple originally could not use many of the more business-oriented CP/M programs. However, a number of companies designed expansion boards for the Apple that, in effect, turn it into an 8080 machine that can use CP/M. Apple Computer's newer machines, Macintosh and Lisa, use operating systems that are extremely complex (and "proprietary": other computers can't use them). This complexity, however, makes these systems exceptionally easy to use. The down side is that program writers shy away from their complexities and Macintosh owners are complaining about the lack of software.

TRS-DOS (for Tandy Radio Shack Disk Operating System) originally was designed by Tandy for the TRS-80 Model I. It since has undergone several revisions and upgrades as hardware changed or consumer needs dictated. TRS-DOS also spawned a number of "bigger and better" versions, such as DOSPLUS or NEWDOS, each designed to do something that the original could not do or to do things more efficiently. The result is that TRS-DOS and its run-alikes have a wide variety of commands and utilities and are relatively easy to learn and use. The main drawback of TRS-DOS and the others is that they are confined to Tandy-made machines. Although there are many programs available for the TRS-80, sometimes other software producers might decide not to go to the expense of translating their programs so they can operate with TRS-DOS. It is worth noting that the TRS-80 Model 4 now has its own version of CP/M as well as TRS-DOS, thus providing a wider array of available software and perhaps signaling declining use of TRS-DOS.

SOFTWARE CONSIDERATIONS IN HARDWARE SELECTION

An important consideration in the selection of a computer is whether it will run the applications programs you most desire. The DOS will undoubtedly have a bearing on your selection, because it can determine which programs will work on your machine. It may not be the wisest choice, however, to decide which hardware and DOS to buy solely because they are the ones which will run that one piece of software you especially want. Think it over—there may be other things you'll want to do with your computer later on. And there is no guarantee that a particular operating system will be "supported" by software companies down the road.

APPLICATIONS PROGRAMS

Your genealogy program, your word processing program, your programs for balancing a checkbook or playing a game , all are "applications programs." When people talk about software, most probably they are talking about applications programs—the programs that combine with programming languages and systems programs to tell the computer what you want it to do.

One of the things you likely most want your computer to do is to help you manage your genealogy records. Of the thousands of programs in existence today, about fifty of them are specifically designed to keep genealogical records. Contrast that with figures from 1981, when there were only seven genealogical programs on the market. What this means is that as more and more people start using computers for genealogy, more and more programs will be developed – and those currently on the market will become better and better.

The biggest problem when you buy applications software is knowing precisely what it is you are buying. In the software world, there is no such thing as a "ten-day free trial." The reason? There is as yet no guaranteed way of preventing a disk from being copied. In fact, a program's utility is often based on the fact that you can copy it to "work disks" for various uses. So, in order to take home a program, you have to buy it. (If you didn't, then it would be relatively easy to copy it onto other disks, return the original, and – presto! –"free" software.) And often you have to buy software without knowing for certain if it will do the job you want it to – or even if it will work on your machine.

InfoWorld's Dan Post recently encapsuled the problem in an editorial:

> Selecting and using software is not – and probably never will be – as routine as shopping for other consumer goods or business tools. When considering most products for purchase, you can tell by reading the label, examining it, or trying it out whether it will suit your needs. With computer software, very little can be ascertained from a product name. All are catchy, few are descriptive. You can't make judgments simply by handling the package . . . . The purchaser must determine precisely the criteria to be met, choose the application package that will meet it . . . , find the system software that will accept the application – *then* select the hardware that will accommodate both. This takes conscientious research. There are no shortcuts.[1]

There's no doubt that the computer you might buy today is appreciably better than it was when the first genealogist ventured to try one. The same can be said for the software. But none of the choices you will have to make will be easy, and "there are no shortcuts."

Fortunately for the genealogist, in addition to a number of excellent genealogy programs now on the market, there are other well-accepted "generic" applications programs. These programs, not designed for any specific business or hobby, can be adapted to a variety of tasks.

In fact, if you examine genealogy application software, you will find it is similar in many respects to database management software and word processing software. Your family records are a database, and any freestyle writing (genealogy research notes, source documentation, biographic sketches) is words being processed. A genealogy program is nothing more than a special case of a database management (DBM) or word processing (WP) program.

Before taking a look at some specific genealogy programs, let's examine how database management, word processing, and other programs can be applied to genealogy.

DATABASE MANAGEMENT SYSTEMS

A "database" is simply a collection of records. For the genealogist, it might be all of the vital statistics – births, deaths, marriages – collected over the years. In their present form – in written or typed family group sheets, charts, or lists – they are useful but cumbersome. Finding a particular record depends on an accurate filing system or your memory. Source material can get mislaid, even specific records misfiled and "lost forever" – and duplications abound.

MAILING LIST PROGRAMS

One common database management computer program is a system for managing mailing lists. A typical "file" might be a list of customers for a particular product. The information on each customer is a "record" within that file. The customer's name, his company, telephone number, street address, city, state, zipcode, and other specific information (type of business, last purchase date, account status, and so on) are all "fields" within that record.

Once the file is developed, the computer user can add or delete records or update specific fields. He or she can also list the records, sort them alphabetically or numerically by a specific field (name, city, zipcode), produce sublists (all customers with no purchases since July), print all or defined parts of the file on paper or labels, according to need. The data can be viewed on the system monitor or printed out – or even transmitted by phone to another computer.

If one of your genealogy uses for a computer is maintaining the mailing list for your family association, a program such as the one described would be extremely useful to you. But take this relatively simple program one step further. Suppose you had a program that would do all of those things, but instead of having fields called "company," "address," and so on, you could change them so they were titled "place of birth," "date of birth," or "spouse." Now you have the beginnings of a genealogy manager instead of a mailing list manager. (No doubt the first genealogy programs for microcomputers were adapted by some clever persons from a DBM program such as a mailing list.) Then imagine all your written or typed genealogy records filed away in such a "manager," where any piece of the information could be viewed or printed with a few keystrokes!

ALL-PURPOSE FILE MANAGEMENT PROGRAMS

An all-purpose DBM system is similar to a mailing list program, but more flexible. It is "user defined"–that is, the user is the one who determines in advance what the records and fields will be and how many characters will be allowed in each.

The program is written in such a way that the file you are managing can be created as an address file (precluding the need for a special mailing list program), a family records file, an inventory of phonograph records or a repair shop parts inventory.

If you wanted to create a relatively simple genealogy file, you likely would create fields for surname, first name, middle name, date of birth, place of birth, date of death, place of death, date of marriage, place of marriage, spouse surname, spouse given name(s), parent and notes. The more powerful the computer and the DBM, the more records that can be managed, the more fields that can be included, and the longer these fields can be.

A difficult aspect, at least for most of us, is deciding in advance the number and type of fields and the length of each. Almost all DBM programs require this, since the computer needs to have this information in order to allocate memory and disk space and to tell it precisely where to find the particular field you are searching for. With some programs, once you establish the fields and their lengths, you are stuck with them. Trying to change them might destroy your entire database. Other programs will allow you, for instance, to create a new file with different fields and lengths and then transfer data from your previous file to this new file. In either case, careful thought needs to be given to the initial creation of the file and its parameters.

Some DBMs also restrict the number of "key" fields. In these, you must designate a few, perhaps five, fields in advance, and you can search and sort only on those fields. Again, this requires you to carefully consider how you will be using your database before designating the "keys." Newer, more powerful programs might allow any field to be searched or sorted, eliminating this problem.

ALL-PURPOSE RELATIONAL DATABASE MANAGERS

Most database managers for microcomputers are called "relational" because they allow the user to set up relationships between bits of information in the file. Some even allow you to relate information between several files. The capability to relate one piece of information to another is what makes a DBM a useful genealogical tool. The trick is in knowing what to tell the computer so that it will "relate" your bits of information in a way that is useful to you.

Note that "relational," in this sense, does not mean that you can determine genealogical relationships between given individuals in a database created with a DBM program (without an elaborate coding method or a "subprogram"). However, programs specifically developed for genealogy purposes can show genealogical relationships. We will describe such "genealogy software" later.

Another critical feature of a DBM is its reporting capability. Some managers allow you to design report forms quickly and easily; others practically require you to learn a new computer language before you can get information in a usable form.

A DBM can be a wonderful tool—once you get all your information in it. Unfortunately, setting up the system to do all you want and then entering all your data is a time-consuming task. Be prepared for several false starts (it's a good idea to test your structure with only a few records before embarking on entering all your data), and be prepared for long, boring hours of data entry (which is true no matter what kind of program you use for genealogy). Also be aware that no matter how fantastically a particular database manager has performed with your stamp collection or your neighbor's phonograph collection, genealogy databases are the most complex of databases, bar none. And as the file grows larger and larger, the indexes come out more and more slowly.

Be warned that one of the "diseases" commonly contracted by computer users is manifested by a complete loss of tolerance for "slowness." Even if it used to take you days to create and type an index for your files, you'll find yourself irritated when your computer takes as long as twenty minutes to do the same job. This disease gets progressively worse. One computer user decided to scrap his "old" machine in favor of a faster one. He was quite pleased with the result, although several thousand dollars poorer. A colleague later calculated, using manufacturers' performance standards, that if our afflicted soul used his new computer every hour of every working day for his normal tasks, by the end of the day the new "faster" computer would have saved him about five minutes! The reason for this, briefly, is that the computer's central processing unit can work infinitely faster than the peripherals often brought into use.

You'll find many genealogists who swear by using generic database managers for their record keeping, but it takes more artistry than you might suspect to operate them. Many require that you learn a whole new lexicon of commands or a new programming language to operate them. Few of them are "menu driven" (meaning that the precise task you want done can be selected from a list of options), and those that are might lack the flexibility you want. Remember, too, that a database manager capable of handling a sizable genealogy database is going to be expensive—usually more than five hundred dollars.

All this is not intended to tell you not to buy and use a generic database manager. We just wanted you to be aware that they do have their drawbacks (as do other types of programs you can use to keep your genealogy records).

WORD PROCESSING SOFTWARE

The most wonderous — and often the most useful and relied upon — program for a genealogist with a microprocessor is a word processing program. Besides making your computer the smartest typewriter in the world, a WP program acquaints you with file handling and other features of your system.

Files created by a WP program are usually called "text files," as opposed to the "data files" created by DBM programs. The beauty of WP files is that they require no elaborate planning or setting up in advance. Just enter your data in free form, using as many or as few words as needed to tell the story. Later, you can "magically" combine your files, rearrange them, change their contents or formats, search them for any combination of letters or characters that you desire, print them, or refile them. You may even decide you want to change all occurrences of "December" in your file to "Dec." It can be done with only a few keystrokes.

WP files can be organized in almost any manner you wish, and this organization can be relatively easily changed. You can have boxes of diskettes labeled according to the information each contains. One disk might be the descendants of the progenitor of a particular branch of a family. Another might be your ancestors. Still another might have blank group sheets, pedigree charts, or research notes.

With a minimum of planning, you can create WP text files with enough uniformity to allow you to later extract (with a simple BASIC program) information needed for a name index or a list of birthdates. This information can later be sorted in alphabetical or numerical order by a special program, and can even be "plugged into" a database file.

Creating forms is especially easy with a word processor, as opposed to a typewriter. You can see the form on your screen and change the position of blanks or other features quickly and with no fuss. Contrast that with creating a similar form by trial and error on a typewriter. With a word processor, it takes minutes and the form can be adapted into a new form in minutes. With a typewriter, it takes hours (and a ream of paper!), and if you want a new form you have to start from scratch.

The forms you create can be stored on disk, then called up and filled in as you acquire information. Suppose the form is a family group sheet. Simply load the FORM (if that's the name you stored it under) from your disk, fill it in with the information on individual number 12345, name the file (H12345, for example, to indicate the person in the Hawn family with that number), and store it as a new file. A collection of these family group sheets could be printed out, bound, and compiled into a family history.

Many genealogists use WP programs extensively rather than DBM programs because they are simple to operate and allow the user to enter information "free form" rather than in a structured manner. If you are more at ease "typing information" than "entering data," then you will appreciate the features of a word processing program. (Both of the authors still largely rely on WP systems to keep their genealogical records.)

For a genealogist, there are other important uses for a WP program. Writing letters, composing a biographical sketch, creating a family book narrative, making source documentation files, cross-referencing files, and transcribing research notes into more readable form are just a few.

An automatic by-product of a word processor is an electronic filing system. Each file created can be saved for later updating or printing. Keeping track of what is in each file and which files are on which disk can be a problem in itself—but one that can be overcome by creating another WP file with this information. Updated and printed after each work session, it can be tacked to the wall by your computer for easy reference.

Want a particular bit of information on a specific individual so you can respond to a letter? Easy. Locate which file the person is on, call up that file, tell the computer to find his or her name. Then use the editing function of your WP to extract the information you want for inclusion as a part of your letter or as an attachment.

A word processing program can be so valuable to a genealogist that when you select your computer you should make certain that it will support a decent WP program. With it you can write letters, address envelopes, create family group sheets and pedigree charts, organize indexes, and write books.

Because of its importance to you, a word processing program likely will be your first software purchase.

PICKING A WORD PROCESSOR

There are dozens—if not hundreds—of word processing programs on the market today. They range from pretty good to terrific. Even the worst of the lot will likely please you—but don't settle for so-so. To help you decide which program may be best for you and your computer, we have devised a series of questions you can ask about them.

A word processing program for which *yes* is the answer to all the following questions is truly "industrial strength" and easy to use. We recommend that you make your decision based on such an evaluation—and that you opt for overcapability (some features you think you might not need or use) rather than facing the prospect of "growing out" of a program and having to buy a new one later.

The questions below are assigned relative point strengths to help you decide which ones are more important in determining the ultimate value of the program.

A WORD PROCESSING PROGRAM ADEQUACY SCALE

(100) Does it run on your computer? No sense in buying a program that won't run on the computer you already own. Look at other WP programs.

(75) Does it run under the operating system you use for genealogy file maintenance? Some computers can run under several DOS; if the WP program runs with DOS "A" and your genealogy database is managed with software running under DOS "B," you won't be able to transfer genealogy files to your word processor or vice versa.

(100) Is the RAM memory of your computer big enough for this WP program? If the WP program is memory-hungry, it may consume your user memory so fully that there is no room remaining for anything but short documents. Add RAM if you can, or choose another program.

(100) Do you have the number of disk drives the WP program requires? DOS and the WP program ought to reside on one diskette, while your text files created with the WP program should be on diskettes you stick in a second drive. This is not only a good idea, it may be an expectation of the WP program developer—there may be no room left for your files if the DOS and WP programs fill a diskette. A two-drive system is necessary for word processing and for genealogy.

(50) Will it support your printer's features? Good printers can have boldface, underlining, subscripts, superscripts, proportional spacing, and type font changes. It would be a shame to use such a versatile printer with a WP program that cannot send signals to use those printer features.

(100) Does your video display have the required screen width? Eighty characters per line is a desirable, standard width for displayed characters. The WP program may be written for narrower or wider displays than your computer monitor's characters per line. Check the match of your screen to the WP expected width.

(10) Does the WP program show you how much usable memory remains while you are creating a text file? It is good to know how fast you are filling RAM memory. You can close out a file, save it, and start a new one at logical breaks if the WP program keeps you informed of memory remaining.

(10) Does the program tell you how many characters and/or pages you have in a file you are creating? The reverse of remaining-memory information, the WP program should also tell you how many characters and/or pages you have created any time you wish to know that.

(75) **Does the screen display keep up with fast typing?** It is maddening to know you hit an "e" and see the screen displaying a character you typed a second or two earlier. The screen ought to keep up, or else it is a WP program you will never be happy with.

(75) **Can you type quickly without losing characters?** This is not the same as the screen falling behind. One WP program was infamous for missing the letters you were typing while it was jumping down to the next line and moving to the left end of it. You shouldn't have to slow down just so the machine can catch every keystroke.

(25) **Can you change the width of the video display?** If you have an eighty-character line and are typing something that is going to be printed forty-five characters wide—such as a newsletter column—you ought to be able to see your file in that width while you are writing. A good WP program allows setting viewed line lengths to less than or greater than the normal eighty-character length. Longer lines will "wrap around," hanging the line end on the next line. Even so, you can see these or short lines as they will appear when printed and even while you are composing.

(50) **Can you program selected keys to trigger often-used words or phrases?** Programmable keys in a WP program let you designate certain letters or numbers on a keyboard to stand for longer character strings. You can strike such a key while holding down a "control key" to cause a repeatedly used word or phrase to be automatically typed for you. This is extremely helpful when, for instance, the genealogist has to repeat "Warsaw, Kosciusko County, Indiana" over and over in a family history.

(75) **Can you search text to locate a word?** Imagine having a multi-page file loaded and needing to insert a word way down in the text just after the occurrence of "Martin." If your WP program allows you to instantly leap to "Martin," you can get the insertion finished in a hurry.

(50) **Can you globally search to find each occurrence of a word?** If "Martin" occurs several times in your long file, you ought to be able to tap a key and jump to the next "Martin." This is a global find feature—finding every occurrence of a word or phrase if you must look for "the right spot."

(50) **Can you globally replace one word or phrase with another in every instance?** If you have used "Pallatine" five or six times in a document and then discover it should be spelled "Palatine," can you express something like Pallatine > Palatine and have all of the changes made with a command to "global replace?"

(50) Is the maximum document size sufficient? If you have little files that add up to a chapter and want to put them all together in one file, is the WP program capable of handling the combined file size?

(75) Can you save a file under another name? If you revise a draft of a saved file and then decide you want to keep the original *and* the revision, could you disk-save the new version under another name and then have a choice of either version later?

(100) Do you have control of margins, page length, and number of lines? Independent of the computer file's manner of composing, can you print the file in any of a variety of formats according to how you decide to set margins and other parameters such as double spacing?

(25) Can you automatically number the pages of a document? If a long document will print on several pages, can page numbers be made to print automatically on successive pages? Can you control where they appear—top center, top right, top left, bottom center, and so on?

(25) Can you justify the right-hand side of the type? The left ends of printed lines always line up unless you deliberately indent. Right-hand justification makes the right ends of lines line up, too. This is automatic if you choose to do it.

(25) Can you automically hyphenate? You can improve the appearance of printed copy by hyphenating words at line ends. When you have composed and edited a file, auto-hyphenation presents you the lines which can have their last words hyphenated.

(75) Can you elect to stop at page end to change paper or to continuously print? If you are feeding single sheets like stationery, the WP program can stop printing after each page so you can load the next sheet. If you have a long, multipage chart of document draft, you may want to load continuous-form paper and walk the dog while the printer keeps on until it finishes the document.

(75) Are the editing commands easy to use and easy to remember? Some WP programs require holding down some control key while striking another key in order to give a command to insert, delete, or otherwise edit a file. Other WP programs have very easy command-giving procedures—such as hitting "d" to delete and "s" to save. These mnemonic codes are easy to remember.

(50) Can you advance the cursor by character, word, sentence, line, and screen? The cursor ought to be easy to move by leaps to the end

of any unit of text: character, word, sentence, paragraph, or screenful —
and backwards in those increments, too.

(25) Can you look at a disk directory while in the word processor?
If while you are working on a text file you want to merge files, can you
call up the disk directory and look over the names of your stored files
without having to leave the WP program?

**(10) Can you look through another file from the disk while in the
word processor?** Suppose you are writing a letter and wish to see how
you said something in another letter. You should be able to depart from
your text, look at another file, and then return quickly to what you were
working on.

(75) Does the end of a line automatically word-wrap? On a typewriter, you hit a carriage return and line feed to move to the next line
on your typing paper. A WP program should give you automatic line feeds
and carriage returns without your having to worry about word divisions.
The sentence continues on the next line; you will not need to specify a
carriage return and line feed except at paragraph ends.

(10) Can you automatically center headings or paragraphs? You
should be able to decide the line lengths and let the WP program center
the copy.

(75) Do you have full screen editing (cursor roving)? A WP program
should allow you to spot a typographical error a few lines back and let
you move the cursor to it for deleting an error, inserting the right spelling, or "overwriting" a word with the right word.

**(50) Are there commands to go instantly to top, bottom, or any
place?** Even if you can tap arrow keys to move your cursor up, down, right,
or left, you should be able to jump to top of file, end of file, next screen,
last screen, left end of a line, right end of a line, and to other locations
in your text file with a swift command.

**(100) Can you delete a character, word, sentence, line, paragraph,
block, or whole file?** Text amounts ought to swiftly disappear at your wish
and, if you goof, the deleted material should reappear so you can redo
it correctly.

(100) Can you insert a character, word, paragraph, or block of text?
You should be able to move the rest of your text file out of the way so
you can make these inserts. You should also be able to mark the begin-

ning and end of a stretch of text and have it inserted into a new location within the file.

(**75**) **Can you move and copy blocks of text?** The block of text might be something you want to repeat in your text file. This is a "copy block" action. Block moving is the feature you need for reorganization of something you have drafted.

(**75**) **Can you insert or append another file?** Eventually, little files can be brought together to form the whole stretch of prose by "appending" one file to another or inserting a disk-saved file in the middle of a text file you are creating.

(**10**) **Can you create automatic headers and footers?** It is nice to label each page with the document name or chapter title. These are called "headers" when they appear at page tops and "footers" if at the bottom.

(**10**) **Are there on-line helps?** When you are typing with your word processor and decide you want to do some editing but have forgotten the commands, an "on-line" help file can be invoked to quickly show you the commands and what they do.

(**10**) **Can you print a range of pages as opposed to a whole file?** Perhaps you only want another copy of page 3 of a document and not the whole file. Can you print only designated portions of a document?

(**10**) **Can you abort printing?** There will come a time when you do not like the margin settings or you need to change the printer ribbon. The print process should have a quick-abort routine to allow going back to square one in printer setup.

(**25**) **Can you merge address files with text files?** A WP program feature called "mail merge" might have an address file for a group and cause that file to be merged with the text file which contains a form letter. This gives you an "inside address" at the top of each letter.

INTEGRATED USAGE

Each kind of software program should do very well the kinds of things it is specifically intended to do. But this does not mean that different programs cannot work as complementary tools that take over the "product" (family data, for instance) at different times or for different work aspects. A typical integration of software packages in genealogy computing occurs when you have formed the family records with a genealogy program and have put in those records the footnote citations without having entered the actual footnotes. For example, a genealogy program might provide room for a paragraph or more of source documentation or brief comments on a person's life (for example, Will Book A, page 45, county clerk's office, Woodstock, Shenandoah County, Virginia, or served as a private in the 35th Infantry Division under Captain Farmer at Verdun Battle in WWI). Suppose you have the text of that will in your genealogy research copy of the will. Or you may have used your WP program to computer-file the text of the will and store it as file "W423" on a diskette; the file may have a cross-reference to the records for which the will is an information source. Your file W423 is a word processing text file that starts out with something like this: "Records 45, 320, 780, 1034, and 1121 . . . . " The long passages describing the possessions and bequests of a family member probably won't fit directly into the genealogy program. Use your word processing program to create complementary and supplementary text files. They can be called up and printed under WP program control kind of best use most genealogists practice when they own both kinds of programs for genealogical records management. Often researchers have biographical sketches that run for many pages, diaries that are small books in themselves, or company rosters of all those other men who fought at Verdun alongside an ancestor. Those are wordy, free-wheeling narratives and descriptions that ought to be stored in word processing files rather than within other genealogy records.

You ought not to try pounding square pegs into round computer-program holes. While your genealogy records program is written to handle distinct information pieces (dates, places, names, and so on) and may do that very well, it is your WP program that can meet your needs for variable length, very long, and freestyle written text or special forms. While your computer hardware may handle any of several kinds of software well, the software should be suited to the jobs you are doing and the jobs the programmer intended it to do.

GRAPHICS SOFTWARE

Drawing maps of family property (for example, showing the outline of an old family farm described in a will by poles and chains and saplings on a rocky knoll) is a genealogical use of graphics; so is computer-drawing a family crest. But the cost and complexity of computer graphics relegates this kind of software to the advanced-uses category.

Roots II by Commsoft, Inc., is genealogy software that has graphics capability as an adjunct to the usual family data management and reports generating. You can even store pictures in a computer with this capability.

The Apple MacIntosh is a terrific graphics computer, and its best feature is the ability to send the video displayed pictures you draw to the printer. You can have illustrations in your family history book with this kind of feature. But *any* graphics making requires special peripherals and circuit boards and as much artistic talent as drawing on paper. To prepare *one* graphics display on a computer is likely to take about 100 times the amount of time it would take you to draw the same thing on paper. We recommend you draw your maps, crests, and other graphics on paper and not on your computer. Besides, graphics data take an awful lot of computer and disk memory. Are they worth computerizing?

TELECOMMUNICATIONS SOFTWARE

When we were covering computer hardware we included the modem — the phone coupling device which permits you to transfer family data from your computer to another or vice versa. A modem is a piece of hardware. As you have learned, the computer and peripheral hardware require software to make them work. Similarly, communications software is needed to make the modem work.

With smart-terminal software, you can "download" programs and files from the computer you are remotely operating; it is the *host* computer. You can also "upload" programs from your smart-terminal (your personal computer) to that remotely located other computer and store them in that distantly located computer's external memory (disk files). The files you download can be sent to your own computer's external memory device during the link-up. When you end your session, those files (programs or family data files) are in your computer and you can subsequently use them without further contact with the host computer. Similarly, when the phone-link is ended, the host computer you have been operating possesses disk copies of your files or transmitted software.

With modems and the accompanying software, any two genealogists can swap files by phone. Smart-terminal software can run as high in price as $200; $150 is not a surprising price. There are, however, simple "public domain" (free) programs for some modems and operating systems.

As with the modem, telecommunications software is something you can defer until later (when you are ready to swap family files with someone). One day we will all be downloading data from master computers containing genealogical databases. We will also be contributing our own data to such central file systems. This is when research will be given a new dimension because of genealogical computing.

In addition to files and programs, messages can be telecommunicated by modem and communications software:

> Electronic mail . . . is a method of electronically transmitting a message from a person at one computer to one at another computer, via a routing mechanism contained in a central or "host" com-

puter . . . . Most electronic mail messages do not take the place of old-fashioned letters – rather, they replace short telephone calls . . . . Instead of trying to call an associate, one can send a message to his or her electronic mailbox. The message is immediately available to the other person, who can read it when convenient and reply by the same means. It also allows one to receive messages while away.[2]

THINGS YOU CAN DO
WHEN NOT DOING GENEALOGY

You are wasting computer capability if you do not use a genealogy computer for things other than genealogy when not doing your genealogy work.

Playing computer games may seem a most trivial other use for your computer. Think twice about that. Almost all huge computers (even Pentagon computers) have computer games squirreled away somewhere. Playing games on an expensive business computer may be an improper use and an expense to taxpayers, but it is also the ingredient that tantalizes some nonexperts to learn more about computers – giving commands to access the game, interacting with the computer to play the game, and so on. By a process close to osmosis, one who plays computer games is learning a lot more about computers and computing than he or she consciously knows. Most educational programs for children are game styled. Shooting the grinch-monster by spelling words correctly on the keyboard or finding the picture of a telephone in a maze you must follow with a light-pen are the essence of entry-level computer uses (for children five to ten years old). Don't overlook the learning as well as enjoyment of owning a few computer games if you have a computer. (When grandchildren come to visit, they *expect* to find computer games if you own a computer.)

Since a genealogy computer and its peripherals will have most of the characteristics found on educational or business computers, the other uses to which you can put your idle computer are as varied as there are applications programs in those fields. Consult your local computer store, pick up a handful of computer magazines at the drugstore, and browse the now-bulging sections of bookstores to find what other computer uses you can implement when genealogy files have been computer-stored, or when you are simply weary of pounding in family data from your boxes of records.

Your nongenealogist friends and fellow members of a local computer club are good sources of help in finding computer uses in fields beyond genealogy. You can write letters or even novels with your word processing software. Running a small home business (the bookkeeping, transactions processing, payroll, mailing labels, and so on) is simplified if you use your computer to substitute for labor (yours or that of hirelings).

Use your imagination. The more you use a computer for other things, the less your genealogy computer costs you! You can rationalize the expense by distributing it over other uses.

If you do plan to engage in nongenealogical uses, you will need to consider the hardware and software requirements of those other uses. However, those will be relatively inexpensive requirements that should need only minor add-ons; your genealogy computer *is* a general purpose computer. It is the usage you make of it (through the applications programs you choose and the special input/output devices you add as peripherals) that gives a computer its personality. Changing its nature is as simple as swapping disks and "rebooting" (bringing other software into your RAM memory).

FOOTNOTES

1. Dan Post, "Editorial," *Interface Age* 7, no. 11 (November 1982): 6.
2. "What Is Electronic Mail," *Infoworld* 6, no. 27 (July 2, 1984): 29.

CHAPTER 6

Picking Genealogy Software

A genealogy program is written to cause the computer to do specific things (such as alphabetizing the family members and listing them with the computer's printer). When several related jobs are involved (entering, changing, searching, and linking your family as well as alphabetizing it), each job is programmed as a *routine*. Collectively, these routines (which may be programs themselves) are called "a genealogy program" or "genealogy system." One might buy a genealogy program that does one job or a few useful jobs. The jobs performed by such programs and the associated computer equipment might be done very well, or done poorly, or done differently from the way you would like to have them done. (For example, the program might cause the computer to vary from your own preferred way of expressing dates of events. Perhaps the program forces you to express a date as "1912/05/16" while your preference is for "16 May 1912" as a format.)

Programs are the creative-writing product of an author (a programmer) just as this book is the product of Andereck and Pence. Computer program or book, the story goes the way the author wrote it; take it or leave it. Just as we put down books that quickly prove unsatisfying, we can reject computer programs that don't do genealogy jobs the way we want, don't do all the jobs we want, or do poorly the jobs we want done.

Besides following the author's perception of what jobs are to be done and how, programs are written to fit a medium. That medium is a specific kind of computer with certain capabilities and limitations. Just as a motion picture film will not run on a videotape player (and vice versa), distinctions between computer programs might make them run only on one kind of computer. And just as books can become movies or television programs (by adaptations to those media), computer programs can be adapted to run on any of several kinds of computers. However, successful transformation of a computer program to versions that run on any computer a genealogist might buy is unlikely. For example, the *Personal Ancestral File* genealogy software is "too big" to run on a lot of computers. It and some other programs are so full of instructions that they require big-memory computers of the kind for which the program was written. If its size is not restrictive, a program might be unusable in a given computer because it is written in a language (or dialect of a language) that is "foreign" to the computer. Programs must give instructions to a computer in exactly the language variant for which the computer was designed.

You can appreciate how languages used in speaking or writing can "lose something in translation" to foreign languages; computer programs can be rewritten to run on a variety of computers with varying degrees of success.

Rather than detailing further the reasons you cannot blithely buy a genealogy program and use it on any computer you might buy, we will simply declare that computer programs must be matched to computers for which they were written. Obviously, the more customized a program is to a given computer's unique characteristics, the less broadly it can be marketed and used. Genealogy is a small marketplace compared to the education, business, or games markets. Though there are half-a-hundred genealogy programs currently being sold, you have to match each to the jobs you want done and to the computer on which it will run.

Genealogy software is getting better all the time. New programs are being introduced almost monthly—and some programs are withdrawn from sale every few months. This is as dynamic a marketplace as that of other software. You have to keep track of the changes.

Genealogical Computing (P.O. Box 2367, Fairfax, VA 22032 703-978-3532), publishes a directory to genealogy software in each bimonthly issue. At the end of this chapter you will find a copy of a recently published directory. You can obtain manuals, demo disks, brochures, and printout specimens—often at little or no cost—from various genealogy software sources. Inquire directly from the sources listed in the directory.

A genealogy program is a specially written database management program. Whereas other managers of databases are interested in auto-part inventories, mailing lists, stamp collections, personnel records, or membership records, *you* are interested in family record database building and managing. You might buy a database management program and adapt it to managing family records. But genealogy files have management requirements far more complex (linking all family members is complex!) than most small-business database requirements. No computer software or hardware salesman will grasp genealogical requirements without having a genealogy background; almost always, the requirements are underestimated and understood only superficially.

Any pedestrian programmer can write data entry, data change, data storing, data finding, and data display programs. Few are competent enough in programming *and* genealogy to link individuals by bloodline or marriage bonds. The ways in which genealogy database programs differ from other databases are not many—but they are significant.

If you could study the fifty-plus genealogy programs found in the directory at the end of this chapter you could see the variance they display in programmer competencies, program adequacy, and value for dollars spent.

The practical alternative to trying out all of the many genealogy programs being sold is to measure any you might consider buying against an "adequacy yardstick." We have tried our hand at creating such a yardstick, which we call a "scale of adequacy."

So many features are equally important that we can't list them in order of importance. Instead, we have weighted each test of adequacy with a point value. The items can be answered yes or no. If the answer is an unconditional yes, award the genealogy program all the points we have indicated as that test item's weight. If the answer is a qualified yes, knock off a few points. And, if the answer is no, the points earned in that test of adequacy would be zero. To our knowledge, no program on the market could earn all the possible points by having unqualified yes answers for each test question. Apply the scale to several alternative programs and pick the one which earns the highest number of points. (You might even photocopy the pages of the following scale and send the copies to vendors with a request that they rate themselves on items you mark.)

Note that some adequacy test questions are critical — so much so that a zero there should outweigh all other points. An example of such a question is, "Does this program run on your computer?" If the answer is no, nothing else matters. We have given 100 as the weight for this and certain other critical test items. Special features of a more optional nature are low in weight so that they have only a nominal effect on the total score.

A GENEALOGY PROGRAM ADEQUACY SCALE

(100) Will the program work on your computer (assuming you have one)? Many genealogy programs are written for a specific model of a specific computer brand. Is the program one that runs on your computer?

(100) Does the amount of required RAM match your computer's memory size? Some program modules are so memory-hogging that a computer having the minimal amount of RAM may be too small to hold even a program that was written to run on that computer. Buy more memory chips or choose another program.

(100) Does the number of disk drives required match your computer's drives? Two disk drives — not one, and not three or four — is the par requirement for the genealogy or business software course. Typical software must have a disk drive dedicated to the program and operating system and another into which you can put family data disks.

(50) **Is the disk operating system required the same as your computer's?** Perhaps a program will run on an Apple IIe computer but not under AppleDOS; must you buy a special circuit board and CP/M DOS to use this program on your Apple computer? The DOS difference may require changing DOS when you run this program.

(50) **Is the disk operating system the same one you use with your word processing software?** Following the previous point, if you run a word processing program for some family files under AppleDOS and your genealogy program under CP/M, you won't be able to flow data files from the genealogy program to the word processing program. Stay with one kind of DOS for all your genealogy-related programs.

(50) **Does the program require use of a printer which is like your printer?** You may find a genealogy program that is incapable of creating a family group sheet or pedigree chart in an 80-character line printout. You might have to buy another printer to handle 132-character lines. Since genealogy reports and charts frequently have lots of data crammed into classical formats, you are likely to need a dot-matrix printer for the chart work and a letter-quality printer for correspondence or book preparation.

(20) **Is it easy to understand the instructions in the user manual?** User manuals or "documentation" are usually after-programming products that have far too little thought and effort put into their preparation. Also, good programmers are not always good teachers. The instructions are at least as important as the program. Be severe in judging them.

(50) **Does the program vendor give buyers good after-sale assistance?** Although you are buying software rather than consultation or training in the purchase price, you should expect follow-up help in getting started or deciphering bad user-manual instructions. Check the seller's reputation for reasonable "hand holding," problem solving, and advice.

(20) **Do many other genealogists use this program?** If the vendor is unwilling to tell you how many other genealogists have bought this software, be wary. Either it is new and probably not wrung out by extensive use in big-family handling, or no one else has found that the program suits his needs. Something new may be the best yet, but you don't want to be a "test pilot" for it.

(50) **Can this program handle an unlimited-size family?** There is no reason a genealogy program or computer has to restrict your family size to 150, 1000, or 5000 members in a file. It is the programmer's choice if a file-size limit occurs. There is no good excuse for diminishing the amount and kind of family data you keep – although "it runs faster" or "you don't have to swap disks" are the kinds of excuses you will get from some vendors.

(50) **Do you consider the things the program does to be genealogically adequate and genealogically sound?** You are the authority in this instance. It is your records system, and no one but you should decide if the fields, field lengths, manner of expressing data, and style of printouts are acceptable.

(10) **Is it easy to make backup copies of the program disks?** You buy one disk copy of the program. Any of many things can destroy its usability – including power outages while computing, or your dog chewing on it. Can you make backup copies on other diskettes, or must you buy a replacement? Is the process of making backups clearly explained and reasonably easy?

(10) **Is it easy to create data disks and safety backups of data disks?** Data disks are the ones on which your family records will reside. Laboriously typing into the computer everything that is in your family files is hard work. Can you prepare diskettes for family data easily, and can you quickly make disk copies to keep at the office, in the neighbor's house, or in other safe places? You won't want to redo days and weeks of data entry!

(10) **Does the program vendor create utility programs that add ways you can massage the created files?** Utility programs might include calculating the average lifespan of each family line or showing the relationship between any two family members in your file. Your vendor ought to be as interested in genealogy as you are and ready to grow with your needs.

(50) **Does the program vendor promise to provide error fixes, upgrades, and additional program features at nominal or no cost?** Watch out for "warranty notices" that say, in effect, you have no recourse if the program bombs, harms your computer, offends your sensibilities, or otherwise is a problem. Unless there is a specific statement of intention that assures you that bugs will be fixed, new features will be forthcoming, and revised versions will be made compatible with the version you bought, you may find yourself out on a limb.

(50) **Have you seen and liked specimens of charts and indexes and reports generated by the program?** Since you are probably going to buy the software without running it yourself, at least look at the computer-produced printed products that result from using the program. See them *all*, and know what the program produces, because computer output is the bottom line of data entry and data maintenance.

(10) Do you know someone who knows the program and will help you when you have a problem? If at all possible, line up a person who is willing to teach you, solve problems with you, and otherwise support you in the likely event that your hardware salesman and software vendor will be too busy or unwilling to help you.

(50) Can you add footnotes and short freestyle comments for any field and in any record? Every record should have room for proof of facts and other small commentaries, even if a life story won't fit in the computer records. A method of citing footnotes and entering footnotes should be present in a good program.

(10) Is there a way to integrate files made with your word processing program with files from this program? Although the genealogy program may limit you to citing sources rather than reciting the text of a source document, it should be able to take files that were made by the word-processing program and stick them in between group sheets and pedigree charts made by the genealogy program.

(10) Are there quick-entry routines that allow abbreviations of long and repetitious place names and character strings? You are going to have to copy all your family files into a computer through the keyboard, character by character. If you have many same-place references for birth, christening, marriage, death, burial, and/or residence, you'll appreciate being able to create an abbreviation file that can automatically enter "Minneapolis, Hennepin County, Minnesota" in response to your hitting something like "#M".

(10) Will the program run on any other model of computer than the one for which you bought it? Over the long haul—and genealogy is a long-haul pastime—you are likely to change computers. Will the genealogy program and family files transfer? If possible, buy software that is "transportable" from one to another kind of computer.

(10) Does the program vendor supply user names for you to check user satisfaction? Perhaps a vendor will give you phone numbers of satisfied customers. Even if this is a hand-picked user sample, it is good to talk with them—and if they are genealogists first and customers second, they'll give you candid views of the vendor and the software.

(10) Is there a user's group formed around use of this software? Some genealogy software has thousands of users and that puts enough of them in close proximity that they have formed veritable user's clubs for mutual help. Other groups are national and handle interactions by mail or newsletter to overcome the distances separating the members. You will find such a group the *best* source of advice, help, and criticism.

(75) Does the program allow you to designate a subject and then create an automatic search of ascending and descending bloodlines? If you can't leave it to the program to climb up or down your family tree and print out charts and records and indexes to subsets of your family, it isn't much of a program. You should be able to pick out a family member and leave the rest to the program – but you may have to change data diskettes when the screen message tells you to.

(25) Can the program handle any number of marriages and any number of children from each marriage? There's one in every family! Ten marriages per person? At least thirty children per marriage? Hope for no-limit capabilities.

(25) Are there church-related fields in the records that match your own needs? Whether you are a member of The Church of Jesus Christ of Latter-day Saints or some other church, you may wish to keep track of certain church-related dates and events.

(25) Can you buy a demonstration disk and a user manual and apply their costs to the software price if you decide to buy the whole package? A demo disk lets you run sample-family data to see what the workings and products are like – but it is not a working program. Buying a user manual is a good way of previewing a genealogy software package. You are going to spend months and years with this program; approach it carefully. Most vendors credit you with this cost when you buy the rest of the package, that is, the operational disks.

(50) Can you return the software and manual with a reasonable or total refund if it does not satisfy your requirements? You *might* buy genealogy programs and return the ones you don't want if the vendors give you full refund. That wouldn't be a very nice thing to do. On the other hand, any vendor who will not refund money for an expensive package that falls short of advertising claims or user expectation is not nice either. Expect fair play; give fair play; and make big noises when you find a vendor is not nice. You'll be heard!

(25) Are the record-keeping differences between this program and your manual system minor and negotiable? Be willing to change the way you have done things for years and years. Presumably, the computer way is better. But don't give away the farm. You do not have to lose family data, document citation, or information bits you keep just because you are computerizing. You will find something you can be satisfied with if you are reasonable and flexible.

(50) Will the program vendor help you to convert data files made on another computer and under another program to this program's control? Changing computers or software never forced a business to reenter all the payroll, inventory, and personnel records; why should you have to redo all your files when upgrading equipment or switching software? Expect file-transfer assistance; vendors must face this need.

(25) Is the vendor prompt in answering your letters and filling your order? Your first warning is poor service; second warning is a poor user manual; and the third warning is no answer to your calls and letters. How many will you need before making loud noises? Rip-offs become known — like certain family research services who send computer-made cards to the whole of America and insist they have searched your family for you.

(25) Will the program create acceptable pedigree charts (ascending and also descending)? Some charts made by computers are inventive and confusing. A good program ought to be able to duplicate the classical, symmetrical charts of ancestral lines found in preprinted forms you can buy. Once a family is computer-entered and linked, a good program should be able to provide a variety of formats and trees in either direction.

(50) Will the program create individual records and family records of an acceptable style? You don't have to put up with unusual printouts and assume they are necessary "because the computer made them." The programmer can be as traditional in format designing as any printed-form maker can be.

(25) Can you create indexes of spouses, individuals, and family groups? Special indexes come from sorting on selected fields and/or selected groups of records. You *can* get this flexibility.

(10) Can you use your own numbers or your old numbering system? Many programs computer-assign person or family-group record numbers; others let you choose your own ID numbers. You can at least put that old number in the footnote place or some user-designated field — or can you?

(25) Can you search files on any word in any field? You should be able to find "Cody," "ody," "Cody, Wyoming," or "John Cody" in any part of any record and have the record printed or displayed on the screen.

(10) Can you use *and, or,* and *not* in search term combinations? The genealogist will love the search power of true Boolean Logic. This lets you search for "Cody" *and* "1790" *not* "Wyoming" and find any records bearing those Cody names with 1790 in some date field, but not if the word *Wyoming* is present. The *OR* term is very useful, too: You can search "Cody" *OR* "Codie" *OR* "Codee" and "1790" *not* "Wyoming." The combinations are endless and the search power is useful.

(25) Can you sort records by chosen fields? If you want to arrange records by date of birth, state where died, or any of many other orders, a good program will help you create such lists.

(10) Can you print or screen-display records in a variety of formats? If one record layout can be shown, others can, too. Does the program allow you options or allow user design of layouts? It should.

(100) Does the program have all the fields you want and with adequate field lengths? Good programs have all the "basic fields" and then let the user create other fields—such as Occupation, Military, Education, Hobbies, and so on.

(75) Can you have records spread out over many disks and still treat them as a single file? This is the same as asking how big a family the program will handle. Partitioning your family into program-limited groups is not necessary. Goals of programmers may include faster running and avoidance of disk swapping; those aren't genealogy goals and they aren't even important sales pitches. The program shouldn't partition the family or indexes to it.

(75) Is a field easy to edit during or after the record-entry process? If you see you have made a spelling error while entering a record, you should be able to correct it quickly and easily. Once the record has been disk-filed, you will be correcting data, adding data, changing data, and deleting data in many records over many years. Be sure this is a quick and painless process.

(10) Can you add fields later? A good program lets you discover needs and add fields even after you have entered many records. Only when you are accustomed to computing will many notions occur to you. The program ought to let you add new fields even in old records.

(50) Can you easily locate records for individuals? Some programs let you enter names or record numbers for many persons and then sit back while their records are found, displayed, and printed. Other than swapping disks in a disk drive, you should be able to let the program do the finding work.

(10) Does the program prevent putting death dates earlier than birth dates? Among the nice features of some programs is a date-validating routine that makes it impossible to have a death date or marriage date or birth date out of the chronological order natural to those events.

(25) Can you express dates in any of several format styles? A program should let you choose your date-expressing style from such variations as "June 16, 1923," "16 June 1923," "06/16/1923," or others. It should also let you make such annotations as "ABOUT," "CIRCA," "?," or even "Mar or May 15, 1789 or 1790." The flexibility should be there.

(50) Will the program protect you from errors if the data diskette is full? Nothing is quite so disastrous as losing a whole disk's file without having the contents in a backup copy. Programmers can save you from yourself if they anticipate common errors. Such user protection could even count the number of records you've made since the last disk-copy was made, and cause a kind message to be displayed: *Don't you think it is time to make a backup?*

This adequacy scale will, at least, help you separate the wheat from the chaff in the genealogy software marketplace. It is not comprehensive of *all* the desirable things to look for in a good program. Try modifying the scale with criteria and weights of your own making.

SEPTEMBER 1984
GENEALOGY PROGRAMS DIRECTORY

1. *Roots/M*. Apple II (CP/M), Kaypro, Heath/Zenith, and 8-inch disk CP/M $49.95. Commsoft – 2452 Embarcadero Way, Palo Alto, CA 94303 (415) 493-2184. Orders only: (800) 227-1617; California calls (800) 772-3545.

2. *Family Roots*. Apple II, IBM PC, Commodore 64, and selected CP/M systems, $185.00 plus $3.50. Quinsept, Inc.– P.O. Box 16, Lexington, MA 02173, (617) 641-2930.

3. *Gensystems*. TRS-80 I and III, $128.45. Armstrong Genealogical Systems – John J. Armstrong, 5009 Utah Drive, Greenville, TX 75401, (214) 454-8209.

4. *Computer Assisted Indexing*. TRS-80 III, $25.00. Run-ready additional $5.00. Brian Harney – Route 2, Louisville Road, Frankfort, KY 40601.

5. *Genealogy: Compiling Roots and Branches.* TRS-80 II, 4, 4P, 12, 16, and 16B, NEC PC8000, $195.00. Armstrong Genealogical Systems – John J. Armstrong, 5009 Utah Drive, Greenville, TX 75401, (214) 454-8209.

6. *Roots/89.* Heath/Zenith, $39.95. Commsoft – 2452 Embarcadero Way, Palo Alto, CA 94303, (415) 493-2184. Orders Only: (800) 227-1617, California Calls: (800) 772-3545.

7. *Genie.* IBM PC, IBM XT, and Tandy 2000, $195.00, plus add-on modules. Central Research of Utah – Box 808, Bountiful, UT 84010.

8. *Family for CoCo.* TRS-80 Color $14.95. TWM – P.O. Box 232, Lititz, PA 17543.

9. *The Genealogist's Right Hand.* Apple II, IIe, and Apple compatibles, $99.95. User Friendly Systems, Inc. – 6135 Ross Road, Fairfield, OH 45014, (513) 874-4550.

10. *Treesearch.* IBM PC, Compaq, Columbia, and Epson HX-20 collector, $200.00. Array Systems, Inc. – P.O. Box 295, Brigham City, UT 84302, (801) 723-7679.

11. *Genesis-80.* TRS-80 III, $139.00. Anthony J. Skvarek – 1514 W. Mission #14, Pomona, CA 91766.

12. *Ancestry I/III.* TRS-80 I and III, $69.95 plus $2.00. Soft-Gene – 11 John Swift Road, Acton, MA 01720, (617) 263-0431.

13. *Genealogy Program.* TRS-80 III, $48.00, Frank Lerchen – 2950 Espana Ct., Fairfax, VA 22031.

14. *Your Family Tree.* TRS-80 III and 4, IBM PC, $29.95. Acorn Software Products – 7655 Leesburg Pike, Falls Church, VA 22043 (703) 893-0868.

15. *My Roots.* Apple II Plus and IIe, $49.95. Mark Peters – 1513 Towhee Lane, Naperville, IL 60565.

16. *Apple Tree III.* Apple II and IIe, $79.95. Cyber Services, Inc. – Risdon W. Hankinson, 701 Sooner Park Drive, Bartlesville, OK 74006.

17. *Roots/34.* IBM System/34, $250.00. Northvale Systems – 507 Crest Drive, Northvale, NJ 07647.

18. *The Family Connection.* Apple II, IIe, and Apple compatibles, $99.50. Discovery Software – P.O. Box 68821, Indianapolis, IN 46268, (317) 639-2621.

19. *Family Records File System.* TRS-80 II, $250.00. Hierarchal Systems Group – P.O. Box DB, College Station, TX 77841.

20. *Genealogy Workshop.* TI 99/4A, $49.95. Tenex – P.O. Box 6578, South Bend, IN 46660, (800) 348-2778, Indiana (219) 277-7726.

21. *Geneas/Base.* TRS-80 I, III, and 4, $109.95 plus $2.50. Praxisoft Computer Enterprises – P.O. Box 1221, Muskegon, MI 49443.

22. *Fretware Family Tree System.* Apple II and IIe, $49.95. The Fretwells – 2605 Highview Avenue, Waterloo, IA 50702.

23. *Family Reunion.* IBM PC, PC-XT, PCjr, Compaq, Eagle, Corona, and others, $99.95 plus $2.50. Personal Software Company – P.O. Box 776, Salt Lake City, UT 84110, (801) 943-6908.

24. *Genealogy on Display.* IBM PCjr, PC, PPC, and PC/XT, $35.00. Send SAS mailer and two disks. Melvin O. Duke – P.O. Box 20836. San Jose, CA 95160, (408) 268-6637.

25. *Patriarch I.* Apple II and IIe, $195.00. Cyclone Software – 3305 Macomb Street NW, Washington, DC.

26. *FGS and PEDC.* Commodore 64, $57.95. Byteware – 906 West 6th Avenue, Monmouth, IL 61462. (*FGS2* and *PEDC*, $59.95.)

27. *Heritage*. TRS-80 I, III, and 4 (in III mode), $23.95. Creative Services— P.O. Box 580, Oak Harbor, WA 98277.

28. *Generations III*. TRS-80 I, III, and 4 (III mode), $29.95. Micro-80, Inc.—2665 Busby Road (GC), Oak Harbor, WA 98277, (206) 675-6143.

29. *Your Ancestors*. Timex 1000, Sinclair ZX-81, T/S1000, and T/S1500 $10.00; Commodore VIC-20 and C-64, TI 99/4 and 4A, $15; *Companion Chart Fill-in Program*, $10.00. Jim Mc Dermott—P.O. Box 140, Great Falls, MT 59403.

30. *Arbor-Aide*. Commodore 64, $100.00 plus $2.50. Software Solutions—7378 Zurawski Ct., Custer, WI 54423.

31. *Text Indexing System*. TRS-80 II, $100.00. Hierarchal Systems Group— P.O. Box DB, College Station, TX 77841.

32. *Lineages*. TRS-80 Color, $30.00. Cassette; $20.00, Listing only. Ervin A. Madera—P.O. Box 1746, Rohnert Park, CA 94928-1241.

33. *Family Generations*. Apple II, II¢, IIe, IIc, and compatibles, $100.00. Rosalie Scharen—12126 SE Sequoia Avenue, Milwaukie, OR 97222.

34. *FamilyFile*. IBM PC, PCjr, and IBM PC compatibles, $175.00 plus $5.00. Compugen Systems—P.O. Box 15604, Fort Wayne, IN 46885.

35. *Family Tree*. Commodore 64, and VIC-20, $39.95, $49.95 Canada. Genealogy Software—P.O. Box 1151, Port Huron, MI 48061, (519) 344-3990; and 1046 Parkwood Avenue, Sarnia, Ontario, Canada N7V 3T9.

36. *Genalog II*. Apple II, $69.50. Genalog Software—111 Woodgate Road, Middletown, NJ 07748, (201) 671-9211.

37. *Genalog 80*. TRS-80 I, $69.50. Genalog Software—111 Woodgate Road, Middletown, NJ 07748, (201) 671-9211.

38. *Ancestor File Programs*. IBM PC, $10.00, $5.00 listings only. J.P. Davis—10650 Hickory Ridge Road, Columbia, MD 21044, (301) 964-6063.

39. *Genieology*. Twenty computers using CP/M, CP/M-86, or MD-DOS, $359.00. Warner Enterprises—P.O. Box 6276, Glendale, CA 91205-0276.

40. *Port for Genealogists*. IBM PC (using port operating system), $400.00, $500.00 Canada. Team Approach Limited—4 Abingdon Drive, Ottawa, Ontario, Canada K2H 7M3, (613) 829-7848.

41. *=Ancestors=*. Atari 800, $39.95, with your disk. Ancestors—Box 2434, Harbor, OR 97415.

42. *Ancestors*. TRS-80 Color, $39.95. Christopher Meek—4132 Lay Street, Des Moines, IA 50317.

43. *Gene-Pro*. Timex 1000 and Sinclair ZX81, $12.95. D. Labue, DML Software—14 Wick Road, E. Brunswick, NJ 08816.

44. *Genealogical Record Programs*. IBM PC and IBM PC compatibles, $50.00. Roderick H. Payne—100 Villa Avenue, Buffalo, NY 14216.

45. *Personal Ancestral File (PBGS 1019)*. IBM PC and XT (DOS 1.1 and 2.0), $35.00. Salt Lake Distribution Center—1999 West 1700 South, Salt Lake City, UT 84104.

46. *Tafel 1.0 (Utility for Commsoft's Roots Basefiles)*. Heath/Zenith CP/M, $24.95 plus $2.00. H. Michael LaFleur—4415 Emory Lane, Charlotte, NC 28211, (704) 364-9667.

47. *Names*. Timex 1000 and 2068, Sinclair ZX-81, $30.00. Virginia Lake— P.O. Box 351, Hockessin, DE 19707.

48. *Family Ties*. CP/M-80, MS-DOS, and PC-DOS, computers including: IBM PC, Kaypro 2, 4, 10, Osborne DD and EXEC, Xerox 820; Superbrain; Televideo; Morrow MD; Heath/Zenith 8, 89, Z100; Apple/Franklin; NEC PC-8001A, 8801A;

Access; HP-125; Epson QX-10; Magic; Otrona; Toshiba T-100. $75.00 plus $2.00 (other formats as demand warrants at extra cost; run-ready at extra cost). Computer Services—1050 East 800 South, Provo, UT 84801, (801) 377-2100.

49. *Family Tree*. TRS-80 I, III, and 4, $29.95. Michtron Corporation—1691 Eason, Pontiac, MI 48054, (313) 673-2224.

50. *The Soundex Computer Program*. TRS-80 I and III, $18.95. Mod I disk, $14.95; cassette Mod I/III. C.& M. Systems—P.O. Box 22807, San Diego, CA 92122.

51. *Roots II*. IBM PC, XT, PCjr, and IBM PC compatibles, $99.00. Commsoft—2452 Embarcadero Way, Palo Alto, CA 94303, (415) 493-2184. Order only: (800) 227-1617; California calls: (800) 772-3545.

52. *Computerized Genealogy*. TRS-80 I, $18.95. Lou Pero—P.O. Box 488, Bend, OR 97709.

53. *Branches*. Atari 400 and 800, $45.00. Sysco Software—3595 Cloverleaf Drive, Boulder, CO 80302, (303) 651-3936.

54. *Calendar G/J*. IBM PC and IBM compatibles, $45.00. Edward R. Swart—276 Beechlawn, Waterloo, Ontario, Canada N2L 5W7.

55. *Roots and Relatives*. Apple II and compatibles, $225.00, Canadian dollars. M. A. Harrison—639 Consol, Winnipeg, MB, Canada R2K 1S9.

CHAPTER 7

Stepping Through the Use of a Genealogy Computer

T he quickest way to explain how a genealogist can use a computer, what a computer program does, and what is expected of a computer user is to give a guided tour through the user manual that accompanies a good genealogy program. We will use *Family Roots*, written by Steve Vorenberg. *Family Roots* costs $185 and runs on Apple II, IBM PC, Commodore 64, and selected CP/M systems (for example, the Radio Shack TRS-80 Model 4 running under the CP/M operating system). We chose *Family Roots* because its features and operations are illustrations of excellence in genealogy as well as computer programming.

With the express permission of Quinsept, Inc., P.O. Box 16, Lexington, MA 02173, the rest of this chapter is largely quoted directly from the user manual of *Family Roots* copyright 1982. We are indebted to Mr. Vorenberg for allowing us to use his work as an excellent example of how you would use a genealogy program with your computer.

From the amount of information quoted, you might think the user manual is reproduced in full. Not so. Many subtle and specific instructions were left out and provide the answers to most questions that may remain after you have toured the covered topics. There are utility programs left unexplained, nuances and options left unmentioned, and many examples skipped. The numbers following each quotation indicate the page on which the material appears in the user manual for *Family Roots*.

OVERVIEW TO FAMILY ROOTS

There are six main capabilities supplied by these programs. Storage of birth, death, marriage, occupation, offspring, and notes for each person is supported by one program. Another prints automatically generated genealogy charts for both predecessors and descendants. A third program provides formatted outputs of your information for individuals or family groups. The fourth program allows you to make indices of your people in a wide variety of ways. The fifth program allows you to search through your data for a large variety of information. Finally, there is a program that allows you to store massive amounts of textual data (notes, etc.) that can be retrieved by name. In addition to the six major capabilities, there are several utility programs to satisfy special needs. (1-1)

EDIT is the data entry program. It allows you to set up a record for each name that you want to keep data on and later modify it. Each name can have up to four components and each name is associated with a record by number. Records can be accessed for additions or changes either by name or by number. Each record can be used to store date of birth, place of birth, date of death (if applicable), place of residence or death, mother, father, children, notes/footnotes, and number of marriages. For each marriage, the spouse, date of marriage, place of marriage, and marital status can be entered. You may also define up to nine fields of your choice. . . . The menu allows you either to step through portions of the list of possible items or to selectively change as many items as you wish. When you are finished with your entries for one person, the program fills in obvious complementary information in other records, e.g. if you enter marriage data for a person, EDIT also puts that data into the spouse's record to save you the trouble of entering it twice.

CHARTS prints four different types of genealogy charts for you. A free-form chart, well-suited to computer generation, allows you to include only names or both names and other selected data for each person on the chart. This type of chart is available for both predecessors and descendants. In addition, the standard 4 generation pedigree chart may be printed. There is also a special pedigree form that compresses 6 generations onto one page with detailed information included for each person.

SHEETS prints or displays your data organized by individual or family group. Information on individuals can be displayed or printed in an easy to read format; the printed form is often used for binding into family books. The family group sheet uses the Mormon format, which includes husband, wife, critical dates and places for each, other marriages, the children from this marriage, spouses of the children, and sources.

LISTS constructs indexes of your names in a wide variety of ways. Any list may be printed or displayed in either alphabetical or numerical order. You may select people to include in your list by diskette, by number range, by supplying your own list of numbers, by common name elements (such as everybody with the same first name), or by surname SOUNDEX (names that sound alike). Merging of lists from different sources (for example, multiple diskettes) is supported. (2-1)

SEARCH allows you to search through records for information of your choice. You can search for embedded character sequences, e.g. you might want to find all people having a mention of Omaha or everyone who was a teacher. You can search dates in various ways, e.g. you can look for all people with the same birthday or everyone living in a certain year. You can search for all mentions of a person. You can search for blank fields. Finally, you can search for all people who have a certain number of children or certain number of marriages. Each of the searches noted above is controlled by you . . . you can search for virtually anything you have stored.

TEXT allows you to store an arbitrary amount of free-text notes, descriptions, or even a small report or book. Access to text is by name or number. Text is stored on a disk in 128 character segments, and as many segments are used as are needed. Each text diskette is independent of every other, so that as many diskettes as are needed can be used. Text can be added, changed, or deleted at any time.

Several utility programs are also provided. CREATE is used to prepare empty data diskettes. BLANKS prints a conventional blank pedigree chart on a single page, in case you want to use such forms. CONFIGUR is used to set up information in the master control file used by all the programs. That information includes your hardware configuration, formatting parameters, and the starting values for all other parameters mentioned above. RENUMBER allows you to reassign the numerical ID's for selected people. ADDRESS will make an address list for living relatives whose addresses you have included in your data. WHAT will tell you the identity and contents of a *Family Roots* diskette. And READER allows you to put a previously generated list of names that had been saved on diskette back into the computer's memory. (2-2)

Family Roots is supplied both for systems with single sided disk drives and for systems with double sided drives. Single sided drives write on one side of the diskette, while double sided ones write on both sides; a single sided diskette may have a capacity of 160,000 characters while the double sided one may hold 320,000 characters or more. (3-1)

INITIALIZING YOUR SOFTWARE

The first of the five formatting parameters is the maximum number of characters per person. The value we supply (called the default value) is 320 characters. This must be large enough to accommodate all the "structured" information you want to store for each person . . . not includ[ing] the characters in the person's name since this is stored elsewhere. (3-17)

If you choose a value too small, you will get messages from the EDIT program occasionally saying there is not enough space to store your information. You can usually cope with that by using abbreviations. If you choose a value too large, you will waste a lot of space on your disk but will seldom have any problems storing . . . .

The second of the five formatting parameters is the number of characters available on one diskette. The number of characters available on 5 1/4 inch floppy diskettes depends on whether you have single or doubled sided drives and on the density—single, double or quadruple . . . .

The third through the fifth formatting parameters are used to define the space for name storage. Names are stored in groups of consecutive ID's, usually 25 names per group. There is a limit on the total number of characters for every group of names, but no limit on individual names within the group . . . .

The default value for the average length of a name is 26 characters . . . . The character count should include first names (can be many), last name, married last name, title (if any), and 5 characters of overhead. If you plan to use the "title" part of the name for something like alternate spellings or your own custom ID number, you should account for that in selecting the average name length. (3-18)

It is unfortunate that these difficult choices must be made before you are familiar with *Family Roots* and how it works. The best way around this is to make a set of "test" data when you first start. In other words, don't get in a big rush to get everything stored as soon as possible. Enter information for 25 to 50 people with the view that you are just trying things out to see how they work. Then if it turns out you aren't satisfied with the results of your choices, you can return to CONFIGUR and start anew, but with a better understanding of the consequences.

The first choice on the Records Parameters menu is for defining user fields. This is for defining up to 9 fields of your own choice. Typical fields might be SEX, OCCUPATION, DATE OF BURIAL, PLACE OF BURIAL, or DATE OF CHRISTENING. It is *not* critical that you choose all your fields at this point. New fields can be added at any time. However, once you have added a field and stored data for it, it will be difficult to change or delete it; this would involve manually changing all the information you entered. (3-19)

You should review the maxima. It is not critical that these be set large enough at this point, since you may change them at any time. For example if you find that 15 children as a maximum limit is not large enough while entering your data, you would run CONFIGUR again to reset this to, say, 18.

The final Records Parameter menu choice is 4. Changing [these values] later may cause you problems, even though it is still possible to change them. The first item is a parameter that establishes the storage order for dates, i.e., day/month/year or month/day/year. This does not affect what you are allowed to enter for dates, but does affect validity checking (e.g. Is the month number between 1 and 12?), date formatting for printout, and recognition of dates in SEARCH . . . . The second item . . . controls whether an "Auto Date" field is used or not. If you have one, every time you change a piece of information for a person, this field will be changed to contain the date that you made the change. (3-20)

The next thing to do in getting started is to run the CREATE utility in order to make blank data diskettes. You need to prepare the diskettes that will be used for your genealogy data before you can store anything on them. There are two steps. First you must format each diskette, then you must set up the *Family Roots* files using the CREATE utility. After doing this for one diskette you may find it easier and shorter merely to copy the first blank data diskette until you have enough blanks. (3-21)

CREATE puts empty data files onto your data diskettes. The empty files that are created are for your names and family information, along with a control file. The control file allows each program to determine the identity of the data diskette (its number) and . . . to prevent incorrectly writing on it, i.e. to prevent destroying your data. (3-22)

How many blank diskettes will you need? At least one, but it won't hurt to make several others now. You can add others later as you need them. There is no limit to the number of data diskettes possible. (3-23)

You must run CONFIGUR utility as one of your first operations. This program writes a "data file" . . . onto the program diskettes. The . . . file contains all the information on what hardware you are using and how to use it, plus many items that affect how much space you have available for your genealogy data storage . . . . You will be led through a series of questions that allows the program to determine how to set its internal values for your hardware . . . . The series of questions about your printer are needed for the program to know (1) whether you have a printer and where it is, (2) how to start and stop it, (3) what your character sizes are and how to control them, and (4) how wide your paper is. (3-11)

The disk drive question establishes how many drives you have. Up to 6 drives are supported, and they are referenced as A: through F: when a program tells you to load a diskette into a drive. (For example, a program may tell you to place diskette 6 into drive C:) . . . . The questions about your display establish how wide it is and how to clear the screen. (3-16)

SETTING THE SOFTWARE TO YOUR UNIQUE NEEDS

Getting Into *Family Roots* Under MS DOS: *Family Roots* should always be "booted" at the start of your working session. This means that you should insert a *Family Roots* program diskette into Drive A: and . . . turn the power on . . . . When you do this the Disk Drive's "In Use" light will come on, the drive will whirr, and the Quinsept *Family Roots* logo will appear on your screen after a few seconds. (3-5)

It (the logo) will remain there for about half a minute if you do nothing, or you can "get on with it" by tapping any key on the keyboard. On your screen you will see PLEASE WAIT . . . followed by various messages that tell you what is happening at the moment. After several such messages, a menu will appear on your screen. A "menu" in general is a list of items from which you must make a choice in order to continue.

This menu gives you a list of the programs you may choose to run. (3-7)

In a system with single sided drives, the program diskette labelled as "Main" will typically have the EDIT, CHARTS, SHEETS, SEARCH and TEXT programs for you to choose from, while the diskette labelled as "Auxiliary" will have all the others, including the LISTS program and the utilities. In a system with double sided drives, everything is, typically, on one program diskette . . . . After finishing each program you are given the choice of ending your session or executing a different program. If you choose to end, you will be returned to BASIC with a BYE . . . followed by the BASIC prompt "A." At this point you can run any other software. (3-8)

Here is the MAIN MENU of *Family Roots*:

CHOOSE WHICH PROGRAM TO RUN, BY LETTER:

A)	EDIT	(DATA ENTRY)
B)	CHARTS	(PEDIGREES/DESCENDANTS)
C)	SHEETS	(PERSON AND GROUP SHEETS)
D)	SEARCH	(EXAMINE FAMILY DATA)
E)	TEXT	(FREE TEXT)
F)	PROGRAMS	(INSERT THE OTHER DISKETTE)

CHOOSE WHICH PROGRAM TO RUN, BY LETTER:

A)	LISTS	(LISTS OF NAMES)
B)	WHAT	(ANALYZE DISKETTE)
C)	READER	(PUT LIST INTO MEMORY)
D)	CONFIGUR	(SET UP PARAMETERS)
E)	CREATE	(MAKE EMPTY DISKETTES)
F)	ADDRESS	(MAKE ADDRESS LIST)
G)	BLANKS	(EMPTY CHARTS)
H)	RENUMBER	(REASSIGN ID'S)
I)	KEYDEF	(DEFINE FUNCTION KEYS)
J)	PROGRAMS	(INSERT OTHER DISKETTE) (3-9)

ENTERING INFORMATION ABOUT YOUR FAMILY

EDIT is the data entry program. Names of people for whom you want to keep records and a standard set of information can be entered and changed using this program. Begin by booting into *Family Roots* and selecting EDIT when the menu of programs is presented.

If you are just starting, place an empty data diskette . . . in at least one drive and press any key . . . . EDIT will read the diskette in each drive to find the location and identity of all the data diskettes. When it finds a new data diskette, it will ask you to identify the diskette . . . . You may supply the diskette number. If you are just starting, you probably will want to call your first diskette number 1. (4-1)

The EDIT main menu will be displayed. The menu gives you five choices.

(1) EDIT RECORDS
(2) EDIT NAMES
(3) CHANGE PROGRAM PARAMETERS
(4) CHECK DISKETTES
(5) EXIT PROGRAM

The "records" referred to . . . contain your family information, one record per person . . . . The display of data for one person will usually reference a wife, parents and several children, and these names are retrieved from the name storage location instead of stored in every record where they are referenced. An identification (or ID) number gets associated with every name that you store . . . and it is this ID number that is usually saved in a record rather than a name.

It is usually better to enter a batch of names at the same time using item 2 first. The difference between . . . menu choices, when working with names, is . . . . For item (1), editing records, you may store only the name of the person the record is for, e.g. if you are entering birth, death, spouses, etc. for Millie Acorn, you can only enter the 4 parts of Millie Acorn's name while you are doing this, and not her parents, spouses or children. For item (2), editing names, you may store the 4 name parts of a large number of people at the same time, but not their family data (until you return to the main menu). (4-2)

After names have been set up . . . you can return to the main menu . . . and select (1) for putting your family information in those records . . . . In the EDIT NAMES mode, a menu is put on the screen to allow you to select whether you want to add a name, change a name, reinitialize a name/record or save your names on disk. Each time you select one of the name editing options, you will sequence through a few questions and "fill-in-the-blanks" type of operation and then return to this menu for your next selection. For example if you choose to add a name, you will supply one complete name and then return to the menu; this allows you to correct the name or erase it immediately in case you made a mistake.

When you add a name, an ID number gets associated with it that is used extensively by all of the *Family Roots* programs. There are two ways that an ID number can be assigned: you may choose each one yourself, or you may select ID's sequentially starting at some number of your choice.

The method that is used is controlled by a parameter that you can set on the CHANGE PROGRAM PARAMETERS menu . . . . If this is your first session with EDIT, it will probably be set . . . starting with 1 . . . . You should choose the "add a name" option (from the "edit names" menu) by pressing   1 . The program finds the next available ID number and assigns the new number to the name and record you are about to enter. (4-3)

The first name you enter (yourself?) will become associated with the number 1 hereafter. The next name you enter (your wife?) will become associated with number 2 . . . . The EDIT program (and the others as well) views all names as having four parts: (1) last name at birth, (2) first name(s), (3) married last name, (4) title. When you enter a new name . . . you will be asked to enter each part separately. If one of the parts . . . doesn't apply (e.g. married last name) or you don't know it, just press the "enter" key. There is no limit on the length of a name . . . . Any character except an "enter" and the name separator character (%) can be in a name.

First names can be entered separated by spaces . . . . We have sometimes included nicknames in parentheses as part of the first name . . . . Another practice . . . is to put in a descriptive word or phrase where the name isn't known, e.g. "(BOY)" or "(JOHN'S FATHER)." Such imprecisions can be easily corrected later when you find the more exact information. "Married last name" will normally be entered only for married females. Title is intended for such things as "JR.," "SR," . . . . However, since "Title" is only printed/displayed and is not used when searching on names, you may put almost anything you want here, e.g. an alternate spelling for the last name.

When you press "enter" after finishing with the title field, you will be returned to the "Edit names" menu.

Family Roots does not restrict the ID numbers you can choose. However, you should consider the consequences of choosing numbers that are far apart for people that are relatively closely related. . . . If you choose numbers that are on different diskettes, you may have to do a lot of diskette switching in the drive(s) in order to print out a chart, family group sheet, or even an individual sheet if it has a lot of name references . . . . For example if you have one drive, and put yourself on one diskette, your father on a second, and your mother on a third, you will need to . . . unload and load each of the diskettes 6 (yes six) times in order to print 3 entries on one of the predecessor charts. By placing all three people on the same diskette, you can start that same chart, walk away, and have it done when you return from your doughnut break . . . . Thus we suggest that your guiding factor should be to place relatively closely related people on no more diskettes than you have drives.

A few comments about other identification schemes. The one used by *Family Roots* is necessarily numeric and you must use it in some form in order to have the programs recognize relationships. However, if you want also to preserve another favorite scheme of yours, you may define a user field (using CONFIGUR) and keep your own ID there. (4-5, 4-6)

If you want to change a name, correct a typing error, or even check on the entry you just made, you should press 2 to select the "change a name" option. . . . The program asks you for the number associated with the name that you want to change. . . . EDIT gives you the opportunity to change each of the four components separately; it also tells you which part of the name you are looking at . . . . For those parts you don't want to change, simply press "enter" and the old entry will be preserved. Similarly, to change a part, just type in the new part. (4-7)

Suppose you had entered JR. in the title and wanted to delete it. When you are asked CHANGE JR. TO: type a CTRL E (for "Erase," i.e. hold down the CTRL key while typing the E key) followed by "enter".

The reinitialize option . . . assumes that the name/record number has been previously assigned. . . . You might use this option if you accidentally entered duplicate names . . . . Be careful with this option! . . . . anything you may have entered for that person . . . will be irretrievably erased. . . . You are given the opportunity to enter a new name for the slot . . . . If you wish, you may leave the slot as temporarily unused by pressing "enter" for each of the four name parts . . . . You will be able to find your blank slots easily since the LISTS program has several ways to expose them. (4-8)

If you added or changed any names, EDIT will save them before returning to the main menu. . . . You will notice a fair amount of disk activity . . . . This is sets of names moving back and forth from the diskettes.

At the end of your session of editing names, there may be several (perhaps as many as 75) that are still in memory and not yet on diskette. You can force the names to the diskette at any time by typing 4 from the "edit names" menu. It is good practice to do this occasionally while you are editing names in order to avoid losing your work due to a power failure or some such problem. . . . EDIT keeps track of what has been saved and will write names onto the diskettes when you exit to the main menu. (4-9)

Dates can be entered in various formats, and the program converts recognized ones to a standard format to facilitate display and searches. Footnotes on dates can be entered and are recognized by the program when printing or displaying . . . . There are four date formats the program recognizes . . . . The order is governed by the Day/Month/Year control parameter set in CONFIGUR . . . . The recognized formats are:

month/day/year, e.g. 1/18/1968 or 1/18/68
or day/month year, e.g. 18/1/1968
or 18/1/68 month-day-year, e.g. 12-9-1949 or 12-9-49
or day-month-year, e.g. 9-12-1949 or 9-12-49
month day, year, e.g. May 9, 1963 or December 6, 1958
or June 15 48 (comma is optional)
day month year, e.g. 9 MAY 63 or 6 DEC 1856
or 15 JUN 1948.

In the last two formats it makes no difference whether you enter the month names in upper case, lower case, or mixed. You don't have to type the entire name of the month, but if you shorten it too much, the conversion uses the first month satisfying the abbreviation, e.g. J is January, JU is June. The spaces that separate the numbers and month names are necessary if you want EDIT to recognize them.

If you enter only two digits for the year, EDIT adds 1900 to it. The value "19" for the century is stored in the CONFIGTN.DAT file and can be reset using the CONFIGUR program. The passing of the century mark is not the only use for this—you might be entering a lot of dates from the 19th century, where it would be convenient to abbreviate 5/7/1836 to 5/7/36. The recognized dates are converted to an eight digit string before storage. The order within the string depends on the order control mmddyyyy for month-day-year, like 11031901, or ddmmyyyy for day-month-year, like 03111901, where the examples represent 3 November 1901. This example could be printed by CHARTS or SHEETS as either 3 Nov 1901 or the slashed format in the same order as stored (e.g. 11/03/1901 for the first one), depending on a parameter setting in those programs. (4-20)

The use of the standard format minimizes the storage required and makes it easy to do searches on years, months, and days. The conversion to the standard format also facilitates validity checking on the ranges for days and months . . . . THE MONTH IS OUT OF THE VALID RANGE . . . is your signal that the date may need to be reentered . . . . When the EDIT menu for a record is displayed and a date value is present, the value is displayed in the standard format so that you can see exactly what is present in the record.

You are not constrained to entering one of the standard date formats in date fields, and indeed such entries can be useful. For example, a date of birth could be entered as "ABOUT 1833." . . . If you know some part of the date precisely, it is usually better to allow the program to store it in the standard format using an entry such as ??/??/1833. This allows the SEARCH program to use it. When you use a non-standard format, EDIT stores exactly what you enter, rather than converting it. (4-21)

You may use footnotes on dates. You would add a footnote to a date to indicate source, uncertainty about year, or numerous other reasons. You enter the footnote indicator on the date by entering a date as described above (standard or non-standard), followed by the carat and a number, e.g. 3/13/1916(carat)1 . . . . The number that you use refers to the note that you will add later in a note field . . . . There is no limit to the number of characters you can enter in a date field.

The Auto Date field, if you are using it, is not set using the methods described above . . . . This field is set automatically any time you choose to edit a record, i.e. any time you answer ANY CHANGES TO BE MADE HERE (Y/N/S/P)? with either Y or S. You can see the value in the field displayed immediately below the name in the record menu as (Last Updated 5/15/1983). The value for the date can come from your clock, if you have one, or from the date you entered when prompted upon booting. (4-22)

ADDING OR CHANGING INFORMATION LATER

Having set up the names that you want to keep information on using the name editing feature, you are ready to store information for those people: select <1> for EDIT RECORDS from the main menu. (4-10)

You would choose to edit records by number list when you want quick access to the records for one or more people . . . . You don't have to enter the numbers in any particular order . . . . The data in the records you selected are shown to you in the order you selected, and you are given the chance to change whatever you want.

Accessing records by name works somewhat differently . . . . You might use this to review and edit everybody with the same surname, the same first name, or the same married name. Alternately you may not have a person's number handy so you might ask for the records using a person's name. In any case the program asks you for three name parts . . . LAST NAME AT BIRTH? FIRST NAME(S)? MARRIED NAME? (4-11)

For each part of a name you supply, the program finds all records having all the supplied name parts . . . finds all records for names of people born MASON . . . finds all records for people having ANN as part of their first name, including, ANN, BETTY ANN, ANNIE, ANN MARY, etc. . . . finds everybody who married a HARRIS . . . finds everybody named JO ACORN at birth, including JOSEPH ACORN, JOSEPHINE AMANDA ACORN, EDDIE JOE ACORN JR., etc. . . . finds all ladies born ACORN who married somebody named HARRIS. (4-12)

Hopefully that gives you an idea of the power of this device. It also has its limitations. Every name on all the data diskettes in the drives is searched to see if it meets your specifications, which means you will experience some delays while the search goes on . . . . Another limitation is that you can't search for everybody born an Acorn or married an Acorn at one time, but you can make two (or more) passes through the search . . . . You [c]ould use SEARCH to find all people having certain common features in their data. In the process of doing that, SEARCH accumulates a list of those people in the computer's memory. When you exit SEARCH, one of your options is to run any of the other programs, including EDIT. If you did that, when EDIT started operating it would still have a list of names in memory that was generated by SEARCH. There are a wide variety of ways to use this . . . . Suppose . . . you wanted the opportunity to review and fill in . . . those with missing date of birth. You would execute the SEARCH program and have it locate everybody . . . with blank date of birth. Now you would return to EDIT and use the list of names in memory to edit only those records for people with the missing information. That means that your computer does the "sifting" for you, and lets you look at and change only the information of immediate interest to you. (4-13)

If you've made a choice of records to access, you are now shown a display of the data in a record and asked if you want to change anything. The permanent fields in a record are . . . (4-14)

For everyone:

1)   BORN ON:
2)   BORN AT:
3)   DEATH DATE OR "LIVING":
4)   DIED/LIVING AT:
5)   FATHER:
6)   MOTHER:
7)   NUMBER OF MARRIAGES:
8)   NUMBER OF CHILDREN:
9)   NUMBER OF NOTES:

For each marriage:

a)   SPOUSE:
a + 1)   MARRIED ON:
a + 2)   MARRIED AT:
a + 3)   MARITAL STATUS:

For each child:

b)   CHILD #X:

For each note:

c)   NOTE X: (4-15)

You are given four choices in the question on whether you want to change something: Y/N/S/P. If you answer <N> for NO, the program retrieves the next record that satisfies your access selection or returns to the main menu if there are none. Answering <Y> for YES puts you into the normal editing mode, while <S> for STEP allows you to step through each data field in the sequence shown on the screen. . . . Answering <P> lets you change one or more program parameters before returning to consider this same question again . . . . When you answer <Y>, the program asks you CHANGE WHICH ITEM NUMBER? Each data field is preceded by a number, and that is the number you use to tell the program which field to give you. For example, if you answer <2>, the program responds with 2) BORN AT?

When you start entering information for marriages and children, the list expands and the numbers change. If the numbers change, the screen display showing current entries always regenerates itself automatically so you know which number to use . . . . You can answer questions and supply data until you are satisfied. After each number you supply and question you answer, the program again asks you which number you want to change. You can supply numbers indefinitely, even repeating ones previously given (to correct errors or make additions). If at any time you want to see the complete display of what is present, just type any letter . . . except P or S . . . in response to the request for a number.

When you are all done, simply press "enter" in response to CHANGE WHICH ITEM NUMBER and the program will store your data in the FAMILY.DAT file on your diskettes and get the next record that you asked for. (4-16)

Each time you are asked to enter data, you can type in whatever information you want, or you can preserve what was present before by pressing "enter." . . . On the other hand, sometimes you may want to erase some data completely; in this case, respond with a CTRL E. (4-17)

The name of the person associated with the record you're editing is shown at the top of the screen . . . . When EDIT stores data for your record, it also stores the same data in other records assuming certain relationships.

There are three different standard fields in which counts are entered — NUMBER OF MARRIAGES, NUMBER OF CHILDREN, and NUMBER OF NOTES. Each time you make an entry in one of these fields, the total number of fields and the field numbering may change, so the record display is regenerated if you're not in the step mode. (4-18)

When NUMBER OF MARRIAGES is blank, all of the *Family Roots* programs assume the information is unknown. If you enter 0 (zero), then that is different from being blank and is essentially saying the person is now single or was never married. If you enter 1 or more, then four new fields are added for each marriage, one for spouse, marriage date, marriage place and status.

When NUMBER OF CHILDREN is blank, the programs assume the information is unknown. This is different from entering 0, which would say that the person has no offspring now or never had any children. When you enter 1 or more, the program adds one field for each child, e.g. if you entered 14, then 14 new fields would be added.

For NUMBER OF NOTES, leaving the field blank is equivalent to entering 0, but the latter uses one character of storage in the record on the diskette. When you enter 1 or more, then one field is added for each note.

You may add a footnote indicator to NUMBER OF MARRIAGES, NUMBER OF CHILDREN or your own count fields with the indicator referring to one of the notes. The program recognizes the carat "(up-pointing vee)" as the footnote indicator; this character was selected since it often prints as a vertical arrow, which is a common indicator for footnotes. The entry with footnote indicated would look like NUMBER OF CHILDREN? <3(carat)2> which means "3 children, refer to note number 2."

There are two "permanent" date fields and another one for each marriage . . . . In addition you may have defined your own date fields, like Date of Burial. (4-19)

QUERYING YOUR COMPUTERIZED FILES

The SEARCH program searches through the records you created (using the EDIT program) looking for whatever information you have selected. There are five types of searches which, when used singly or combined, enable you to find records satisfying almost any search criteria you wish. Use of SEARCH won't be very useful until you have a considerable number of records, although you may use it even when there is only one record. Choose SEARCH from the programs menu . . . . When SEARCH is ready you will see the main menu with the following choices:

1) PERFORM A SEARCH	4) CHECK DISKETTES
2) OUTPUT SEARCH RESULTS	5) EXIT PROGRAM
3) CHANGE PROGRAM PARAMETERS	

Each time you set up a search, you are asked to define . . . what to search for (the character, data, etc.) . . . where to search for it (what fields) . . . and . . . which records to search (what people). SEARCH then methodically proceeds to look in the fields of every record you selected to see if what you're looking for is there. When it finds something, the person's ID is saved in memory and the name is shown on your screen. After the search is completed you are returned to the main menu. (8-1)

Note that the result of your search is a list of names stored as ID's in the computer's memory. In order to preserve or view the list you must specifically choose to output it. If you want to examine the records to see what was found, you must run another of the *Family Roots* programs to do so, but the list will still be available in memory after moving to the other program, making that a simple matter. You may save the list on diskette and load it into the LISTS program to alphabetize or print it nicely. And the list remains in memory to be used as the choice of records for more searches . . . . Only the records having non-blank names are searched.

Let's examine the implication of reusing a list in memory for another search. Each of the five searches available is an OR search. This means that you can specify a large number of items to look for on any one pass through the records, and if any *one* of the items is found, the record is said to have satisfied the search. You do AND searches by specifying searching for one value, then reusing the results to search for another value, and so on until you're finished. This type of search means that the records found must satisfy *all* of the criteria you set up, not just *one*.

Suppose you wanted to find everybody who was born in LAS VEGAS and died in CALIFORNIA between 1960 and 1970. You would first set up a search of all the records for "born in Las Vegas." All the records would be searched and several would be found; the numbers for those would be saved in the computer's memory, say 13, 27, 59, 81 and 428. You would then set up another search for people who "died in California." You instruct the program to search only the five record numbers saved from the last search. Suppose three of those satisfy the search, 27, 59, and 428. Finally you set up a search for "people who died between 1960 and 1970." Again you specify to the program to search only the three records whose numbers were saved, and only one record satisfies your search, number 59. You can output that number to your printer, the screen, or a diskette; or you might use SHEETS just to see what's there or print a group sheet for that person.

The actual search of records can take a while since many records are usually retrieved and examined. Typically about ½ second would be needed for each record searched. If you watch your display, you will see a message showing what record is being searched. When a record is found to satisfy your criteria, the name is displayed. (8-2)

You initiate a search by selecting <1> on the main menu. The result of that effort is another menu, which we'll call the SEARCH menu:

1) SEARCH CHARACTER STRINGS   4) SEARCH FOR NUMBERS
2) SEARCH DATES   5) SEARCH FOR
3) SEARCH FOR NAMES   EMPTY FIELDS

When you make one of these choices, you are asked to specify which fields to search and what values in those fields are of interest.

You choose to search for character strings by typing <1> from the SEARCH menu. You will first select which fields you want to be searched in each record and then you choose the character strings to be found. The search is for embedded strings, e.g. if you're looking for YORK, then YORK, NEW YORK, and YORKY would all satisfy the search. (8-3)

The IGNORE UPPER/LOWER CASE parameter affects the results of the search. If the parameter is off, New York and NEW YORK are considered to be different because, for example, the "e" and "E" are distinct. Conversely, with the parameter on, those two forms would be the same. Your choice of which to use depends on how you entered your data and on how long you're willing to wait – the search with the parameter on takes much longer. It may often be faster to include both (or multiple) forms to search for, rather than using this parameter. For example, searching for New York, NEW YORK, and NEW York is faster than using one of them and asking that upper/lower case differences be ignored.

You are first shown a list of all the variables you can choose. You select up to 10 of these by number. (You can increase that limit using CONFIGUR.) . . . The list of variables includes all fields . . . . Once you have selected your variables, SEARCH shows you the list you have chosen and gives you a chance to do it again, in case you made a mistake. (8-4)

The next step is to pick up to 10 character strings to search for. You type each string of interest then press "enter." When you have enough, type only the <"enter">. The program again asks you for confirmation by showing you your list. If you reject it you return to select the entire list of strings again. (8-5)

You choose to search dates by typing <2> from the SEARCH menu. You are then faced with a decision on one of three different types of searches:

1) SEARCH FOR DATE BETWEEN TWO YEARS
2) SEARCH FOR YEAR BETWEEN TWO DATES
3) SEARCH FOR APPEARANCE OF MONTH/DAY

where "date" refers to something in a record and "year" means a number you will supply.

An example of the first type would be a search for "everybody born between 1775 and 1850." You would use the second for "everybody alive in 1863" or "everybody married after 1927." You would use the third to find everybody born in a certain month or certain day, e.g. "everybody born in March" or "everybody who was married on June 6." Note that if you want to search for a specific date including year, you should use the search on character strings. Also note that only dates in the standard format . . . are searched; the others are ignored.

You will first be asked the fields (variables) you want to search, followed by the values you want to search for. (8-6)

You choose to search on people by typing <3> from the Search menu. You first choose the variables to search and then the people you want to search for. SEARCH shows you the variables that you can search, namely:

1) MOTHER
2) FATHER
3) SPOUSES
4) CHILDREN

plus any person fields you may have defined for yourself. Since person searches often use all the fields, you are asked DO YOU WANT TO SEARCH ALL NAMES IN EACH RECORD? A <Y> answer bypasses the further choice of variables. If you want particular fields, answer <N> or <"enter"> for the question, and supply numbers to pick the fields; answer <"enter"> when you have enough.

Next you choose the names to search for. You may do this by name or number, but number would be the usual choice. When you supply a name, the program searches for the exact name as entered. This search is slightly faster but less general than searching for embedded character strings; you should use the "Character String" search if you are unsure of the name or spelling . . . . You may search for up to 10 names at the same time. When you supply a number, the program displays the name corresponding to that number and asks for confirmation.

The access menu then appears and the search begins after you make your selections. (8-8)

The search on counts is quite similar to the search on names, except that there is no confirmation of names needed. You elect to search on counts when you type <4> from the SEARCH menu. SEARCH shows you the variables you can search on, namely

1) NUMBER OF MARRIAGES
2) NUMBER OF CHILDREN
3) NUMBER OF NOTES

plus any count fields you may have defined yourself.

Next you supply the actual values to search for. You type these one at a time until your list is complete, then press <"enter">. You can supply up to 10 numbers . . . . (8-10)

You choose to search for empty fields by typing <5> from the Search menu. This kind of search is quite similar to searching for strings except that the string in this case is empty.

You will probably use this type of search to help you find where to fill in missing information. (8-11)

The results of your search or searches are now stored in memory and you want to have a look at them or save them . . . . Type <2> from the main menu to get the choice of three places to put the names:

1) OUTPUT TO SCREEN
2) OUTPUT TO PRINTER
3) OUTPUT TO DISKETTE

The printed output includes a header and the names for people who satisfied your searches. . . . The standard header shows what selections you made to arrive at the list, i.e. the type of search, variables searched, and values used. (8-12)

The output to diskette is quite similar to saving a list of names on diskette using the LISTS program, and, in fact, the format in which they are stored is identical. You would use this type of output to pass your results to LISTS for alphabetizing or printing. SEARCH needs to know which diskette to store on and what to call its output . . . . There are eight parameters available, with default values; the default values can be reset using the CONFIGUR program. (8-14)

COMPUTERIZING NOTES, DOCUMENTATION, AND BIOGRAPHIES

The most unacceptable flaw widely found in genealogy programs a few years back was the total lack of a place to cite sources of data. You can still find genealogy programs that shrug off the responsibility for documenting family data with a cavalier instruction like this: "Use your word-processing program to keep track of source documentation, footnotes, biographical sketches and other narrative-style information." Then the program seller could ignore the subject of source citing and get on with gathering facts by computer.

Before looking at how *Family Roots* accomodates data notations, let's read what genealogists say about the importance of such notations. If you buy their urgings, don't buy a genealogy program that doesn't give adequate fact-documenting capability.

Noel C. Stevenson: "In 1928, Neal F. Mears, a professional genealogist, wrote that 'There are nearly 10,000 family histories and compilations in print and probably not more than ten percent of them are worth the paper on which they are written. This is due solely to the fact that the worthless ones were compiled by persons who had no knowledge of the science of genealogy and particularly no comprehension of what constitutes proof. Anything they heard or saw from any source whatsoever, was good enough.'"[1]

National Society Daughters of the American Revolution: "Before apply-ing for membership in a hereditary society, do your homework! Those societies expect applicants to have researched their lineages thoroughly enough to be aware of the problems which might arise during the verifi-cation process, and to have documentation to resolve such problems. You, as the applicant, will be required to submit data to prove the parentage of each person from whom descent is claimed, and to prove each date and place of birth, marriage and death given on the lineage papers."[2]

"Regardless of how thorough you are in research and how good you are at correct analyses, if your notes are poorly kept and your records poorly documented the work you do will never be appreciated by any competent genealogist who views it or reviews it. He will probably repeat the same searches because he is not sure what you have done. Then, if he finds your work was good, he will condemn you the more for not keeping a good record. It will cost time and money to duplicate your work if you do only half the job."[3]

Price, Thorndale and Eakle: "It is remarkable how quickly you can forget the meaning of even your own notes! Most researchers can tell you a personal horror story of neglecting to copy a vital fact or its source and then spending years searching for it again."

"To summarize what is known about a couple and their children, the researcher usually uses a family group sheet, with spaces for names, par-ents, dates, places of events, children, spouses, sources, and other infor-mation to help identify members of one particular family."[4]

We return to *Family Roots* to see how it handles documentation of family facts:

There are a number of fields in which you can enter textual data such as names of places. These are free-form form fields that can contain any information you want to put there. (4-22)

Each text field is only limited in length by the size of the record, i.e. the sum of the length of all the fields can't be more than the record length limit (320 or whatever you set it to). It is advisable, however, to limit text fields to about 25 to 30 characters since they are printed in genealogy charts (when you elect to do so); overly long lines go to the edge of the printer paper or continue on the next lines, which doesn't keep the chart neat . . . . For footnotes you can use the carat "(up-arrow)" followed by a number to refer to a note field, as for dates. You could enter the supplemental information directly into the text field . . . . You would use a footnote to indicate sources, possible alternatives, etc.

Entering Birthplace . . . for example RENO NEV RENO; NEVADA3 RENO NEVADA (3) RENO, NEV. USA (UNCERTAIN) RENO NEV– FARM 7 MILES SOUTH would all be acceptable entries . . . . Entering Address Or Place of Death . . . entries that can be made here are almost the same as described above . . . except that there is some special processing to allow recognition of a complete address. A complete address, including phone number, is useful for living persons. (4-23)

If you enter a full address for a deceased person, no formatting or city/state extraction is done by CHARTS or SHEETS . . . . If you defined any fields for yourself, they will appear starting at menu item 5. The ones that you defined as free-text can have anything you choose in them. You may use footnotes on these fields by ending your entry with a "carat3" or something similar. (4-24)

YOUR CHOSEN FIELDS: Likely fields of this type would be OCCUPATION, SEX, PLACE OF CHRISTENING, PLACE OF BURIAL, and RELIGION. If you were entering information for OCCUPATION, that could be any of the following: FARMER, DIETICIAN, COLONEL IN THE ARMY, INVENTED THE PHONOTEL, or even IRASCIBLE OLD GOAT.

After number of marriages is entered . . . the menu will show a field labeled as (8) MARRIED AT for each marriage. After you select the number (for example, 11, 15, 19, etc.) the program will display (11) MARRIED AT (MRG #1)? The last item in parentheses shows you the marriage number, since there can be several such entries . . . . After number of marriages is entered . . . the menu will include one or more items labeled as #) MARITAL STATUS. This one does have some unique processing. Marital status is viewed as the current or final status of a marriage (or potential marriage). EDIT recognizes four usual status values MARRIED, WIDOWED, DIVORCED, ENGAGED, and abbreviates these to the first letter in order to save diskette space. (Note that a person is recognized as SINGLE from your entry of "0" in the NUMBER OF MARRIAGES field.) The CHARTS and SHEETS programs expand these to the full word in their displays and printing. You are not limited to these four values and could enter anything else you want; if you do this, your entire entry will be stored. (4-25)

After you enter something larger than 0 for number of notes . . . you can enter text for each of the notes. The program asks in the form #) NOTE 1? where "#" is a field number and depends on whatever else you have entered. The note fields are intended for short notes of interest and for long footnotes. Long passages of textual information should not be put here since they rapidly use up the available space and may not print or display very nicely in the CHARTS and SHEETS programs. Use the TEXT program or your word processing program for storage of significant textual data. (4-26)

If you use a note as a footnote, there is no distinction in the entry of the note itself as to what kind of note it is . . . . The only difference with footnotes is that they are referenced from other fields, as described above about the use of the carat "up-arrow." Footnotes would generally indicate sources of information (the same note could be referenced from several other fields) or qualifications of some other field (e.g. "date not necessarily exact"). (4-27)

Suppose you had the following notes: (1: National Archives) (2: History of Arkansas by Tyler) (3: I'm not sure about this) (4: Worked as engineer at World's Fair) (5: Look for more info on this) (6: Adopted).

If you were printing a chart that was to include some notes, you may not want the 3rd and 5th notes to appear. You could suppress them by placing 6(carat)110101 in the NUMBER OF NOTES field for this person, and setting a program parameter . . . . The "110101" means "print" for each 1 and "don't print" for each 0, by position. The leading "6" is the number of notes, of course. (4-28)

Footnotes are used in people fields in the same way as for others. For example entry of 6) MOTHER? <27carat1> would be recognized as record 27 with a reference to note number 1.

Complementing refers to the automatic entering of inferred data in records other than the one you are editing . . . . In general complementing saves you considerable entry of data, because you enter the information once and EDIT puts it in all the appropriate places.

The following are the inferred automatic entries done by complementing:

(1) If marriage information is entered for a record, the MARITAL STATUS field is filled-in in the same record if blank . . . . (2) When a FATHER and MOTHER field is entered for a record, the CHILD field is completed in the parent's record. (3) When a CHILD field is entered for a record, the appropriate parent field is completed in the child's record. (4) When any marriage information is entered in a record, the same information is placed in the record for the appropriate spouse. (5) When a CHILD field is entered for a record, that same child is placed in the record of the appropriate spouse; this inference is not always possible. (6) When a CHILD field is entered for a record, the opposite parent field in the child's record is completed if it can be determined from the spouse information. (7) When a DIED/LIVING AT field is entered for a parent, EDIT asks if the same place should be saved for each spouse and each child. (4-31)

The TEXT program stores, retrieves, edits, prints and displays free-form textual information on the people in your list of names. It is not a general text editing or word processing program, but rather a "card file" system with retrieval based on the names you have set up using the EDIT program. The TEXT program doesn't use the FAMILY.DAT file set up by EDIT but needs the (numbered) data diskettes from EDIT in order to retrieve names. In addition you will need to format one or more blank diskettes for use as text storage media before you begin . . . . Data diskettes used for text will be called "text diskettes" or "text data diskettes" . . . these are distinct from the numbered data diskettes used by the EDIT program. . . . Select the TEXT program from the Programs Menu.

The initial access to the data on the diskettes is similar to the EDIT and other main programs, but after that you'll find TEXT is quite different . . . . The textual information is stored in the SUPPMENT.DAT file on each diskette. Also on each diskette there is a DIRECTRY.DAT file that keeps track of whose information is in SUPPMENT.DAT on this particular diskette, and a COUNTERS.DAT file that keeps track of how space is used in SUPPMENT.DAT. The structure is such that every text diskette is independent of every other, but the program helps you in determining who is on which diskette.

There is no automatic splitting of information on one person across diskettes, but there is nothing to prevent you from having information on the same person on different diskettes. You could use this to advantage by keeping different sets of diskettes for different purposes . . . . One set could record facts for a person, the second could record notes to yourself on research progress and work to be done, while a third might contain anecdotes. (9-1)

The entire file (SUPPMENT.DAT) is partitioned into 128 character segments. These segments are allocated to text for a particular person one at a time as needed. This means that a person's whole record (i.e. the full text) in a file is of somewhat arbitrary length and is bounded only by the space in the file, which in turn is only bounded by the space on the diskette. This scheme allows efficient use of the space on the diskette, since very little of that space will normally be blank or wasted.

The independence of the files from diskette to diskette, coupled with the efficient use of space on each, gives you an essentially unlimited capability to store data about your family. Retrieval by name or number helps you to find the information easily and quickly.

When you look through a person's record, you do so in 128 character segments, although there is also a command to print an entire record as a unit. Additions to a record are done in 128 character segments, which you can select to have done each time you press "enter," or you may hold these additions until a longer section of text is ready to store.

Changes and deletions to a record are also on a 128 character basis, rather than on individual words. (9-2)

When you have text stored on the diskette, you can move through the record in single-segment (128 character) steps, or reposition yourself at the beginning of the record. You would do this to examine content or to position yourself to change something or print something . . . . You position yourself at the start of the record by typing S. You move forward in the record by typing F and backward by typing B. (9-6)

You use the P command to print a single segment on the printer and the L command to list the entire record for the person on the printer . . . . The start segment is preceded by a line telling who the printed output is for and date generated, unless you choose to define your own header. This is controlled by a parameter. (9-7)

You use the M (Modify) command to reenter the text in one segment of the record and the D (Delete) command to eliminate one segment. The affected segment is the one you last passed over using the F/B commands . . . . When you modify a segment you may shorten or lengthen it. It doesn't have to be the same length as before. TEXT automatically adjusts the succeeding segments for any significant change in length. (9-9)

Any text entries may be printed using the SHEETS program . . . . It does cause significantly longer delays to do it this way however. (9-13)

CREATING INDEXES FROM YOUR FAMILY FILES

Before we look at the way *Family Roots* is used to create indexes, we will display indexes created by several genealogy programs. An index is an arranged list. Remember, if you don't like the looks of a list because it is faintly printed, that flaw is a fault of reproduction or worn-out printer ribbon; if you don't like the style of the print itself, that flaw is attributable to the printer used and not the genealogy program; and, if you don't like the blurry image or tiny size of a printout, that's poor photocopying or our necessary size reduction. All of these specimens were originally 8 ½ by 11 inches unless otherwise noted; please judge these printouts for *substance* and not the failings in printing and reproduction.

By Surname — A common index need is by surname. Plate 13 shows M.A. Harrison's variant from *Roots and Relatives*; Plate 14 is an example of *Genealog II* from Genealog Software; Plate 15 is from Discovery Software's *Family Connection*; Plate 16 is Armstrong Genealogical System's display from *Genealogy: Compiling Roots and Branches*; Plate 17 is Array Systems' *Treesearch* version; Plate 18 is from *Ancestor File Programs* by J. P. Davis; Plate 19 shows Software Solutions' *Arbor-Aide* variant; and Plate 20 is from our walk-through study program, *Family Roots* by Quinsept.

You may find one or another printout to your liking. Note that all of these surname-index lists contain an identification number as well as the names in alphabetic order by surname! This is how you find a computerized record when you know a name — in most genealogy software, the "RIN" (record identification number) is the search term to use for quickly accessing a person's record. Some of these indexes carry additional information (such as dates, for example). Do not fault a surname index for *not* having additional information; you asked for a list by *name* in alphabetical order, and that is what you get. Another kind of index may carry the other information you may want to see.

By First Name — The need to look up family members named "John Henry" or "Agatha Ann" is served by an index arranged by first-name. Here are some illustrations of such indexes. Plate 21 is the J.P. Davis version from *Ancestor File Programs* and Plate 22 is from Armstrong Genealogical Systems' *Genealogy: Compiling Roots and Branches*.

By Numeric Order—The "numeric order" of records indexing refers to the identification number the computer program uses to file away a given person's record. Frequently, a person's computerized record will refer to a father or mother by record identification number (RIN). You will need an index by number in order to see who is being referenced. Plate 23 shows Discovery Software's *Family Connection* version of a numeric-order index; Plate 24 is from *Family Tree* by Genealogy Software, and our study program, *Family Roots* by Quinsept, Inc., shows its number index in Plate 25.

Special Indexes— If you want to see what records are on a single disk, you can get a by-disk index as illustrated in Plate 26 from *My Roots* by Mark Peters. You can have an index of footnotes as shown in Plate 27 taken from Armstrong Genealogical Systems' *Genealogy: Compiling Roots and Branches*. That same program generates indexes by birthdate, by marriage date, and by death date, too. See Plates 28, 29, and 30 for examples. The genealogy software by Array Systems, *Treesearch*, is unique in many ways. Because of its uniqueness, it can generate by-event indexes as seen in Plate 31 and Plate 32.

Your-Choice Indexes—We showed how *Family Roots* can be used to find all records having certain data in them. This search process produced lists of records that contained the search terms. Plate 33 shows a multiple-terms search using *Family Roots*. In this illustration, the terms which had to be in any record (if it was to match the search terms) were "1800," "1899," "GERMANY," "GERM," "WAGON MOUND," "WAGON," and "MOUND." The years were to be found in DATE OF BIRTH or CHRISTENED ON fields; the search strings (the words or word-parts) had to be in one of these fields: PLACE OF BIRTH, PLACE OF DEATH/LIVING, PLACE(S) OF MARRIAGE, BURIAL PLACE, or CHRISTENED AT. Now, *that* is quite an order! Nowhere will you find the power of genealogy computing seen so dramatically as in a multiterm search of records having so many search-term parameters as this. Only the very best genealogy software has the capability to produce indexes of so complex a nature as is seen in Plate 33. In *Genealogy Program*, Frank Lerchen has search-term indexing of a simpler nature. Plate 34 shows two of his search-index lists; they are by parent and by child's name. In the illustration, we find "Mary" must be the parent name for the search and "Frank" must be the child's name. The Array Systems *Treesearch* program provides us an illustration of picking out all of a given surname from a family file which contains more than one surname; see Plate 35. Another version of this by-surname search/index capability is from Software Solutions' *Arbor-Aide* software; see Plate 36 (which shows an index resulting from a search for "DeL").

These are but samples from genealogy software you might buy. We regret being unable to show all the variants from all the different packages.

FAMILY RECORD INDEX

FRN	NAME	LIFE-SPAN
295	????, ????	-1939
194	????, AUDREY	-
318	????, CAROL	1943-
171	????, CAROL	-
184	????, EMILY	-
326	????, GRACE	-
327	????, KAREN	-
199	????, PATRICIA	-
275	????, SARAH	1830-
306	ALCANBRACK, ELMIRA	-1957
149	ANDERSON, JOHN	-
302	ANDERSON, MARIAN (MARY)	-
155	ARMSTRONG, ISABEL EMILY	-
127	ARNOLD, WILLIAM	-
170	ASHTON, HERMAN	-
217	ASSELTINE, GEORGE	-
269	AUSTIN, STANLEY	-
285	BACON, SUSANNE MARIE	1953-
325	BAKER, DENNIS	-
11	BALDWIN, ARTHUR HENRY	-
101	BALDWIN, BEATRICE	-
100	BALDWIN, EDITH MAY	-
54	BARKLEY, JAMES(JIM)	-
10	BARKLEY, MARTHA HELEN	1893-1975
135	BARNES, GORDAN RICHARD	1947-
102	BARRETT, JANE P	-
63	BARROWS, ANNIE SAFFORD	1859-1926
60	BARTLEY, ALZINA	-
59	BARTLEY, CECILIA	-
57	BARTLEY, EMMA	-
56	BARTLEY, GEORGE	-
55	BARTLEY, JOSEPH(JOE)	-
58	BARTLEY, JACK	-
53	BARTLEY, JOHN	1841-1941
101	BATES, GEORGE H	-
215	BAXTER, RALPH	-
145	BEAMISH, THOMAS	-
311	BECKEDAHL, LESLIE WALTER	-
296	BERRY, LEONE	-
305	BLACK, ELLA	-
201	BLIECH, STAN	-
4	BOYCE, ALBERT EDWARD	-
13	BOYCE, ALICE	-
11	BOYCE, ALICE	-
1	BOYCE, FLORENCE	1883-1950
9	BOYCE, MARGARET RHODA	1889-1971
138	BOYD, ERNEST JOHN	1915-
173	BOYLE, ALLAN	-
176	BOYLE, ALLAN (SR)	-
176	BOYLE, GRANDMA	-

Plate 13. M.A. Harrison *Roots and Relatives* Index

SALLEE1 FILE INDEX

(1)	0035	BINFORD BETSEY KINSEY	1739
(2)	0065	BONDURANT FRANCOISE	1715
(3)	0130	BONDURANT JEAN PIERRE	
(4)	0073	BRUCE ANN	
(5)	0044	CHASTAIN BARNETT SR.	1774
(6)	0011	CHASTAIN CYNTHIA ANN	1841
(7)	0176	CHASTAIN PIERRE JR.	1708
(8)	0352	CHASTAIN PIERRE SR.	1662
(9)	0088	CHASTAIN WILLIAM	
(10)	0022	CHASTAIN WILLIAM	1797
(11)	0076.2	COX RHODA	
(12)	0515	FORTIER JUDITH	
(13)	0013	HAMILTON JEMIMA	1825
(14)	0045	HIXON SARA	
(15)	0003	JOHNSTON JEMIMA	1893
(16)	0012	JOHNSTON JOHN	1830
(17)	0006	JOHNSTON SAMUEL	1860
(18)	0514	MARTIN JACQUES	1590
(19)	0257	MARTIN MARIE	1634
(20)	0077	MARTIN SARAH	
(21)	0132	MAXEY EDWARD SR.	
(22)	0033	MAXEY JEMIMA	
(23)	0067	MAXEY MARY (SUBLETT?)	
(24)	0133	MAXEY SUSANNAH (?)	
(25)	0066	MAXEY WILLIAM	
(26)	0009	MCCOY CHRISTIANA POUND	1814
(27)	0072	MCCOY JAMES	1720
(28)	0018	MCCOY ROYSE (RICE)	1789
(29)	0036	MCCOY WILLIAM	1754
(30)	0513	MESTAY SUZANNE	1610
(31)	0136	PANETIE JEAN PIERRE	
(32)	0136*	PANETIE JEAN PIERRE	
(33)	0017	PANKEY JUDITH	1767
(34)	0034	PANKEY SAMUEL	1758
(35)	0068	PANKEY STEPHEN	
(36)	0129	PERRAULT OLIVE	1680
(37)	0020D	PIERSON ABRAHAM N.	
(38)	0010	PIERSON GOWAN B	1834
(39)	0020	PIERSON JACOB	NOTE
(40)	0020B	PIERSON JOHN A.	
(41)	0020F	PIERSON MARY F	
(42)	0021	PIERSON TERESA	1812
(43)	0005	PIERSON TERESA (POLLY)	1858
(44)	0304	POUND JOHN	
(45)	0076*	POUND JOHN	1735
(46)	0608	POUND JOHN	1690
(47)	0076	POUND JOHN	1735
(48)	0038	POUND JOSEPH	1770
(49)	0019*	POUND MALINDA	1796
(50)	0019	POUND MALINDA	1796
(51)	0152	POUND THOMAS	1708
(52)	0037	ROYSE ELIZABETH	1758
(53)	0028	RUSSEL JOHN	
(54)	0014	RUSSELL JOHN	
(55)	0128	SALLE ABRAHAM	1674

Plate 14.   Genealog Software *Genealog II* File Index

INDIVIDUAL NAME	CPN
Cannon, Nora Louise	A210
Christensen, Bertha Mae	A176
Clabaugh, Amos Henry	A132
Clabaugh, Andrew Wesley	A159
Clabaugh, Benjamin Perley	A170
Clabaugh, Byron E.	A172
Clabaugh, Elizabeth	A168
Clabaugh, Estella Jane Black	A131
Clabaugh, Esther Ellen (Ella)	A 24
Clabaugh, Eugene	A160
Clabaugh, Harry Collier	A174
Clabaugh, Henry S. (Claybaugh)	A129
Clabaugh, John	A162
Clabaugh, John	A169
Clabaugh, John N. (Nash?)	A133
Clabaugh, Mary Etta (Mollie)	A134
Clabaugh, Nancy	A167
Clabaugh, Nancy (Nettie)	A135
Clabaugh, Nicholas	A164
Clabaugh, Nicholas	A166
Clabaugh, Nicholas Riley	A137
Clabaugh, Robert	A165
Clabaugh, Rosemary	A173
Clabaugh, Thomas	A171
Clabaugh, William P.	A136
Cox, Cynthia	A145
Cox, Sarah Peterson	A139
Crawford, Lydia	A 64
Cruse, Maud Lou	A 47
Dysert, Lillian	A184
Elmore, Harriet	A 26
England, Maudie Bilbrey	A185
Evans, Vinnie	A189
Gearheart, Abigail	A 51
Graham, Charles Jr.	A105
Graham, Florence	A104
Graham, Helene	A103
Harper, George Dwain	A179
Henry, Elizabeth	A130
Hill, Mary Jenny	A119
Huffman, Harriet Jane	A123
Huffman, Job	A140
Huffman, Mary Ann	A141
Hull, Altha Luetta	A 61
Hull, Amanda	A 70
Hull, Barbara Ann	A 56
Hull, Calvin	A 71
Hull, David	A 66
Hull, Elmer Ellsworth	A 55
Hull, Gertrude Florence	A 53
Hull, Henry	A 65
Hull, Isaac	A 50
Hull, John	A 62
Hull, John	A 69
Hull, John William	A 57
Hull, Lillian Pearl	A 52
Hull, Lydia Ann	A 60

Plate 15. Discovery Software *Family Connection* Alphabetical
Record Index

ARMSTRONG-GORANSON GENEALOGY
==
Page 1   LAST NAME..(MARRIED LAST NAME),..FIRST NAME INDEX part 1   11 Feb 1981
==

```
ID #                              Name
====    ========================================================
 120    ???????? (ARMSTRONG), ANN
  86    ???????? (ARMSTRONG), BRENDA
 324    ???????? (BEEBE), HENNIE
 390    ???????? (JACOBSON), SYLVIA
 328    ???????? (MATSON), KATHRYN
 247    ???????? (VINCENT), BESS
 372    ???????? (ZIMMERMAN), FLORENCE
 231    ???????? (ZIMMERMAN), MARY
 190    ADAMS (BURCHFIELD), GRETTA MAE
 189    ADAMS (BURCHFIELD), ZELMA MAUDE
 421    ADAMS (HELD), HARRIET JEAN
 330    ADAMS, WILLIAM EDWARD
  71    ARMSTRONG (BOHME), DOROTHY GRACE
 126    ARMSTRONG (BURCHFIELD), MARY ELIZABETH
  54    ARMSTRONG (CASPER), CAROL JUNE
  78    ARMSTRONG (CHISHOLM), MARILYN JEAN
 123    ARMSTRONG (DANIELS), SABRA ELIZA
 140    ARMSTRONG (GIERUCKI), MARY LOUISE
 121    ARMSTRONG (HUBBELL), MARILLA MARGARET
  46    ARMSTRONG (LOCKE), CAROLYN
  68    ARMSTRONG (MOORHEAD), JEAN MARIE
  61    ARMSTRONG (OKKERSE), NANCY ANN
  59    ARMSTRONG (WEINBRENNER), DONNA RUTH
 127    ARMSTRONG (WILSON), MARGARET ADELTA
 125    ARMSTRONG (WILSON), MARGARET ELEANOR
  55    ARMSTRONG (WIMMER), ELAINE GLADYS
 283    ARMSTRONG, AARON
 280    ARMSTRONG, ALEXANDER
   1    ARMSTRONG, ALICE ANN
 136    ARMSTRONG, ALTON ROBERT
   9    ARMSTRONG, AMANDA SUE
 148    ARMSTRONG, ANDREW
  50    ARMSTRONG, BEVERLY
 106    ARMSTRONG, BLAKE EDWARD
 102    ARMSTRONG, BRENT ALAN
  12    ARMSTRONG, BRYAN MARCUS
 214    ARMSTRONG, CAROL ANN
  65    ARMSTRONG, CHARLES CEDRIC
  19    ARMSTRONG, CHARLES LEO
  84    ARMSTRONG, CHARLES RAY
   5    ARMSTRONG, DAVID ARTHUR
   6    ARMSTRONG, DAVID CLINTON
 138    ARMSTRONG, DAVID KEITH
 217    ARMSTRONG, DAVID KEITH JR.
 141    ARMSTRONG, DAVID S.
 113    ARMSTRONG, DAVID SAMPSON
  77    ARMSTRONG, DELLA MAY
  56    ARMSTRONG, DURRELL WAYNE
 286    ARMSTRONG, ELEANOR
 287    ARMSTRONG, ELIZA JANE
```
==
part 1 continued...

Plate 16. Armstrong Genealogical Systems *Genealogy: Compiling
Roots and Branches* Index

ALPHABETICAL LIST OF JONES AND HARRISON FAMILIES
09-05-1984

31	HARRISON 000000	EDWIN LEWIS 01 AUG 1859 17 MAY 1904	BANGOR, PENOBSCOT, ME 000002/000003 PARK CITY, SUMMIT, UT	
32	HARRISON 300003	EDWIN LEWIS 23 DEC 1946	LEHI, UTAH, UT 000006/000007	
33	HARRISON 900003	ELLIE LOUISE 13 JUL 1959 03 AUG 1962	SALT LAKE CITY, SALT LAKE, UT 000006/000007 SALT LAKE CITY, SALT LAKE, UT	
34	HARRISON 00000C	GILBERT DONALD 28 APR 1887 8 FEB 1951	EUREKA, JUAB, UT 00000D/00000P SALT LAKE CITY, SALT LAKE, UT	
35	HARRISON 000006	JAMES PATRICK 04 APR 1920 12 SEP 1977	SALT LAKE CITY, SALT LAKE, UT 00000C/00000D PANAMA CITY, BAY, FLA	
36	HARRISON 400003	KATHLEEN 25 JUN 1950	MURRAY, SALT LAKE, UT 000006/000007	
37	HARRISON 000003	NANCY RUTH 24 OCT 1941	SALT LAKE CITY, SALT LAKE, UT 000006/000007	
38	HARRISON 500003	PATRICIA ANN 26 MAR 1954	SALT LAKE CITY, SALT LAKE, UT 000006/000007	
39	HARRISON 200003	PAULA 19 DEC 1943	SALT LAKE CITY, SL, UT 000006/000007	
40	HARRISON 200003	PENNY LYNN 08 MAR 1945	PROVO, UTAH, UT 000006/000007	

Plate 17. Array Systems, Inc. *Treesearch* Index

```
---------------------------------------------------------------------------
                    INDEX OF THE RAY FAMILY FILE                    Pg  2
---------------------------------------------------------------------------


                                      Generation    Identity No.   Ancestor No.

              SOPHIA      STEELMAN        4              92             13
              STILLMAN                    3              61
              SUSAN       G               3              70
              WARREN                      4              97
              WILLIAM                     2              11

              WILLIAM                     3              80
              WILLIAM                     1               1            104
              WILLIAM     COLLINS         3              19


BROWN         (POSSIBLY)  WARREN          3              75
CAMPBELL      MARGARET    F.              2               9
COLLINS       BETHIA                      2               4             53
COLLINS       MARY        C.              3              32
COLLINS       RICHARD     JR.             2              16

COLLINS       SOPHIA                      2              12
COLLINS       WYMAN       (WILLIAM)       3              50
CRAIG         MARIA                       3              63
DINSMORE      FRANCES                     3              59
DYER          EZEKIEL                     3              25

FICKETT       MARY                        3              20
FOSTER        JAMES                       3              54
FOSTER        LYDIA                       3              30
FOSTER        WILLIAM     G.              3              52
GRACE         MARY        M.              3              69

GRIFFIN       ELIAS                       3              84
HALL          SOPHIA                      4              94
HINKLEY       ANNA        JANE            3              27
JACKSON       HENRY       ANDREW          4              87
JOHNSON ?     CAROLINE                    4              98

LEIGHTON      EDWARD                      3              82
LORD          JERUSHA                     2               6
MEANS         AUGUSTA     A.              3              77
MITCHELL      EUNICE      DELILAH         3              81
NASH          AMBROSE                     3              40

NASH          LIVONIA     A.              3              42
PARRITT       WOODBURY    L.              3              79
PRATT         JULIA       A.              3              68
REED          JOHN        O. C.           4              93             12
RIFENBERGH    FREDERICK                   4              91

SAWYER        EBEN                        3              56
SAWYER        ELBRIDGE                    3              44
SAWYER        STILLMAN    DYER            3              73
SMALL         MARIA                       3              66
SMALL         MOSES       HINKLEY         3              71
```

Plate 18. Joyce P. Davis *Ancestor File Program* Index

Alphabetic Chart
Sandra Lee DeLisle Disk
(All Ancestors)

ID	1st Name	Middle Name	-------------Last Name------------	Birth Date
135	Angelique	Marie	Aide-Crequy	13 Oct 1740
153	Marie	Clotilde	Aide-Crequy	13 Oct 1740
138	Jean	Baptiste	Bertrand	13 Mar 1706
069	Therese		Bertrand	11 Mar 1751
141	Elisabeth		Biguet-Nobert	06 Apr 1722
013	Laura		Bishop	19 Apr 1882
026	William		Bishop	01 Jan 1863
260	Jane		Blaeser	
031	Mary	Elizabeth	Boyer	01 Jan 1841
023	Mary		Burke	
158	Alexis		Cailler	16 Jun 1756
079	Madeleine		Cayer	
265	Arthur	Benedict	DeLisle	03 May 1920
259	Daniel	Eugene	DeLisle	01 May 1947
263	Deborah	Mary	DeLisle	07 Oct 1959
262	Diane	Marie	DeLisle	06 Dec 1955
002	Eugene	Daniel	DeLisle	30 Aug 1918
008	Eugene	Joseph	DeLisle	15 Jan 1848
032	Jacques		DeLisle	30 Mar 1782
064	Jacques		DeLisle	20 Jun 1755
128	Jacque		DeLisle	18 Mar 1718
016	Jacques		DeLisle	00 Jan 1800
264	Julie	Ann	DeLisle	05 Jun 1961
004	Peter	Eugene	DeLisle	05 Jul 1888
001	Sandra	Lee	DeLisle	21 May 1951
067	Clotilde		Dussault-Toupin	19 May 1764
159	Marie	Josette	Dussault	09 Mar 1753
019	Salome		Dussault	13 Mar 1836
015	Fidelia	L	Fellows	13 Mar 1863
030	Oliver		Fellows	12 Jun 1837
130	Jerome	Thierry	Fiset	00 Unk 1725
065	Marie	Elisabeth	Fiset	18 Jun 1757
029	Elizabeth		Fritz	
025	Adelia	H	Furney	22 Sep 1837
011	Sarah		Garvey	25 Mar 1853
022	Thomas		Garvey	
137	Marie	Catherine	Gaudin	24 May 1706
037	Marie	Therese	Gauthier	
140	Jacque	Alexis	Germain	14 Apr 1713
035	Marie	Angelique	Germain	18 Sep 1776
070	Pierre	Etienne	Germain	19 Dec 1743
027	Ann	Rose	Gormlay	00 Sep 1859
078	Augustine		Houde	
156	Francois		Houde	
039	Marguerite		Houde	
071	Angelique	Marie	Langlois	
139	Marie	Joseph	Letellier	06 Apr 1713
017	Francoise		Leveille	
068	Jean		Leveille	27 Dec 1738
136	Jean		Leveille	08 Jan 1707
034	Jean	Baptiste	Leveille	11 Aug 1771
154	Augustine		Matte	08 Nov 1748

Plate 19. Software Solutions *Arbor-Aide* Alphabetical Chart

```
         INDEX TO NAMES           03/07/1983

    RECORD
    INDEX      NAME

     411   BECKER, HERMANN
     429   BOOKEY, SAMUEL
     426   BRENT, JAMES
     428   DUVALL, SAMUEL
     437   EGE, JOHANN

     412   FISCHBACH, THEIS OF OBERFISCHBACH
     431   FOSTER, JAMES W.
     403   GREEN, GILBERT HUNTON
     439   HAGAR, JOHN HENRY
     418   HEIMBACH, JOHANN

     424   HEIMBACH, JOST
     402   HUNTON, ANNIE
     407   HUNTON, CHARLES HENRY
     404   HUNTON, CHARLES
     410   HUNTON, CHARLIE

     408   HUNTON, EPPA
     420   HUNTON, EPPA (4TH EPPA)
     419   HUNTON, EVA
     425   HUNTON, FRANCES
     421   HUNTON, GEORGE B.

     416   HUNTON, MARGARET L
     433   HUNTON, MARTHA
     423   HUNTON, MILTON KIRK
     432   HUNTON, MOSS
     427   HUNTON, PRISCILLA

     422   HUNTON, ROBERTA
     417   HUNTON, SARAH LUCELIA
     406   HUNTON, THOMAS EDWARD
     405   HUNTON, THOMAS LOGAN
     401   HUNTON, THOMAS

     434   KEYSER, CHARLES HAMPTON JR.
     415   MC NISH, ELIZABETH
     413   MOSS, GEORGE
     438   RIXEY, FRANCES JANE ELIZABETH
     435   RIXEY, PRESLEY MOREHEAD

     436   RIXEY, RICHARD LEWIS
     440   RIXEY, SAMUEL TURNER
     414   SORRELL, AGNES
     430   STRICKLER, ABRAHAM
     409   VANCE, MARY
```

Plate 20.   Quinsept, Inc. *Family Roots* Name Index

```
-------------------------------------------------------------------------------
                          INDEX OF THE RAY FAMILY FILE
-------------------------------------------------------------------------------


                                      Generation    Identity No.   Ancestor No.
RAY
        ABIGAIL                           3              49
        ADRIAN       JUDSON               3              41
        ALEXANDER    CAMPBELL             3              58
        ANNIS        CLARK                4              86
        BELINDA                           3              28

        BETHIA                            3              74
        BETSEY                            2              14
        CAROLINE                          3              55
        CATHERINE                         3              51
        CHARLES      W.                   3              31

        DAVID        A.                   3              45
        DOLLY                             2              15
        ELEANOR                           3              83
        ELIZABETH                         3              53
        ELIZABETH    (BETSEY)             3              39

        GEORGE       F.                   3              29
        JAMES                             2               8
        JAMES        JR.                  3              57
        JOHN                              3              47
        JOHN                              2               5

        JOSEPH                            2               3             52
        JOSEPH       W.                   3              67
        LEWIS        JOSEPH               3              17             26
        MARCIA                            3              37
        MARGARET                          3              60

        MARTHA                            2              13
        MARTHA       ANN                  4              99
        MARTIN       LUTHER               3              65
        MARY         ANN                  3              43
        MARY         COLLINS              3              24

        MARY         JANE                 4             100
        MULL                              4              88
        NANCY                             3              72
        NANCY        G.                   3              35
        PETER        STEELMAN             4              89

        RICHARD      COLLINS              3              22
        RUBY                              3              33
        SAMUEL       MERRILL              3              76
        SIMEON       BROWN                3              26
        SOPHIA                            3              78
```

Plate 21. Joyce P. Davis *Ancestor File Program* First Name Index

ARMSTRONG-GORANSON GENEALOGY
==
Page 1   FIRST NAME..LAST NAME..(MARRIED LAST NAME) INDEX part 1   11 Feb 1981
==

ID #	Name	ID #	Name
396	'BABY BOY' GROAT	203	BONNIE SUE BEEBE (BLANDING)
153	'BABY BOY' WILSON	86	BRENDA ???????? (ARMSTRONG)
423	???????? BIELKE	45	BRENDA JEAN SMITH
424	???????? KELM	458	BRENDA KAY BALDWIN
425	???????? PERIS	102	BRENT ALAN ARMSTRONG
426	???????? SCHULTE(SCHUTH)	37	BRIAN SMITH
427	???????? WIETZKE	109	BRIAN LOGAN LOCKE
283	AARON ARMSTRONG	12	BRYAN MARCUS ARMSTRONG
31	AARON STEPHEN GORANSON	380	BURTON EUGENE MOORHEAD
401	AGNES STEVENSON (GROAT)	257	CARL JOHAN GORANSSON
154	AGNES CECELIA O'BRIEN (HOFFMAN*	14	CAROL GUNN (ARMSTRONG)
391	ALAN JACOBSON	481	CAROL HIGHFILL (RUSCO)
300	ALBERT HORTON	214	CAROL ANN ARMSTRONG
402	ALBERT LESTER GROAT	206	CAROL ELIZABETH BEEBE (MATZ)
280	ALEXANDER ARMSTRONG	54	CAROL JUNE ARMSTRONG (CASPER)
182	ALFRED HUBBELL	333	CAROL P. KROPF (BURCHFIELD)
350	ALFRED BENSON RUSCO	482	CAROLEE JOYCE RUSCO (DENNING)
450	ALFRED WAYNE RUSCO	491	CAROLINE SMITH (BAILEY)
1	ALICE ANN ARMSTRONG	46	CAROLYN ARMSTRONG (LOCKE)
382	ALICE E. ROGERS (LUCAS)	477	CAROLYN KAY RUSCO (OBORNY)
136	ALTON ROBERT ARMSTRONG	197	CAROLYN MARIE BURCHFIELD (GROH*
483	ALVIN LEANDER DENNING	274	CATHERINE YARGER
486	AMANDA SMITH (DECKER)	185	CECIL RHODES CUMMINGS
312	AMANDA ZIMMERMAN	387	CEDRIC HOWARD
9	AMANDA SUE ARMSTRONG	433	CHARLENE MAE HELD (STEPHENS)
308	AMY ZIMMERMAN	175	CHARLES HUBBELL
186	AMY PAULINE POWELL (BURCHFIELD*	65	CHARLES CEDRIC ARMSTRONG
32	ANDREA JUDITH GORANSON	222	CHARLES DAVID LUCAS
148	ANDREW ARMSTRONG	191	CHARLES JOSEPH SCHREIBER
120	ANN ???????? (ARMSTRONG)	19	CHARLES LEO ARMSTRONG
298	ANN KELLY	253	CHARLES R. SKINNER
494	ANNA DECKER	84	CHARLES RAY ARMSTRONG
263	ANNA TEMPLIN (WIETZKE)	142	CHARLES SHERMAN BURCHFIELD
258	ANNA CHARLOTTA LARSSON (GORANS*	196	CHERYL JEANNE BURCHFIELD
7	ANNA MARIE GORANSON (ARMSTRONG*	416	CHRIS ALLEN SMITH
163	ANNIE WILSON	415	CHRIS E. SMITH
82	ANTHONY BRUCE CHISHOLM	33	CHRISTOPHER MARTIN
248	APRIL DAWN CHISHOLM	266	CLARA ANNA TEMPLIN (PERIS)
484	APRIL LEANN DENNING	334	CLARENCE POWELL
15	ARTHUR JOHN GORANSON	348	CLARENCE ALFRED LUCAS
499	ASHBY GRAY	356	CLARENCE ALFRED JR. LUCAS
418	AUGUST TEMPLIN	352	CLARENCE COMFORT RUSCO
500	BECKY GRAY	475	CLARK DAVID RUSCO
150	BENJAMIN FRANKLIN WILSON	176	CORA HUBBELL
403	BERTHA TIMMONS (BROWN GROAT)	195	CRAIG CHARLES BURCHFIELD
247	BESS ???????? (VINCENT)	100	CYNTHIA ANNETTE WIMMER
392	BEULAH PEARL WARREN (GROAT)	293	DANIEL RHODES
50	BEVERLY ARMSTRONG	325	DAVID BEIRIGER
462	BILLY JEAN PIKE	227	DAVID CONOLY
106	BLAKE EDWARD ARMSTRONG	291	DAVID SMOOTZ

==
part 1 continued...   asterisk denotes name shortened to fit on page

Plate 22. Armstrong Genealogical Systems *Genealogy: Compiling Roots and Branches* Index

```
INDIVIDUAL NAME                        CPN
------------------------------------------------
Wyatt, Allen Lee Sr.                ▲  1
Peas., Debra Mae                    ▲  2
Wyatt, Allen Lee Jr.                ▲  3
Wyatt, Eric Christopher             ▲  4
Wyatt, James Allen                  ▲  5
Hull, Virginia Lee                  ▲  6
Wyatt, Martin Henry                 ▲  7
Sorter, Harriet Marie               ▲  8
Hull, Richard Harold Sr.            ▲  9
Lowder, Helene Larue                ▲ 10
Wyatt, Sandra Elaine                ▲ 11
Winward, James Wallace              ▲ 12
Wyatt, April Lynne                  ▲ 13
Wyatt, Martin Richard               ▲ 14
Wyatt, Nora Jean                    ▲ 15
Wyatt, Daniel Martin                ▲ 16
Hull, Richard Harold Jr.            ▲ 17
Hull, Norma Jean                    ▲ 18
Hull, Wilma Ann                     ▲ 19
Winward, Jana Alysse                ▲ 20
Wyatt, Daniel W                     ▲ 21
Woody, Emma                         ▲ 22
Sorter, Homer Hill                  ▲ 23
Clabaugh, Esther Ellen (Ella)       ▲ 24
Wyatt, Jacob                        ▲ 25
Elmore, Harriet                     ▲ 26
Wyatt, James                        ▲ 27
Wyatt, Millie                       ▲ 28
Wyatt, John Sr.                     ▲ 29
Trembell, Sarah                     ▲ 30
Hull, Orion Ferdinand               ▲ 31
Peas., Cecil Lee                    ▲ 32
Rasmussen, Wilma Pearl              ▲ 33
Peas., Wilmot Lee                   ▲ 34
Peas., Bruce Kay                    ▲ 35
Peas., Danny Ray                    ▲ 36
Peas., Isaac Lee                    ▲ 37
Wilkins, Vera                       ▲ 38
Peas., Vera                         ▲ 39
Peas., William Kief                 ▲ 40
Peas., Irvin Leroy                  ▲ 41
Peas., Ernest Lavon                 ▲ 42
Peas., Erleen                       ▲ 43
Peas., Lois                         ▲ 44
Peas., Betty                        ▲ 45
Peas., Asa Jr.                      ▲ 46
Cruse, Maud Lou                     ▲ 47
Peas., Asa Sr.                      ▲ 48
Keefer, Isabelle                    ▲ 49
Hull, Isaac                         ▲ 50
Gearheart, Abigail                  ▲ 51
Hull, Lillian Pearl                 ▲ 52
Hull, Gertrude Florence             ▲ 53
Hull, Ruth Ann                      ▲ 54
Hull, Elmer Ellsworth               ▲ 55
Hull, Barbara Ann                   ▲ 56
Hull, John William                  ▲ 57
```

Plate 23. Discovery Software *Family Connection* Numeric Index

INDEX OF NAMES

```
1   HILLMAN      RICHARD GORDON
2   HILLMAN      MARK ANDREW
3   HILLMAN      STEVEN JAMES
4   HILLMAN      THOMAS PETER
5   HILLMAN      CHRISTOPHER MICHAEL
6   HILLMAN      MICHAEL JOHN
7   HILLMAN      JAMES PHILLIP
8   HILLMAN      MELISSA KATHERINE MARGARET
9   SABADOS      MARGARET ALICE THELMA
10  HILLMAN      GORDON PAYEN
11  HILLMAN      FRANK ERNEST
12  BOURNE       EMMA
13  HILLMAN      ERNEST PETER
14  HILLMAN      GEORGE HERBERT
15  HILLMAN      LILLIAN MARY
16  HILLMAN      BERTHA
17  HILLMAN      ETHEL LINDA
18  NICOLA       LEANORA LOUISE DIANA
19  BOURNE       CHARLES
20  SHARP        RACHEL AMY
21  HILLMAN      PETER
22  NICHOLSON    ESTHER
23  NICOLA       FRANCESCO
24  MORGAN       EMILY
25  BOURNE       ALFRED
26  COOPER       EMMA
27  SHARP        CHARLES
28  PURDY        LAVINA ADELAIDE
29  HILLMAN      THOMAS
30  HAMPER       ELIZABETH
31  NICHOLSON    NELSON
32  HOTSTONE     MARY
33  NICOLA       LUIGI PAYOLA
34  PAGUENNE     GIULA
35  MORGAN       HENRY
36  HAYWARD      MARIA
37  BOURNE       WILLIAM
38  POND         SARAH
39  COOPER       DANIEL
40  PIDGEN       MARY ANN
41  SHARP        JOHN
42  ELLSWORTH    MARY
43  PURDY        NEHEMIAH
44  ELLSWORTH    ELIZABETH
45  HILLMAN      THOMAS
46  MITCHELL     SARAH
47  HAMPER       JOHN
48  UNKNOWN      EMMA
49  NICHOLSON    JOHN
```

Plate 24. Genealogy Software *Family Tree* Number Index

NUMERIC LIST   03/07/1983

RECORD
INDEX   NAME

    401   HUNTON, THOMAS
    402   HUNTON, ANNIE
    403   GREEN, GILBERT HUNTON
    404   HUNTON, CHARLES
    405   HUNTON, THOMAS LOGAN

    406   HUNTON, THOMAS EDWARD
    407   HUNTON, CHARLES HENRY
    408   HUNTON, EPPA
    409   VANCE, MARY
    410   HUNTON, CHARLIE

    411   BECKER, HERMANN
    412   FISCHBACH, THEIS OF OBERFISCHBACH
    413   MOSS, GEORGE
    414   SORRELL, AGNES
    415   MC NISH, ELIZABETH

    416   HUNTON, MARGARET L
    417   HUNTON, SARAH LUCELIA
    418   HEIMBACH, JOHANN
    419   HUNTON, EVA
    420   HUNTON, EPPA (4TH EPPA)

    421   HUNTON, GEORGE B.
    422   HUNTON, ROBERTA
    423   HUNTON, MILTON KIRK
    424   HEIMBACH, JOST
    425   HUNTON, FRANCES

    426   BRENT, JAMES
    427   HUNTON, PRISCILLA
    428   DUVALL, SAMUEL
    429   BOOKEY, SAMUEL
    430   STRICKLER, ABRAHAM

    431   FOSTER, JAMES W.
    432   HUNTON, MOSS
    433   HUNTON, MARTHA
    434   KEYSER, CHARLES HAMPTON JR.
    435   RIXEY, PRESLEY MOREHEAD

    436   RIXEY, RICHARD LEWIS
    437   EGE, JOHANN
    438   RIXEY, FRANCES JANE ELIZABETH
    439   HAGAR, JOHN HENRY
    440   RIXEY, SAMUEL TURNER

Plate 25. Quinsept, Inc. *Family Roots* Number Index

DISK INDEX

ID	NAME
1-0009	BAUDHUIN, Marceline
1-0025	BOSMAN, Katherine/Marie Catherine
1-0001	DESTREE/DETRY, Marie-Therese
1-0005	DEWARZEGGAR, Eugene
1-0008	HERLACHE, August
1-0022	HERLACHE, Desire Joseph
1-0015	HERLACHE, Gilbert Joseph
1-0000	HERLACHE, Jean-Baptiste
1-0013	HERLACHE, Jean-Baptiste
1-0006	HERLACHE, Jean-Baptiste
1-0004	HERLACHE, Marie-Josephine
1-0002	HERLACHE, MarieTherese
1-0021	HERLACHE, Ralph
1-0011	HERLACHE, Rosalie Francoise
1-0017	HERLACHE, Sylvester
1-0014	HERLACHE, Vital Joseph
1-0010	HERLACHE, Zeno
1-0007	JENQUIN, Adele
1-0019	JONIAUX/JUNIO, Jean Baptiste
1-0018	JUNIO, Mary
1-0020	LAURENT, Lizzie
1-0012	LIBERT, Nicolas
1-0016	MACCAUX/MACCO, Euphrasie/Frasie
1-0023	MACCAUX/MACCO, Jean-Baptiste
1-0003	NEUVILLE, Henry
1-0024	QUINARD/KINNARD, Eufrazie

Plate 26. Mark Peters *My Roots* By-disk Index

ARMSTRONG-GORANSON GENEALOGY

```
================================================================================
Page 1                            FOOTNOTES                        11 Feb 1981
================================================================================
  #       Footnote text
 ===      ======================================================================
  1       FARMER, SELF-TAUGHT PILOT
  2       TEXAS A & M GRADUATE, VETERINARIAN
  3       TEXAS A AND M GRADUATE, B.S. MECHANICAL ENGINEERING 1969
  4       WAS IN WAR OF 1812
  5       IN CIVIL WAR FOR SOUTH
  6       UNIVERSITY OF TEXAS GRADUATE, B. S. PHARMACY 1972
  7       UNIVERSITY OF TEXAS GRADUATE, B.A. 1976, M.D. 1980
  8       HOUSEWIFE
  9       FARMER
 10       SHOEMAKER
 11       CHIROPRACTOR
 12       WEST TEXAS STATE UNIVERSITY GRADUATE,B.S. 1976
 13       NICKNAMED ALIAS J, BLACKSMITH, BEEKEEPER, GOLD-PROSPECTOR
 14       MOVED ON FOOT FROM VIRGINIA TO ILLINOIS ABOUT 1860
 15       COLLEGE INSTRUCTOR
 16       EMIGRATED FROM SWEDEN WHEN    YEARS OLD
 17       COMPUTER HOBBYIST
 18       TEXAS A & M GRADUATE, EDUCATION
 19       TEXAS TECH UNIVERSITY GRADUATE, HOMEMAKING
 20       UNIVERSITY OF TEXAS GRADUATE, B.S. EDUCATION 1974
 21       OKLAHOMA A & M GRADUATE
 22       TEXAS TECHNOLOGICAL COLLEGE GRADUATE
 23       KANSAS STATE LEGISLATOR, 1890'S
 24       NURSE
 25       KILLED BY LIGHTNING
 26       PURDUE UNIVERSITY GRADUATE, M.S. MECHANICAL ENGINEERING 1974
 27       died when young
 28       RETIRED FROM POST OFFICE WITH 32 YEARS OF SERVICE IN 1970
 29       BIRTH RECORD FROM FAMILY BIBLE IN POSSESSION OF J. SMITH 2-7-81
 30       DICOVERED AND NAMED KOTZEBUE, ALASKA IN 1813
 31       THIRD SPOUSE OF FRED SMITH (ID # 599)




================================================================================
end of the list of 31 footnotes
```

Plate 27. Armstrong Genealogical Systems *Genealogy: Compiling Roots and Branches* Footnote Index

ARMSTRONG-GORANSON GENEALOGY

```
==================================================================================
Page 1                    BIRTHDATES by Month, Day, & Year          11 Feb 1981
==================================================================================
```

Date	Person	ID #	Birthplace
1 Jan 1945	MARY LOU SEIBERT (RUSCO)	473	?
2 Jan 1924	HARDY LYNN HULSEY	244	LADONIA,TEXAS
6 Jan 1930	CLARENCE ALFRED JR. LUCAS	356	WICHITA,KANSAS
7 Jan 1881	WILL FLETCHER	543	?
7 Jan 1944	GLEN LAVERNE WILSON	720	LARNED,KANSAS
9 Jan 1970	JONATHAN CLARK WIMMER	101	WICHITA,KANSAS
9 Jan 1974	JAMEE NOELLE SKINNER	254	DENVER,COLORADO
9 Jan 1981	SARA ELIZABETH ARMSTRONG	861	PORTSMOUTH, VIRGINIA
11 Jan 1973	DAVID R. WILSON	749	HUTCHINSON,KANSAS
12 Jan 1914	LEONARD ERIC HOFFMAN	192	PARKSTON,SOUTH DAKOTA
13 Jan 1871	JOHN EHLERS	273	?
15 Jan 1951	CAROL GUNN (ARMSTRONG)	14	DALLAS,TEXAS
15 Jan 1966	SHERRY LYNN WILSON	738	HUTCHINSON,KANSAS
16 Jan 1976	JOHN MATTHEW ARMSTRONG	13	MIDWAY ISLAND
17 Jan 1934	FRANKLIN WAYNE WILSON	706	?
18 Jan 1940	KAREN EDITH RUSCO (BALDWIN)	455	?
22 Jan 1942	HAROLD AMOS WILSON	708	LARNED,KANSAS
24 Jan 1978	JOSEPH DAVID ARMSTRONG	10	PLANO,TEXAS
27 Jan 1860	JOHN ZIMMERMAN	317	?
27 Jan 1870	MARY ELIZABETH ARMSTRONG (BURCHFIE*	126	IDA,MICHIGAN
27 Jan 1961	DAVID GLENN RADENBERG	448	?
30 Jan 1952	KENNETH LEE ARMSTRONG	2	AMARILLO,TEXAS
30 Jan 1952	CAROLEE JOYCE RUSCO (DENNING)	482	GREAT BEND,KANSAS
30 Jan 1973	BRYAN MARCUS ARMSTRONG	12	EUREKA,CALIFORNIA
31 Jan 1980	RYAN LUCAS MCPHAIL	620	HAYS,KANSAS
2 Feb 1968	DOUGLAS DEAN RUSCO	474	HAYS,KANSAS
4 Feb 1941	JUDITH ANN CHUMLEY (RUSCO)	451	?
5 Feb 1845	CHRISTIAN KOOPMAN	664	BADEN,GERMANY
5 Feb 1845	CARL JOHAN GORANSSON	257	ESKILSKUNA,SWEDEN
5 Feb 1880	JOHN DAVID RUSCO	342	?
7 Feb 1913	MATILDA MACCAUGHEY (ARMSTRONG)	108	HONOLULU,HAWAII
8 Feb 1845	REBECCA SMITH (LUCAS)	223	?,VIRGINIA
8 Feb 1877	GEORGE ALLEN LUCAS	343	ASHLAND,ILLINOIS
8 Feb 1904	WAYNE MANLEY ARMSTRONG	21	MENO,OKLAHOMA
9 Feb 1854	SABRA ELIZA ARMSTRONG (DANIELS)	123	UNIONTOWN,PENNSYLVANIA
9 Feb 1948	LYNNA BETH HULSEY (ARMSTRONG)	11	?
9 Feb 1974	BLAKE EDWARD ARMSTRONG	106	VUNG TAU, SOUTH VIETNAM
10 Feb 1942	MARY LYNN WALKER (ARMSTRONG)	104	FREDRICK,OKLAHOMA
14 Feb 1863	BENJAMIN FRANKLIN WILSON	150	BROWN CO.,ILLINOIS
17 Feb 1898	FORREST CHARLES BURCHFIELD	132	NEWKIRK,OKLAHOMA
18 Feb 1959	MONTE JOSEPH MILLER	731	HUTCHINSON,KANSAS
18 Feb 2192	GLENN CARL RADENBERG	446	?
19 Feb 1949	JOHN JAMES ARMSTRONG	3	AMARILLO,TEXAS
23 Feb 1948	BRIAN LOGAN LOCKE	109	SEATTLE,WASHINGTON
26 Feb 1822	LEVI ZIMMERMAN	228	WESTMORELAND CO.,PENNSYL
26 Feb 1960	JEAN MARIE ARMSTRONG (MOORHEAD)	68	FRESNO,CALIFORNIA
28 Feb 1969	ERIC BRIAN LINDER	776	?
1 Mar 1975	HOPE MARIE ARMSTRONG	70	TULARE,CALIFORNIA
3 Mar 1868	CHARLES SHERMAN BURCHFIELD	142	HOWARD CO.,INDIANA

continued...
Asterisk denotes name shortened to fit on page.
```

**Plate 28.** Armstrong Genealogical Systems *Genealogy: Compiling Roots and Branches* Birthdate Index
```

ARMSTRONG-GORANSON GENEALOGY
==
Page 2   MARRIAGE DATES by Year, Month, & Day   11 Feb 1981
==

Date	Person	ID #	Living at
5 Sep 1909	THEODORE CARL HELD	347	deceased 4 Dec 1959
5 Sep 1909	NELLIE CLARA LUCAS (HELD)	346	deceased 12 Nov 1964
20 Oct 1909	IVA DELL WILSON (O'BRIEN)	152	deceased 18 Jul 1949
20 Oct 1909	THOMAS JAMES O'BRIEN	156	deceased 15 Dec 1962
24 Feb 1915	ALICE E. ROGERS (LUCAS)	382	deceased 18 Apr 1918
24 Feb 1915	CLARENCE ALFRED LUCAS	348	deceased 1 Sep 1979
6 Jul 1916	HARRY BIDE GROAT	393	deceased 12 Jan 1966
6 Jul 1916	BEULAH PEARL WARREN (GROAT)	392	deceased 31 Nov 1931
4 Feb 1918	HAROLD JENNINGS BURCHFIELD	131	deceased 30 Apr 1941
4 Feb 1918	AMY PAULINE POWELL (BURCHFIELD)	186	FARMINGTON,MICHIGAN
27 Sep 1919	SOPHIE TEMPLIN (GORANSON)	41	deceased 7 Jan 1968
27 Sep 1919	JOHAN WILHEM GORANSSON	40	deceased 12 Nov 1978
11 Jun 1925	THEO HOLT (STALLINGS)	83	TEMPLE,TEXAS
11 Jun 1925	EZRA ALLEN ARMSTRONG	23	deceased 30 Aug 1950
12 Oct 1925	CHARLES LEO ARMSTRONG	19	COTTONWOOD,ARIZONA
circa 1925	IRENE TIDENBERG (ARMSTRONG)	62	deceased 10 Oct 1929
6 Mar 1926	SOPHIA DENKER (LUCAS)	383	GREAT BEND,KANSAS
10 Aug 1929	WAYNE MANLEY ARMSTRONG	21	WICHITA,KANSAS
10 Aug 1929	ZELMA TAYLOR (ARMSTRONG)	57	WICHITA,KANSAS
4 Oct 1931	FRANK EVERETT WILSON	366	deceased 24 Dec 1967
4 Oct 1931	VERNA MAE SCHREIBER (WILSON)	637	HUTCHINSON,KANSAS
4 Nov 1931	LESTER BUCKMAN	638	LARNED,KANSAS
4 Nov 1931	OLIVE MARY WILSON (BUCKMAN)	368	LARNED,KANSAS
24 Dec 1931	ELMER VRATIL	639	?
24 Dec 1931	HELEN FERNE WILSON (SCHULZ)	369	LARNED,KANSAS
28 Feb 1932	LLOYD CHARLES RUSCO	349	deceased ?? ?? ????
28 Feb 1932	LEONA MAY WILSON (RUSCO)	438	?
1 Jun 1932	FLOYD LUCAS ARMSTRONG	24	MIAMI,OKLAHOMA
1 Jun 1932	DELMA LORENE INGRAM (ARMSTRONG)	103	MIAMI,OKLAHOMA
16 Jun 1932	STELLA TAYLOR (ARMSTRONG)	60	SANGER,CALIFORNIA
16 Jun 1932	GLENN ALTON ARMSTRONG	20	deceased 17 Aug 1977
circa 1932	GRACE VERA WELLS (ARMSTRONG)	53	COTTONWOOD,ARIZONA
22 Jun 1933	EDITH SOPHIA LEBBIN (RUSCO)	439	?
22 Jun 1933	ALFRED BENSON RUSCO	350	GREAT BEND,KANSAS
13 Jun 1934	ORVILLE JOHN RUSCO	351	GREAT BEND,KANSAS
13 Jun 1934	KATHERINE MARY SCHARTZ (RUSCO)	440	GREAT BEND,KANSAS
6 Oct 1936	CHARLES JOSEPH SCHREIBER	191	OTIS,KANSAS
6 Oct 1936	MARY EDNA O'BRIEN (SCHREIBER)	155	OTIS,KANSAS
5 Sep 1937	URSEL SIDNEY ARMSTRONG	22	OJAI,CALIFORNIA

==
continued...

Plate 29.   Armstrong Genealogical Systems *Genealogy: Compiling
Roots and Branches* Marriage Date Index

ARMSTRONG-GORANSON GENEALOGY

Page 3	DATES OF DEATH by Year, Month, & Day		12 Feb 1981
Date	Person	ID #	Place of death
24 May 1947	JANET KAY RUSCO	479	GREAT BEND,KANSAS
18 Nov 1948	JAMES LEE ARMSTRONG	42	PANHANDLE,TEXAS
27 Dec 1948	FREDERICK CHRISTIAN TEMPLIN	241	HAMBURG,MINNESOTA
14 Jan 1949	CHRISTIAN TEMPLIN	585	GLENCOE,MINNESOTA
18 Jul 1949	IVA DELL WILSON (O'BRIEN)	152	LA CROSSE,KANSAS
25 Oct 1949	MARIE BENZ	584	HAMBURG,MINNESOTA
30 Aug 1950	EZRA ALLEN ARMSTRONG	23	AMARILLO,TEXAS
18 Oct 1950	WILLIAM TEMPLIN	587	STEWART,MINNESOTA
29 Oct 1950	EMELIA (EMILIE?) BADE (TEMPLIN)	586	GLENCOE,MINNESOTA
6 Feb 1951	OLLIE ROSS LUCAS (RUSCO)	341	GREAT BEND,KANSAS
25 Nov 1951	AGNES STEVENSON (GROAT)	401	WICHITA,KANSAS
?? ?? 1952	GORDON GLENN ARMSTRONG	89	AMARILLO,TEXAS
17 Dec 1953	LILLIE BELLE LUCAS	345	WICHITA,KANSAS
20 Apr 1954	CATHERINE SOPHIA ELLING (TEMPLIN)	580	GIBBON,MINNESOTA
1 Jan 1956	DWIGHT OWEN BOURBON	629	GREAT BEND,KANSAS
8 Feb 1956	EFFIE MAE LUCAS (ARMSTRONG)	43	AMARILLO,TEXAS
26 Jul 1958	MARIE GRAUPMAN	588	?
4 Dec 1959	THEODORE CARL HELD	347	ANAHEIM,CALIFORNIA
21 May 1962	VERN IRL ARMSTRONG	63	NORTH FORK,CALIFORNIA
15 Dec 1962	THOMAS JAMES O'BRIEN	156	LA CROSSE,KANSAS
?? ?? 1962	LILLIE BAILEY (FLETCHER)	539	?
12 Nov 1964	NELLIE CLARA LUCAS (HELD)	346	ANAHEIM,CALIFORNIA
2 Jun 1965	JOHN DAVID RUSCO	342	GREAT BEND,KANSAS
14 Jun 1965	ESTHER CAROLYN JAERGER (RUSCO)	441	GREAT BEND,KANSAS
12 Jan 1966	HARRY BIDE GROAT	393	WICHITA,KANSAS
9 Jun 1967	LEONARD ERIC HOFFMAN	192	HOLSTEAD,KANSAS
24 Dec 1967	FRANK EVERETT WILSON	366	HUTCHINSON,KANSAS
7 Jan 1968	SOPHIE TEMPLIN (GORANSON)	41	DULUTH,MINNESOTA
10 Sep 1968	RALPH DANA ARMSTRONG	48	LOS ANGELES,CALIFORNIA
21 Jan 1970	RUTH LORENE BURCHFIELD (MATSON)	135	NAPLES,FLORIDA
7 Aug 1970	EMMA CHARLOTTE KOOPMAN (LUCAS)	344	GREAT BEND,KANSAS
7 Aug 1970	WILL FLETCHER	543	?
6 May 1971	EDWIN CRENSHAW BEEBE	187	GRAND RAPIDS,MICHIGAN

continued...

Plate 30. Armstrong Genealogical Systems *Genealogy: Compiling Roots and Branches* Death Date Index

ALPHABETICAL LIST OF JONES EVENTS 1940-1980
09-05-1984

```
1    JONES, ANN CATHERINE                                    F      000001
     BIRTH          12 SEP 1965        MURRAY, SL, UT
     JONES, JOHN EDWARD / HARRISON, NANCY RUTH          000002/000003/000000
                                                       JONES102          (1   )

2    JONES, JOHN EDWARD                                      M      000002
     BIRTH          23 SEP 1965        MURRAY, SL, UT
     JONES, ANN CATHERINE / HARRISON, NANCY RUTH       000001/000002/000000
     JOHN IS THE FATHER                                JONES102          (1   )

3    JONES, JOHN EDWARD                                      M      000002
     MARRIAGE       12 NOV 1963        SALT LAKE CITY, SL, UT
     HARRISON, NANCY RUTH                              000003/000000/000000
                                                       JONES101          (1   )

4    JONES, JOHN EDWARD                                      M      000002
     DIVORCE        3 MAY 1970         SALT LAKE CITY, SL, UT
     HARRISON, NANCY RUTH                              000003/000000/000000
     NANCY FILED ON GROUNDS OF MENTAL CRUELTY          JONES103          (1   )

5    JONES, JOHN EDWARD                                      M      000002
     NEWSPAPER      10 JUN 1980        PARK CITY, SUMMIT, UT
     BAILEY, ELVA FERN / JONES, KARL DAVIS             000005/000004/000000
     KARL KILLED IN HOUSE FIRE                         JONES105          (1   )

6    JONES, JOHN EDWARD                                      M      000002
     WILL           12 APR 1970        PARK CITY, SUMMIT, UT
     JONES, KARL DAVIS / BAILEY, ELVA FERN             000004/000005/000000
     KARL CUT JOHN OUT OF WILL                         JONES104          (1   )

7    JONES, KARL DAVIS                                       M      000004
     NEWSPAPER      10 JUN 1980        PARK CITY, SUMMIT, UT
     BAILEY, ELVA FERN / JONES, JOHN EDWARD            000005/000002/000000
     KARL KILLED IN HOUSE FIRE                         JONES105          (1   )

8    JONES, KARL DAVIS                                       M      000004
     WILL           12 APR 1970        PARK CITY, SUMMIT, UT
     BAILEY, ELVA FERN / JONES, JOHN EDWARD            000005/000002/000000
     LEFT ALL TO WIFE, DISINHERITED SON; DT 9 JUN 1980 JONES104          (1   )
```

Plate 31. Array Systems *Treesearch* By-event Index

JONES AND HARRISON FAMILY EVENTS, BY NAME
09-05-1984

11   HARRISON, NANCY RUTH   F   000003
     MARRIAGE   12 NOV 1963   SALT LAKE CITY, SL, UT
     JONES, JOHN EDWARD   000002/000000/000000
                                                     JONES101   (1   )

12   JONES, JOHN EDWARD   M   000002
     MARRIAGE   12 NOV 1963   SALT LAKE CITY, SL, UT
     HARRISON, NANCY RUTH   000003/000000/000000
                                                     JONES101   (1   )

13   JONES, ANN CATHERINE   F   000001
     NEWSPAPER   12 SEP 1965   MURRAY, SL, UT
     JONES, JOHN EDWARD / HARRISON, NANCY RUTH   000002/000003/000000
     BIRTH TOOK PLACE IN POLICE CAR   JONES102   (1   )

14   JONES, ANN CATHERINE   F   000001
     BIRTH   12 SEP 1965   MURRAY, SL, UT
     JONES, JOHN EDWARD / HARRISON, NANCY RUTH   000002/000003/000000
     FIRST CHILD OF THE MOTHER   JONES102   (1   )

15   JONES, JOHN EDWARD   M   000002
     BIRTH   23 SEP 1965   MURRAY, SL, UT
     JONES, ANN CATHERINE / HARRISON, NANCY RUTH   000001/000002/000000
     JOHN IS THE FATHER   JONES102   (1   )

16   HARRISON, NANCY RUTH   F   000003
     NEWSPAPER   3 MAY 1969   SALT LAKE CITY, SL, UT
     JONES, JOHN EDWARD   000002/000000/000000
     NANCY AND JOHN WERE IN AN AUTOMOBILE ACCIDENT   JONES108   (1   )

17   BAILEY, ELVA FERN   F   000005
     WILL   12 APR 1970   PARK CITY, SUMMIT, UT
     JONES, JOHN EDWARD / JONES, KARL DAVIS   000002/000004/000000
     ELVA IS SOLE BENEFICIARY   JONES104   (1   )

18   JONES, KARL DAVIS   M   000004
     WILL   12 APR 1970   PARK CITY, SUMMIT, UT
     BAILEY, ELVA FERN / JONES, JOHN EDWARD   000005/000002/000000
     LEFT ALL TO WIFE, DISINHERITED SON; DT 9 JUN 1980 JONES104   (1   )

19   JONES, JOHN EDWARD   M   000002
     WILL   12 APR 1970   PARK CITY, SUMMIT, UT
     JONES, KARL DAVIS / BAILEY, ELVA FERN   000004/000005/000000
     KARL CUT JOHN OUT OF WILL   JONES104   (1   )

20   JONES, JOHN EDWARD   M   000002
     DIVORCE   3 MAY 1970   SALT LAKE CITY, SL, UT
     HARRISON, NANCY RUTH   000003/000000/000000
     NANCY FILED ON GROUNDS OF MENTAL CRUELTY   JONES103   (1   )

Plate 32. Array Systems *Treesearch* By-event Index

```
SEARCH FOR DATE BETWEEN TWO YEARS:
   DATE OF BIRTH
   CHRISTENED ON

SEARCH FOR THE FOLLOWING VALUES:
   1800
   1899

SEARCH CHARACTER STRINGS:
   PLACE OF BIRTH
   PLACE OF DEATH/LIVING
   PLACE(S) OF MARRIAGE
   BURIAL PLACE
   CHRISTENED AT

SEARCH FOR THE FOLLOWING VALUES:
   GERMANY
   GERM
   WAGON MOUND
   WAGON
   MOUND

RECORDS FOR THE FOLLOWING PEOPLE SATISFIED THE SEARCH:

   ID    NAME

    8)  VORENBERG, SIMON
    9)  HARRIS, THERESA
   11)  HARBERG, CARL
   12)  MAYER, GOTLIEB FREDRIC
   13)  MAYER, ERNEST JACOB
   93)  VORENBERG, EMMA
   94)  VORENBERG, CLARA (KATHINKA)
   95)  VORENBERG, JULIA
```

Plate 33. Quinsept, Inc. *Family Roots* Data Search

DATE OF REPORT 04/19/82
LIST OF ALL RECORDS CONTAINING THE PARENT'S NAME: Mary

NAME: Susan Mary JONES	REC. NO.:	5
NAME: Mary Isadore LAKE	REC. NO.:	13
NAME: Mary FARIS	REC. NO.:	15
NAME: Mary C. WHEATON	REC. NO.:	27

DATE OF REPORT 04/19/82
LIST OF ALL RECORDS CONTAINING THE CHILD'S NAME: Frank
THE NO. IN PARENTHESIS IS THE MARRIAGE NUMBER.

CHILD'S NAME: Frank Hugh (1)	REC. NO.:	2
CHILD'S NAME: Frank Hugh (1)	REC. NO.:	3
CHILD'S NAME: Frank Hugh (1)	REC. NO.:	4
CHILD'S NAME: Frank Hugh (2)	REC. NO.:	5
CHILD'S NAME: Frank Herbert(1)	REC. NO.:	8
CHILD'S NAME: Frank Herbert(1)	REC. NO.:	9
CHILD'S NAME: Frank Stevens(2)	REC. NO.:	12

Plate 34. Frank Lerchen *Genealogy Program* Search List

4_

```
                    HARRISON FAMILY
                     09-05-1984


1    HARRISON            BRADLEY
     300003             27 JUL 1947        SALT LAKE CITY, SL, UT
                                           000006/000007


2    HARRISON            CINDY
     400003             14 MAR 1976        TEMPE,,AZ
                                           000006/A00006


3    HARRISON            EARL ROBERT
     100003             1 JUN 1943         SALT LAKE CITY, SALT LAKE, UT
                                           000006/000007


4    HARRISON            EDWARD
     000002
                                           000000/000000


5    HARRISON            EDWIN LEWIS
     000000             01 AUG 1859        BANGOR, PENOBSCOT, ME
                                           000002/000003
                        17 MAY 1904        PARK CITY, SUMMIT, UT


6    HARRISON            EDWIN LEWIS
     300003             23 DEC 1946        LEHI, UTAH, UT
                                           000006/000007


7    HARRISON            ELLIE LOUISE
     900003             13 JUL 1959        SALT LAKE CITY, SALT LAKE, UT
                                           000006/000007
                        03 AUG 1962        SALT LAKE CITY, SALT LAKE, UT


8    HARRISON            GILBERT DONALD
     00000C             28 APR 1887        EUREKA, JUAB, UT
                                           000000/00000P
                        8 FEB 1951         SALT LAKE CITY, SALT LAKE, UT


9    HARRISON            JAMES PATRICK
     000006             04 APR 1920        SALT LAKE CITY, SALT LAKE, UT
                                           00000C/00000D
                        12 SEP 1977        PANAMA CITY, BAY, FLA


10   HARRISON            KATHLEEN
     400003             25 JUN 1950        MURRAY, SALT LAKE, UT
                                           000006/000007
```

Plate 35. Array Systems *Treesearch* Surname Search

Alpha Search List
Sandra Lee DeLisle Disk
(All Ancestors)

Search Key - - DeL

ID	1st Name	Middle Name	------------Last Name-----------	Birth Date
001	Sandra	Lee	DeLisle	21 May 1951
002	Eugene	Daniel	DeLisle	30 Aug 1918
004	Peter	Eugene	DeLisle	05 Jul 1888
008	Eugene	Joseph	DeLisle	15 Jan 1848
016	Jacques		DeLisle	00 Jan 1800
032	Jacques		DeLisle	30 Mar 1782
064	Jacques		DeLisle	20 Jun 1755
128	Jacque		DeLisle	18 Mar 1718
259	Daniel	Eugene	DeLisle	01 May 1947
262	Diane	Marie	DeLisle	06 Dec 1955
263	Deborah	Mary	DeLisle	07 Oct 1959
264	Julie	Ann	DeLisle	05 Jun 1961
265	Arthur	Benedict	DeLisle	03 May 1920

Plate 36.   Software Solutions *Arbor-Aide* Search Index

Now that we have seen what computerized indexing of family records is about, let's see how Family Roots does it:

The LISTS program constructs lists of people's names in alphabetic or numeric order and can also be used to make lists of empty name slots or ID numbers. This is really a program for manipulating names in a variety of ways. There are several familiar ways to select the names to be included in a list, as well as a new one, the one to pick out all names that sound alike. Lists can be stored in memory, saved to diskette, retrieved from diskette, and merged. (7-1)

> LISTS Main Menu . . .
>
> 1) MAKE ALPHABETIC LIST
> 2) MAKE NUMERIC ORDER LIST
> 3) MAKE SPECIAL LIST
> 4) CHANGE PROGRAM PARAMETERS
> 5) CHECK DISKETTES
> 6) EXIT PROGRAM

The first two choices produce a list of names, either alphabetic by surname or in ascending ID order, depending on the choice. After selecting one of these you will be asked to select the names to be included using the access menu. Selecting the third item on the above list produces a menu of seven special functions that make lists . . . . The final three items should be familiar by now . . . since they appear on all the main menus.

When you select either of the first two items on the main menu, you will be asked to choose which set of names to include in the list . . . .

> 1) NUMBER RANGE
> 2) NUMBER LIST
> 3) NAME SETS
> 4) SURNAME SOUNDEX
> 5) WHOLE DISKETTE

The first two access choices work exactly as described for EDIT . . . except in this case only the names will be retrieved, not the records . . . . The third choice . . . you can ask that upper/lower case differences be ignored between what you specified and what is selected. This is done with the IGNORE UPPER/LOWER CASE parameter, which can be accessed and changed by typing <P> on the access menu above. (7-2)

If you ask for WHOLE DISKETTE, LISTS checks to see if there is only one data diskette available in a drive. If so, that one is used . . . . Generating a list is not a brief operation.

The SURNAME SOUNDEX choice is what you use to find a set of people whose last names sound alike although they may be spelled differently. When you make this choice you will be asked MAKE ALPHABETIC LIST FOR ALL SURNAMES SOUNDING LIKE: where you must supply a name . . . . When you give a name, LISTS will search all data diskettes that are available in a drive for surnames that sound like it, i.e. LISTS will not ask for any other diskettes. If you want a large search to be done, you will have to start the search several times with different diskettes in the drives, save the results to a diskette . . . , and merge lists from diskettes.

On SOUNDEX searches, the surname at birth is always searched, but others can be searched too depending on parameter settings. (7-3)

We have used the Soundex on our own family names. It properly finds the names sounding like Yeast to be Yaist, Yaste and Jost. Similarly Rectors and Richters all get found properly.

The generation of alphabetic and numeric ordered lists is quite similar, with the major difference being the pause required while alphabetizing takes place. Both types of lists are saved in memory until another list is requested.

If you used a number selection (range, list or whole diskette), LISTS can directly access the names from the diskettes. The only cases where you may need to switch diskettes are when your number list has a person not available on one of the current diskettes, or when your number range advances from the names on one diskette to the next higher one. The name set and Soundex selections must search through all the available names and therefore take longer . . . . LISTS stores the names in the computer's memory until your entire set of names has been retrieved, or until the available memory has been used up. (7-4)

You might think that every name is saved only once, but this is not necessarily the case. In alphabetic lists it is often valuable to include married women under both their maiden and married names, for convenience in finding their ID numbers when you use the list as an index. How a woman will appear in a list is controlled by the two parameters USE MAIDEN NAME and USE MARRIED NAME.

One other parameter affects what is saved in memory . . . . If the SHOW EMPTY NAME SLOTS parameter is on, any blank name found will be saved in memory and included in the final list produced . . . . This parameter is probably more pertinent to numeric order lists but works for alphabetic as well . . . . The only difference between alphabetic and numeric lists as finally output is the order of the names . . . . Then names in the numeric order list appear in the order they are found from your access choice. Alphabetic lists have the names ordered by surname.

LISTS checks the OUTPUT TO PRINTER parameter to see where to send the list. If the parameter is "off," the list will be shown on the screen, and "on" directs it to printer . . . . If the list goes to the screen, you can control the speed of display. (7-5)

When alphabetizing starts, the message on your screen changes to ALPHABETIZING NAMELIST along with an estimate of how long it will take and an indication of progress being made. (7-6)

The actual time depends on how well your names are sorted to start out with and on how similar they are to each other. Example times might be 1 minute for 200 names . . . or 9 minutes for 600 names . . . . After the list is complete, you will be returned to the main menu. (7-8)

Making Special Lists. When you choose item 3 on the LISTS main menu, a new menu of 7 miscellaneous items appears . . . . Not every item actually produces a list . . . . You can perform the following functions from here: merging two alphabetic lists into a longer one . . . showing a list from a diskette without saving all of it in memory (it might be too long to fit) . . . loading a list from a diskette into memory . . . saving a list you just made to a diskette . . . alphabetizing a numeric order list that's in memory . . . repeating the output of a list to your screen or the printer . . . making a list of empty slots on your data diskettes. Each . . . corresponds to one of the menu choices.

An alphabetic list of names in the computer's memory is restricted in size to what will fit there. This depends on many things, but it is usual that only one diskette's worth of people or less can be alphabetized at once. The way you get a longer list is to alphabetize several separate lists, save each to a diskette and then merge them two at a time to build the larger list. A merged list does not get saved in memory but must be directed to your screen, the printer, or a diskette, and you should set the parameters for this before starting.

You need to be aware that the diskette(s) used for this is a scratch one, i.e. this is not your usual data diskette, but is one used to store a list, probably temporary, and may have other "junk" on it. The diskette needs to have been formatted using the usual MS DOS or CP/M procedure described . . . in your operating system reference manual. (7-10)

You use the second choice on the Special Lists menu to review or print a list of names that you previously saved on diskette with either the LISTS . . . or the SEARCH . . . program.

You can use the third choice on the Special Lists menu to load a list from diskette into memory. You would use this to load and then alphabetize a list of names previously saved to diskette, which is especially useful if the list was the result of some work using the SEARCH program. (7-12)

LISTS will tell you soon if this particular list is too big. One diskette's worth of names should almost always fit. (7-13)

The fifth choice on the Special Lists menu will cause a numerically ordered list of names that is saved in memory to be alphabetized.

The sixth choice on the Special Lists menu is for making a printout or viewing a list of names which resides in the computer's memory. The list may have gotten there by a search you just did, or may have been read in from a diskette . . . . This option is used when you want extra copies of a printed list or when you want to reexamine a list on the screen. (7-15)

You should not switch diskettes in your disk drives unless told to do so or unless you are at the main menu. On the main menu you must select CHECK DISKETTES by typing <5> after you switch, so that LISTS can find out where and what everything is. (7-20)

PRODUCING CHARTS, GROUP SHEETS & NARRATIVES

The pedigree chart and family group sheet are standard report forms for expressing what has been found through the genealogist's research. We will show specimens of reports from several genealogy programs, but first we will finish our walk-through of *Family Roots* to see how it handles pedigree chart, family group, and narrative report generating:

The CHARTS program prints pedigree charts and descendant charts from the data you store on diskette using the EDIT program . . . . You can boot . . . and choose CHARTS from the programs menu, or you can get the programs menu after having run one of the other *Family Roots* programs.

The CHARTS main menu:..

1) PRINT DESCENDANTS CHARTS
2) PRINT FREE-FORM PEDIGREE CHARTS
3) PRINT STANDARD PEDIGREE CHARTS
4) PRINT COMPRESSED PEDIGREE CHARTS
5) CHANGE PROGRAM PARAMETERS
6) CHECK DISKETTES
7) EXIT PROGRAM

The titles are fairly indicative of the function to be performed. The first four choices cause one or more charts of the type indicated to be printed on your printer or shown on your screen.

When you select any of the first four options of the main menu, you will need to tell CHARTS which people or record numbers you are interested in. You are given a choice of specifying a number range, a list of numbers or parts of a name, and sometimes a list in memory. (5-1)

Each person you select via the access menu is the starting point for a chart; you do not have to select all the people that you want to have appearing somewhere in the chart. Thus if you choose a pedigree chart for yourself, CHARTS determines all the relationships and includes the appropriate people—your mother, father, grandparents, etc. Similarly a descendants chart for your paternal grandfather includes your father and his brothers and sisters, all their children, and so on.

For each name that satisfies your access selection, the name is retrieved from the diskette. If the diskette isn't available, you will be asked to load it into a particular drive. Once the name is retrieved, you will be asked a question . . . . This gives you the opportunity to verify the selection before continuing with the chart.

It should be emphasized that CHARTS constructs the charts based on the NUMBERS entered in person fields using the EDIT program; if you have entered a name rather than a number in a person field, only that name will appear on a chart and no further ancestors or children related to that name will be found or printed. (5-2)

During the printing of a chart, it will not be unusual for CHARTS to ask you to switch diskettes. This is because a record on one diskette points to a record on another via a person number you used.

A number of the program parameters affect all of the charts, while some affect only particular ones . . . . The ones that affect all charts . . . USE MONTH NAMES . . . to select the date format . . . PRINT ID WITH NAMES . . . the ID number for a person is printed with the name . . . TOP-OF-FORM AFTER PRINTS . . . controls whether the printer will eject a page . . . when it is finished with a chart . . . PRINT SIZE . . . selection for the size of print, in number of characters per inch . . . USE LAST NAME FIRST . . . controls whether the names in the chart are printed as AMANDA HEMMINGBONE or HEMMINGBONE, AMANDA . . . PRINT MARRIED NAME . . . for married women this controls whether their maiden or married name will appear on the chart . . . TAB BEFORE HEADER . . . "header" is the information printed before a chart that shows, usually, who the chart is for and perhaps other information like date of preparation . . . is used to position the header on the left or right so it can be seen if you bind your charts . . . ASK FOR HEADER . . . use this to define your own header if you don't want to use the standard one. (5-3)

The SHEETS program prints or displays the information that you store for one person, and prints a family group sheet in the format used by the Mormons.

Choose SHEETS from the programs menu . . . . The SHEETS main menu . . .

1) DISPLAY INDIVIDUALS
2) PRINT INDIVIDUALS
3) PRINT FAMILY GROUPS
4) CHANGE PROGRAM PARAMETERS
5) CHECK DISKETTES
6) EXIT PROGRAM

As usual, the titles are indicative of the function to be performed. The first two choices are basically the same, the only difference being where the results are placed. The third choice puts together the family group based on a husband or wife selected. The program parameters mainly affect how the data is printed or shown. Checking diskettes is how you swap diskettes under your own volition. (6-1)

If you choose to DISPLAY INDIVIDUALS, the data saved for that person will be put onto your screen . . . while the PRINT INDIVIDUALS puts the same thing to the printer . . . . When you choose to PRINT FAMILY GROUPS, the person found is used as the Husband or Wife in the group sheet. If you access the names of both the husband and wife, two identical sheets will be generated. You do not have to specify the children, their spouses, and other spouses of the husband and wife — these are located for you by SHEETS based on the data you stored.

Individual sheets are particularly useful when combined with a chart into a book. When we do this we choose a particular family line and print one of the free-form charts, either descendants or pedigree, using names only . . . . Then for every name on the chart, or perhaps everybody with the same surname, we print individual sheets, one per page. Finally, the chart and the sheets are bound into a family book. This is a cohesive unit of information that is relatively easy to prepare after your data has been entered. We have found that relatives appreciate them as gifts for any special occasion.

When you show individual records, each record you selected is retrieved from a diskette and all the explicit and inferred information is displayed or printed. (6-2)

All records that you selected are output in succession until the list is complete . . . . You are returned to the SHEETS main menu at the end of the cycle . . . . If a person you selected isn't available on one of the diskettes currently in a drive, SHEETS will tell you which diskette it needs and where to place it.

The presentation of the information in a record is formatted to make it easy to read, and related facts are grouped . . . . Date fields are formatted depending on the value of the USE MONTH NAMES parameter . . . . Person fields containing numbers are converted to the person's name, or are otherwise shown exactly as stored . . . . The record number is also normally shown, but can be suppressed for a "finished" look . . . . Notes are enclosed in parentheses with the note number and a colon preceding the text you entered. (6-3)

The TEXT program is used to save free-text passages for individuals. This might include a description of the person's life or other such pertinent facts, which you might like to have appear on the same page as the standard information stored using EDIT. One of the parameters allows you to do this. If you have it on, after each individual sheet is printed you will be told INSERT TEXT DISKETTE IN DRIVE B: FOR SPUDKNUT PRESS ANY KEY WHEN READY. The text diskette is searched and any text is printed if found. If the person is not there, you will be given another chance. . . . Don't put back the standard data diskette until told to do so – you may damage your data otherwise. (6-5)

A family group sheet collects all the pertinent information for a family unit and prints it. The family unit is a husband and wife plus all the children of that union. Other husbands of the wife or wives of the husband and their offspring would be the subject of different group sheets. (6-6)

The format used for the group sheet is the standard one promoted by The Church of Jesus Christ of Latter-day Saints, the Mormons . . . . The information requested by their standard form will be included in a sheet if you have that information available. In particular, dates and places of christening and burial are used. If you have defined these fields for your own use, SHEETS will know which they are and include the information stored there in the sheet.

One difficulty inherent in the Mormon form is its width, since it packs a great deal of information in a horizontal format. Consequently SHEETS must have at least 120 characters of width available in order to construct a group sheet. If that much is not available, you are given an opportunity to reset character size. If your printer can't support 120 characters of width . . . you won't be able to print group sheets . . . . We will consider adding a group sheet in a narrower vertical format in a future update, if there is a demand for it.

A family group sheet is started by your choice of the husband or the wife to be used . . . . After you verify the name, SHEETS checks to see if that person has exactly one spouse, and uses him or her if so. If there are no spouses with numbers available, the sheet generation is cancelled. If there is more than one spouse, you will be asked which one. (6-7)

Once the question of which husband and wife combination has been settled, SHEETS next needs to figure out which is the husband and which the wife. If you have defined a SEX field for yourself and stored data there for these people, that is how the decision is made. If that can't be done (no SEX field or nothing stored), SHEETS then tries to see which is the woman by checking if a Married Last Name is present for either person. If there is still no success, the last resort is to ask you IS AUBREY WENTWORTH MALE?

The group sheet starts with a header if you define one, as controlled by the ASK FOR HEADER parameter . . . . The top part of the sheet has the husband's name, followed by important date and place combinations like birth, death, marriage. Alternate marriages for the husband are then shown, if any. Next comes a similar section for the wife, with exactly the same possibilities except that the marriage date and place are not repeated. (6-9)

The children of this husband and wife are found by comparing the children you have stored in the husband and wife's records. Those that are in both places are used . . . . It is usually preferable that the children in the sheet be listed in the order of birth, from the oldest to the youngest. SHEETS will attempt to put them in order if you have the PUT CHILDREN IN ORDER parameter on, or will use the order in the husband's record if it is off. SHEETS can do the ordering if all the children's birthdates (in their own records, not in the parent's ones) are in the standard format.

If there are nonstandard birth dates or if there are children without records, SHEETS will still attempt to order the children if you have the parameter on, but it may not produce an order you like — all those with dates that can't be deciphered are put at the end of the list . . . . Each child is printed with a particular set of information. If the person is saved as a name rather than a number, only the name is shown and nothing else. Numbered people have more. First is the person's sex. If you have defined a SEX field for yourself, anything saved there is used. If that isn't available, SHEETS checks to see if the person has a Married Last Name saved; if so F is entered for sex. If none of these work, you are asked IS JUNE WENTWORTH MALE? (6-10)

Next comes the child's name, date and place of birth, first marriage if any, and date of death if appropriate. The first marriage includes the date and the name of the spouse. If there are other marriages for any of the children, they are saved and printed at the bottom of the sheet.

The last section of the sheet is for showing sources. Sources are assumed to be stored in the notes for the husband, wife and children. However, other information might also be present in the notes, and SHEETS has no way to tell other than asking you. The first question is OMIT SOURCES? in case you want to avoid deciding which notes to include in this particular sheet. Otherwise each note is retrieved and shown to you on the screen for your decision as to whether to include it . . . . If you have the same source indicated in different records, this also gives you the control to prevent multiple printing of the same source. (6-11)

Printing a Standard Pedigree Chart . . . . The Standard Chart is probably quite familiar to you, as it is often used by genealogists. The chart is printed on a single sheet of paper and includes a person, parents, grandparents, and great-grandparents . . . . If you asked for ID numbers to be printed with the names, they appear in front of each name. The birth, marriage, and death (if applicable) dates are printed. The corresponding "places" are also printed if there is enough space on the line for something intelligible, i.e. truncation may occur but at least 12 characters will be printed for each place. In the case of multiple marriages, the marriage information shown is only that pertinent to the spouse who appears on the chart. (5-12)

If one or more of the relatives aren't available in your FAMILY file (as generated by EDIT), that space in the chart will be left blank . . . . This makes the chart easy to read, and it is convenient to fill in the chart in longhand if you carry it with you in your familial searches. Note that if the person is living, the "D" is replaced by "Living" along with any data you may have stored about that.

The standard header for a standard chart consists of the words "CHART NO." . . . . This allows you to assign a number of your own choosing to each chart, providing a means of interconnecting them. You can define your own header which will appear instead of the standard one by setting the ASK FOR HEADER parameter.

The advantage of the standard chart is its familiarity and its uncluttered appearance. Its disadvantage is that it is highly structured. This means that the spaces for information are limited.

Beyond the parameters that affect all charts, there is only one unique to the standard chart. This is the one called CASCADE STANDARD CHARTS. When this is on, CHARTS will generate more than one chart if you have enough data available. The "extra" charts are the continuation of the one you selected. For example, if there is at least one parent indicated in the great-grandparents position, a chart will also be produced for that great-grandparent. Furthermore, if parents are found for the great-grandparents in the generation of the extra chart for the great-grandparent, more charts will be composed. This goes on until all of your data of this type is exhausted, or until the memory in CHARTS allocated to this is used up. The latter depends on quite a few factors but could occur for charts containing the ninth generation. No message appears—the chart just isn't printed. (5-14)

There are fifteen parameters used by CHARTS that affect the way things are displayed or printed. A value is normally assumed for each of these parameters (called a default) so you don't have to worry about setting all of them when you're just starting. (You can change the starting values using CONFIGUR.) There is a menu and procedure to change the values. (5-16)

Each parameter:

USE MONTH NAMES . . . MAXIMUM GENERATIONS . . . PRINT ID WITH NAMES . . . TOP-OF-FORM AFTER PRINTS . . . PRINT NAMES ONLY . . . SUPPRESS NOTES ON CHARTS . . . CASCADE STANDARD CHARTS . . . PRINT SIZE . . . PRINT EMPTY FIELDS . . . USE LAST NAME FIRST . . . SELECTIVELY SUPPRESS NOTES . . . PRINT MARRIED NAME . . . TAB BEFORE HEADER . . . ASK FOR HEADER . . . DATE . . . LINES PER PAGE. (5-17)

The compressed pedigree chart is almost not a chart at all. It represents an attempt to squeeze as much information as possible into as little space as possible . . . . The compressed chart can run to more than one page. Its length is determined by how much information you have stored and by how much space is available to generate it. This chart, unlike the others, is generated entirely in the computer's memory before any printing is done. (5-15)

The advantages of the free-form chart are that a great deal of information can be packed into it and that it can show a large number of generations in one chart. Admittedly it may be a little difficult to read until you get used to it. (5-8)

The descendants chart starts with the person you selected and shows all people (from your diskettes) directly descended from that person. This chart may contain only names or you may elect to include all the other information for each person in the chart as well. This choice is governed by . . . PRINT NAMES ONLY, on the parameters menu. (5-4)

There are five parameters which you can select which will affect the printing of a chart, in addition to those that affect all the charts, namely . . . the maximum number of generations (normally 7) . . . the appearance of notes on the chart when you have selected to include everything . . . the selective suppression of notes . . . the inclusion of empty fields . . . whether you want gaps between pages. (5-5)

PEDIGREE CHARTS ILLUSTRATED

Now that we have seen how to create pedigree charts and family group sheets from *Family Roots*, let's look at specimens of such charts and sheets as various genealogy programs produce them. We'll begin with pedigree charts. There are almost as many variations of a pedigree chart as there are genealogy programs! We will try to illustrate the variance and note some differences in them:

SYMMETRICAL ANCESTRY CHARTS

Three Generations—A three-generation chart may contain so much information about the charted persons that there is room for only three generations on a page. On the other hand, a three-generation chart may be the best a program can produce; some genealogy programs don't produce any pedigree charts at all. (Some programmers feel there are better ways of showing ancestry and descent than a pedigree chart, and we'll illustrate those no-chart variants.) First, let's see what Acorn Software produces with *Your Family Tree*. Plate 37 shows a cryptic reference to locations in their three-generation chart. One by Jim Mc Dermott called *Your Ancestors* is the best illustration we have seen of doing pretty well on a shoestring. His program runs on a Timex 1000 or Sinclair ZX81 (the Tinker Toy of computers). Plate 38 shows what Mc Dermott's program can produce. The Creative Services program, *Heritage* (for various TRS-80 computers), makes a names-only pedigree chart but gives detail about the subject of the chart; see Plate 39. Plates 40 and 41 show charts from Roderick H. Payne's *Genealogical Records Program*. These illustrate a common pedigree-chart display technique used in genealogical computing: Where one chart leaves off, the extension (found on another chart) is referenced. Thus, a three-generation chart really is not all that inferior to charts displaying more generations; it simply takes more pages and more computer runs to get sixteen or more generations charted. We wind up the three-generation displays with Mark Peters' s *My Roots* display (see Plate 42); it carries an information load for each person charted.

Four Generations — Plate 43 shows Byteware's *PEDC* printout with some data about each person. Our study software, *Family Roots* by Quinsept, Inc., can produce four-generation charts as you see in Plate 44 .

Five Generations —The five-generation chart is the most common kind produced by genealogy programs, but although the form is common it is not standardized. For example, we can point to Plates 45 and 46 for unique attributes: Discovery Software's *The Family Connection* software produces a blank, symmetrical chart and then lists the family members who would appear in such a chart if they were charted. The "ahnentafel" (family list with numbers coinciding with chart positions) can be read and the mind's eye can place a person in the chart as an intellectual transference process. Interesting! Then there is Genealog Software's *Genealog II* program, which makes a chart that the vendor suggests you polish by adding hand-drawn lines as seen in Plate 47. What happens if you don't draw in lines by hand? Ancestors sells *=Ancestors=* and it has no lines on the chart; see Plate 48 for a no-lines chart example by Ancestors. Lines are usually made by the programmer's choosing certain symbols with which a printer might draw vertical or horizontal lines. Notice the variations in computer drawn lines as you look at these specimens. Another no-line chart can be seen in Plate 49. It is from Software Solutions' *Arbor-Aide* program. (Frankly, we find the odd location of data groups a bit jarring to the eye!) If we were grading pedigree charts, we'd give an "A" to Plate 50 . It is an example from Array Systems' *Treesearch*. Plate 51 is from Commsoft Inc's *Roots/M* program and it deserves an "A +" for the letter quality, symmetry, information shown, and references to the other charts in the set for which this is the first chart. CompuGen Systems' *Family-File* produced the chart in Plate 52 and furthers the opinion that computers can produce very nice pedigree charts. Plate 53 shows the printout from Soft-Gene's *Ancestry I/III* program. The numbers on that pedigree chart are clearly not the usual pedigree-chart numbering; they seem to associate couples with some family-group numbering system.

Six Generations —To get six generations charted on one page requires mirrors! You can squeeze more generations onto a page by using the compressed type capability of a dot-matrix printer. That's how Personal Software Company's *Family Reunion* chart fits on a page; see Plate 54. Or you can do it with a folding-in of one generation's data into the next. *Family Tree* by Genealogy Software made the illustration in Plate 55 that way. Again, the chart has "funny numbers" on it; those are record numbers and may confuse those who expect the usual chart-numbering scheme (subject is #1, father is #2, mother is #3, and so on).

FREE-FORM OR ASYMMETRICAL CHARTS

Predecessor Charts—We've finished with the symmetrical pedigree charts and turn to examples of pedigrees expressed in asymmetrical form. Actually, *Family Roots* produces a symmetrical pedigree chart but it is spread on pages so that you don't see the symmetry of it. Quinsept, Inc. calls it a "dense free-form pedigree chart"; see Plate 56. Plate 57 is another version by Quinsept, Inc.'s *Family Roots*; it has more information in it so they call it "free-form" rather than "dense free-form." Armstrong Genealogical Systems' *Genealogy: Compiling Roots and Branches* is another predecessor chart having asymmetrical appearance; See Plate 58. Some people find these charts hard to read; so do we.

Descendants Charts—You aren't going to get symmetry in a chart of descendants from a selected patriarch! Unless some extraordinary family planning was implemented and carried on in *every* following generation, you will find charting the lineage links very tough. Few genealogy programs try it. Team Approach Limited's *Port for Genealogists* does the job better than any software we have seen. Plate 59 shows the results. Personal Software Company's *Family Reunion* handles descent as shown in Plate 60 . The program from Armstrong Genealogical Systems, *Genealogy: Compiling Roots and Branches*, produced Plate 61. Our study program, *Family Roots* by Quinsept, Inc., created the example in Plate 62.

LISTS OF FAMILY LINEAGE

Ahnentafel—The ahnentafel is a listing of pedigree which might be called a pedigree chart without the white space and symmetry showing. Actually, any of the pedigree charts we've illustrated occupy a lot of page space in trying to give a symmetrical layout, and any given page has more form than substance. See Plate 63 for an example of our study software, *Family Roots* by Quinsept, Inc. It gives a compact view of ancestry in a listing that lacks the symmetry but loads the information in minimum space.

Pedigree Lists—A very nice list of ancestors or descendants can be produced by the *Roots and Relatives* program by M.A. Harrison. See Plates 64 through 68 for a pair of lists that were just too nice to leave out. Frank Lerchen's *Genealogy Program* produces patriarchal and matriarchal lineage lists; see Plates 69 and 70.

We have seen the wide variation in pedigree chart generating in genealogy programs through these displays. Should there be a "standard" pedigree chart that could be created by *any* genealogy program? We do not know; we know there is not yet any standardized display.

INDIVIDUAL AND FAMILY
GROUP SHEETS ILLUSTRATED

Individual Records — We show several individual record displays: Plate 71 shows Software Solution's version created by *Arbor-Aide*. Plate 72 is from *Ancestor File Programs* by J. Davis; and Plate 73 is from our walk-through study program, *Family Roots* by Quinsept, Inc.

Family Group Records — Genealogists are quite familiar with family group sheets. They usually buy blank group sheet forms and use them for their basic records. We'll present without comment some illustrations of family group records generated by a variety of programs. Judge for yourself the acceptability of them:

Plate 74 is from *Roots and Relatives* by M. A. Harrison.

Plate 75 is from *Genealogy: Compiling Roots and Branches* by Armstrong Genealogical Systems.

Plate 76 is from *Family Tree* by Genealogy Software.

Plate 77 is from *Ancestry I/III* by Soft-Gene.

Plate 78 is from *FamilyFile* by CompuGen.

Plate 79 is from *Roots/M* by Commsoft, Inc.

Plate 80 is from *Treesearch* by Array Systems, Inc.

Plate 81 is from *=Ancestors=* by Ancestors.

Plate 82 is from *Genealog II* by Genealog Software.

Plate 83 is from *FGS* by Byteware.

Plates 84 and 85 are from *My Roots* by Mark Peters.

Plate 86 is from *Genealogical Record Programs* by Roderick H. Payne.

Plate 87 is from *Arbor-Aide* by Software Solutions.

Plate 88 and 89 are from *Ancestor File Programs* by J. Davis.

Plate 90 is from *Family Roots* by Quinsept, Inc.

ANCESTRAL CHART

```
                                              JOHN PETER SMITH SR.
                                                   BORN      1890   US/IN/MI
                                                   MARRIED   191?   US/??
                                                   DIED      1960   US/IL/CO
                                                   CAPTAIN - WORLD WAR I
                                                   # 4             + 3

                            JOHN PETER SMITH JR.
                                 BORN      1935   US/IL/CO
                                 MARRIED   1958   US/CA/LA
                                 DIED      1965   US/CA/LA
                                 STUNT PILOT
                                 # 2

                                              ALICIA CAPET
                                                   BORN      18??   EU/FR
                                                   MARRIED   191?   US/??
                                                   DIED      1935   US/IL/CO
                                                   EMIGRATED 1918
                                                   # 5             + 1

PAULINE J. SMITH
     BORN      1960   US/CA/SC
     MARRIED   ----   --/--
     DIED      ----   --/--
     FAMILY GENEALOGIST
     # 1

                                              R.  EDWIN BROWN
                                                   BORN      1915   US/MO
                                                   MARRIED   1935   US/MO
                                                   DIED      ----   --/--
                                                   PHYSICIAN
                                                   # 6             + 5

                            MARGARET RICHARDSON BROWN
                                 BORN      1937   US/CA/LA
                                 MARRIED   1958   US/CA/LA
                                 DIED      ----   --/--
                                 NOVELIST
                                 # 3

                                              FRANCES RICHARDSON
                                                   BORN      1910   US/KY
                                                   MARRIED   1935   US/MO
                                                   DIED      ----   --/--
                                                   LIBRARIAN
                                                   # 7             + 4

GENERATION 1              GENERATION 2          GENERATION 3
```

***Plate 37**.   Acorn Software *Your Family Tree* Ancestral Chart*

Compiled by: Jim McDermott   PO Box 140   Great Falls MT 59403

Hugh Jay Barber
Born 03/31/1883   (No. 8)
at Ellsworth Wis
*Died 11/28/1963   [cont. chart #   ]
* at Tillamook Ore
* Married 21/OC/1908

Glenn Jay Barber
Born 10/24/1922   (No. 4)
at Tillamook Ore====================
*Died   / /
* at
* Married 18/SE/1949

* Annie Ripley
* Born 07/03/1884   (No. 9)
*at Emerson Neb
Died 08/27/1931   [cont. chart #   ]
at Tillamook Ore

Kenneth Jay Barber
Born 09/08/1951   (No. 2)
at Tillamook Ore
*Died   / /
* at
* Married 10/SE/1977

Gregory Croston Lyster
Born 10/27/1879   (No. 10)
at Yorktown Kan
*Died 09/10/1977   [cont. chart #   ]
* at Hill City Kan
* Married 17/AP/1901

* June Hope Doris Maxine Isabelle Ger
* Born 06/16/1925   (No. 5)
*at Vesper Kan=======================
Died   / /
at

* Ella Hansena Henricksen
* Born 04/19/1881   (No. 11)
*at Vesper Kan
Died 01/10/1956   [cont. chart #   ]
at Lincoln Kan

Rebekah Jane Barber
Born 07/29/1980   (No. 1)
at Tillmook Ore
Died   / /   [Same as #   on chart   ]
at

Don David Miller
Born 09/27/1892   (No. 12)
at Dover Mich
*Died 06/28/1941   [cont. chart #   ]
* at Sandpoint Idaho
* Married 13/FE/1911

Gerald Geen Miller
Born JY/10/   (No. 6)
at Sandpoint ID====================
*Died   / /
* at
* Married 23/NO/1951

* Amy Bell Verback
* Born 10/16/1892   (No. 13)
*at St. Johns Kan
Died   / /   [cont. chart #   ]
at

* Jane Kay Miller
* Born 07/21/1953   (No. 3)
*at Sandpoint ID
Died   / /
at

Frederick Wilhelm Porath
Born 05/18/1893   (No. 14)
at Wahpeton ND
*Died 04/22/1967   [cont. chart #   ]
* at Sandpoint ID
* Married 18/JA/1927

* Shirley Jean Porath
* Born 08/16/1932   (No. 7)
*at Colfax ND=========================
Died   / /
at

* Elizabeth Mae Anderson
* Born 08/27/1909   (No. 15)
*at Dolliver Iowa
Died   / /   [cont. chart #   ]
at

-
Born - / /   (No. 0)
at -
Died - / /   [Spouse of # 1]
at
Married - / /

Plate 38.   Jim Mc Dermott *Software by Jim Mc Dermott*
Pedigree Chart

```
                                               -- GERRY TRUHILL
                          -- ERNEST TRUHILL     -
                          -                     -- ALICE SIMPSON
          -- JERRY TRUHILL
          -               -                     -- JOE GARCIA
          -               -- ERSIE GARCIA        -
          -               -                     -- TONI GONZALES
TERRI HANSON TRUHILL
          -                                     -- JACOB L. BURKETT
          -               -- CECIL R. BURKETT    -
          -               -                     -- MAE BELL WILSON
          -- DONNA BURKETT
                          -                     -- LLOYD DOTY
                          -- ALICE DOTY          -
                                               -- MARY ESTHER SMITH
```

```
TERRI HANSON TRUHILL
--------------------
BORN:    3-24-1971  WALNUT CREEK CALIF
MARRIED: UNMARRIED 1984
DIED:    LIVING ISLAND CO WASH  1984
COMMENT: ALL DATA LINES MAY BE 66 CHARACTERS IN LENGTH
```

Plate 39.   Creative Services *Heritage* Pedigree Chart

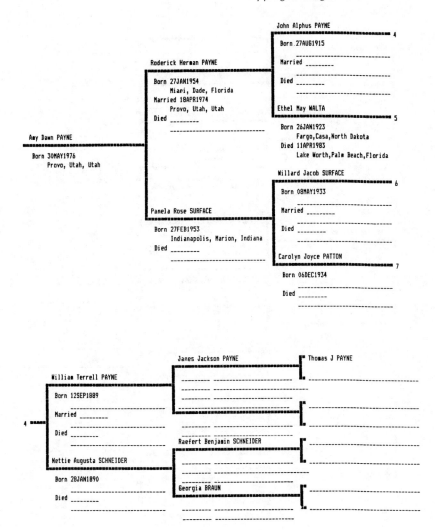

Plate 40. Roderick H. Payne *Genealogical Records Program* Pedigree Chart

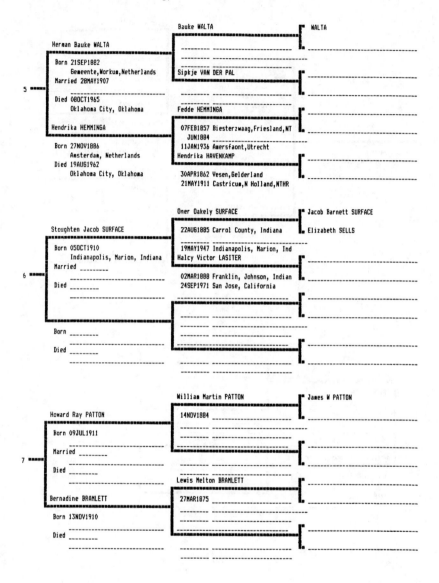

Herman Bauke WALTA
Born 21SEP1882
    Gemeente,Workum,Netherlands
Married 28MAY1907
5
Died 08OCT1965
    Oklahoma City, Oklahoma

Hendrika HEMMINGA
Born 27NOV1886
    Amsterdam, Netherlands
Died 19AUG1962
    Oklahoma City, Oklahoma

Bauke WALTA

Sipkje VAN DER PAL

Fedde HEMMINGA
07FEB1857 Biesterzwaag,Friesland,NT
JUN1884
11JAN1936 Amersfaont,Utrecht
Hendrika HAVENKAMP
30APR1862 Vesen,Gelderland
21MAY1911 Castricum,N Holland,NTHR

WALTA

Stoughten Jacob SURFACE
Born 05OCT1910
    Indianapolis, Marion, Indiana
Married _____
Died _____

Born _____
Died _____

Omer Oakely SURFACE
22AUG1885 Carrol County, Indiana
19MAY1947 Indianapolis, Marion, Ind
Halcy Victor LASITER
02MAR1888 Franklin, Johnson, Indian
24SEP1971 San Jose, California

Jacob Barnett SURFACE
Elizabeth SELLS

Howard Ray PATTON
Born 09JUL1911
Married _____
Died _____

Bernadine BRAMLETT
Born 13NOV1910
Died _____

William Martin PATTON
14NOV1884

Lewis Melton BRAMLETT
27MAR1875

James W PATTON

Plate 41. Roderick H. Payne *Genealogical Records Program*
Pedigree Chart

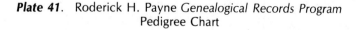

PEDIGREE CHART
HERLACHE, Gilbert Joseph

```
    +-ID 1-8: HERLACHE, August
    ! Born 12 Oct. 1848 (?) at Ceroux-Mousty, Brabant, Belgium
    ! Died 02 Feb. 1929 at Green Bay, Brown Co., Wisconsin
    ! Married 22 Nov. 1887 at Grandlez-Lincoln, Kewaunee Co., Wisconsin
    !
 +-ID 1-17: HERLACHE, Sylvester
 ! Born 03 July 1889 at Town of Gardner, Door Co., Wisconsin
 ! Died 19 May  1961 at Algoma, Kewaunee Co., Wisconsin
 ! Married 29 Jan. 1912 at Lincoln, Kewaunee Co., Wisconsin
 !  !
 !  +-ID 1-16: MACCAUX/MACCO, Euphrasie/Frasie
 !     Born 26 Feb. 1859 at Grandlez-Lincoln, Kewaunee Co., Wisconsin
 !     Died 27 Feb. 1932 at Rio Creek, Kewaunee Co., Wisconsin
 !
ID 1-15: HERLACHE, Gilbert Joseph
Born 12 Nov. 1912 at Escanaba, Menominee Co., Michigan
Died 16 Aug. 1975 at Two Rivers, Manitowoc Co., Wisconsin
 !
 !  +-ID 1-19: JONIAUX/JUNIO, Jean Baptiste
 !  ! Born 04 May  1854 at Corroy-le-Grand, Brabant, Belgium
 !  ! Died 09 Jan. 1919 at Algoma, Kewaunee Co., Wisconsin
 !  ! Married 12 Jan. 1883 at Lincoln, Kewaunee Co., Wisconsin
 !  !
 +-ID 1-18: JUNIO, Mary
    Born 02 Sep. 1892 at Lincoln, Kewaunee Co., Wisconsin
    Died 19 Aug. 1947 at Rio Creek, Kewaunee Co., Wisconsin
    !
    +-ID 1-20: LAURENT, Lizzie
       Born 03 Nov. 1854 (?) at Belgium
       Died 20 Oct. 1923 at Rio Creek, Kewaunee Co., Wisconsin
```

Plate 42. Mark Peters *My Roots* Pedigree Chart

ByteWare

Compiled by   (Your Name)   CHART NO._____

NO. 1 ON THIS CHART IS   8 _ JEROME DOE_____
                                                      | BORN 1 JAN 1900
THE SAME AS PERSON NO._____ | BRIGHTON ENG
                                                      | MARR 1 JUN 21
ON CHART NO._____   4 _ JOSEPH DOE_____| SOMEBURG USA
                                  | BORN 1 JAN 1925 | DIED 15 NOV 81
                                  | HOMETOWN USA | SMALLTOWN USA
                                  | MARR 1 JUN 1946 |
                                  | HOMETOWN USA   9 L JANET JOHNSON_____
                                  | DIED 1 DEC 1970   BORN 1 MAY 1905
                                  | ANYTOWN USA   MUNICH GERMANY
                                  | DIED 1 APR 26
     2 _ JACK L. DOE_____ | SOMETOWN USA
       | BORN 1 JAN 1950 |
       | ANYTOWN USA | 10 _ SAM SCHMITTE_____
       | MARR 1 JUN 1971 | | BORN 1 FEB 1900
       | SMALLTOWN USA | | PITTSBURG PA
       | DIED _____ | | MARR 1 JAN 1918
       | _____   5 L JANE SMITH_____| METROPOLIS USA
       | BORN 1 FEB 1925 | DIED _____
       | ANYTOWN USA | _____
   1 L JOHN J. DOE_____   DIED 15 NOV 65   11 L JEANETTE LE DEUVIENNE__
     | BORN 1 JAN 1975   SMALLTOWN USA   BORN 1 MAY 1900
     | SMALLTOWN USA   CAJUN COUNTY LA.
     | MARR _____   DIED _____
     | _____   _____
     | DIED _____
     | _____   12 _____
     | | BORN _____
     | | _____
     | SPOUSE: | MARR _____
     | _____ | _____
     | | DIED _____
     | 6 _ _____ | _____
     | | BORN _____ |
     | | _____   13 L _____
     | | MARR _____   BORN _____
     | | _____   _____
     | | DIED _____   DIED _____
     | | _____   _____
   3 L _____ |
       BORN _____ | 14 _ _____
       _____ | | BORN _____
       DIED _____ | | _____
       _____ | | MARR _____
                              7 L _____ | _____
                                  BORN _____ | DIED _____
                                  _____ | _____
                                  DIED _____   15 L _____
                                  _____   BORN _____
                                                      _____
                                                      DIED _____
                                                      _____

Plate 43.   Byteware *PEDC* Pedigree Chart

```
                                                                381 WHARTON RECTOR
                                                                .------------------------------------
                                                                !B 1771-3 VA
                                               53 ELIAS (MAJ) RECTOR      !M PRE 1806 VA
                                               .------------------------------!D
                                               !B 28 Sep 1802 MAIDSTOWN VA FAU!
                                               !M 26 Nov 1835 FT SMITH ARK   !409 MARY VANCE
                                               !D 22 Nov 1878 ARKANSAS       '------------------------------------
                                               !                             B  NORTH CAROLINA
                         39 ELIAS RECTOR        !                             M PRE 1806
                         .------------------------------------!             D PRE 1806 ?
                         !B 13 Jun 1860 FORT SMITH ARK  !
                         !M 10 Jan 1889 FORT SMITH ARKAN!                     73 WILLIAM DUVAL
                         !D 18 Apr 1953 FORT SMITH ARKAN!                     .------------------------------------
                         !                             !                     !B --/--/1784 FREDERICK CO. MD
                         !                             !54 CATHERINE JAMIMA DUVAL  !M PRE-1820 WELLSBURG BOONE CO.
                         !                             '------------------------------!D 30 Jun 1851 FT SMITH ARK
                         !                             B --/--/1818 WELLSBURG VA (NOW!
                         !                             M 26 Nov 1835 FT SMITH ARK   !74 HARRIET TABITHA DODDRIDGE
                         !                             D 18 Dec 1891 FT SMITH ARK.  '------------------------------------
                         !                                                          B ??/??/1802 WELLSBURG V VA
33 MARY VIRGINIA (MOSS) RECTOR!                                                     M PRE-1820 WELLSBURG BOONE CO.
.------------------------------!                                                   D 15 Jan 1841 FORT SMITH ARK
B 31 Aug 1897 ARKANSAS        !
M 21 Jun 1931 FORT SMITH ARKAN!                                                    534 THOMAS E. HUNTON GEN.
Living SCHAUMBERG ILLINOIS    !                                                    .------------------------------------
                             !                                                    !B 06 Aug 1772 FAUQUIER CO VA.
                             !                             62 JOHN BRENT HUNTON   !M 20 Aug 1817 VA
                             !                             .------------------------------!D 27 Oct 1836 VA. BURIED IN JO
                             !                             !B 27 Sep 1821 FAUQUIER CO VA !
                             !                             !M 01 Oct 1861              !610 MATILDA BRENT
                             !                             !D 30 Apr 1900 FT SMITH ARK '------------------------------------
                             !                             !                           B 15 Apr 1787 VA
                             !                             !                           M 20 Aug 1817 VA
                             !                             !                           D 19 Apr 1854 VA
                             !50 ANNA LUCILLE HUNTON       !
                             '------------------------------!
                             B 06 Nov 1866 VIRGINIA       !
                             M 10 Jan 1889 FORT SMITH ARK !
                             D 31 Oct 1954 PARK RIDGE ILL !
                             !                             .------------------------------------
                             !                             !B
                             !43 MARY MOSS                 !M
                             '------------------------------!D
                             B ? FAIRFAX VA               !
                             M 01 Oct 1861                !
                             D CA 1884 FT SMITH ARK       '------------------------------------
                                                          B
                                                          M
                                                          B
```

Plate 44. Quinsept, Inc. *Family Roots* Pedigree Chart

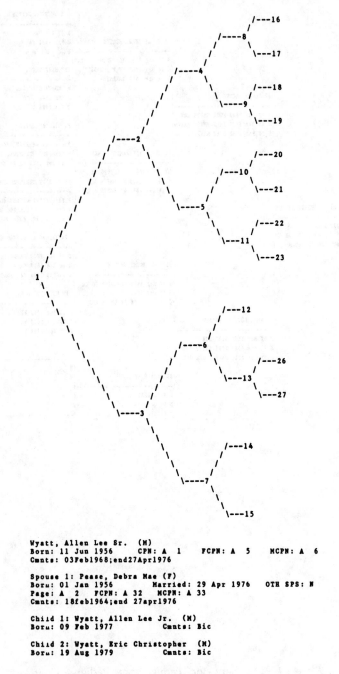

```
                                                   /---16
                                          /---8
                                 /---4            \---17
                                          \---9    /---18
                        /---2                      \---19
                                          /---10   /---20
                                 \---5             \---21
                                          \---11   /---22
          1                                        \---23
                                          /---12
                                 /---6             /---26
                        \---3             \---13
                                          /---14  \---27
                                 \---7
                                          \---15
```

```
         Wyatt, Allen Lee Sr.  (M)
         Born: 11 Jun 1956      CPN: A  1    FCPN: A  5    MCPN: A  6
         Cmnts: 03Feb1968;end27Apr1976

         Spouse 1: Pease, Debra Mae (F)
         Born: 01 Jan 1956       Married: 29 Apr 1976   OTH SPS: N
         Page: A  2   FCPN: A 32   MCPN: A 33
         Cmnts: 18feb1964;end 27apr1976

         Child 1: Wyatt, Allen Lee Jr.  (M)
         Born: 09 Feb 1977        Cmnts: Bic

         Child 2: Wyatt, Eric Christopher  (M)
         Born: 19 Aug 1979        Cmnts: Bic
```

Plate 45. Discovery Software *Family Connection* Pedigree Chart

The following names are depicted in graphical form in the above chart. The
numbers in the chart refer to the number found to the left of each name.

1) Wyatt, Allen Lee Jr. (M) Computer Page Number: A 3
 Born: 09 Feb 1977   Died:

2) Wyatt, Allen Lee Sr. (M) Computer Page Number: A 1
 Born: 11 Jun 1956   Died:

3) Pease, Debra Mae (F)   Computer Page Number: A 2
 Born: 01 Jan 1956   Died:

4) Wyatt, James Allen (M) Computer Page Number: A 5
 Born: 25 May 1932   Died:

5) Hull, Virginia Lee (F)   Computer Page Number: A 6
 Born: 27 Jun 1936   Died:

6) Pease, Cecil Lee (M)   Computer Page Number: A 32
 Born: 25 May 1926   Died:

7) Rasmussen, Wilma Pearl (F) Computer Page Number: A 33
 Born: 28 Feb 1930   Died:

8) Wyatt, Martin Henry (M) Computer Page Number: A 7
 Born: 12 Jun 1903   Died:

9) Sorter, Harriet Marie (F) Computer Page Number: A 8
 Born: 24 Apr 1910   Died:

10) Hull, Richard Harold Sr. (M) Computer Page Number: A 9
 Born: 18 Sep 1911   Died: 21 Dec 1969

11) Lowder, Helene Larue (F) Computer Page Number: A 10
 Born: 29 Oct 1915   Died:

12) Pease, Isaac Lee (M)   Computer Page Number: A 37
 Born: 2 Aug 1904   Died:

13) Wilkins, Vera (F)   Computer Page Number: A 38
 Born: 25 Apr 1909   Died:

14) Rasmussen, Wilmot Earl (M) Computer Page Number: A175
 Born: 20,may 1900   Died: 15,jan.1947

15) Christensen, Bertha Mae (F) Computer Page Number: A176
 Born: 08 Oct   Died:

16) Wyatt, Daniel W (M)   Computer Page Number: A 21
 Born: 25 Jul 1879   Died: 02 May 1910

17) Woody, Emma (F)   Computer Page Number: A 22
 Born: 02 Jan 1877   Died: 20 Mar 1960

18) Sorter, Homer Hill (M) Computer Page Number: A 23
 Born: 18 May 1885   Died: 04 Apr 1961

19) Sharp, Fanny Viola (F)   Computer Page Number: A114
 Born: 4 Apr 1887   Died: 3 May 1959

20) Hull, Orion Ferdinand (M) Computer Page Number: A 31
 Born: 8 Jan 1864   Died: 27 Nov 1921

21) Clabaugh, Esther Ellen (Ella) (F) Computer Page Number: A 24
 Born: 29 Dec 1868   Died: 19 Mar 1933

22) Lowder, Theodore Warren Sr. (M) Computer Page Number: A 72
 Born: 20 Sep 1886   Died: 22 Dec 1935

23) Mitchell, Allie Ina (F)   Computer Page Number: A 73
 Born: 27 Mar 1889   Died: 14 Jun 1972

26) Wilkins, Joseph David (M) Computer Page Number: A148
 Born: 25 Apr 1877   Died: 16 Apr 1962

27) Lark, Clara Ellen (F)   Computer Page Number: A149
 Born: 07 Jun 1888   Died: 25 Sep 1959

Plate 46. Discovery Software *Family Connection* Pedigree Chart

PEDIGREE CHART FOR SALLEE CLAUDE HOWARD, GEN.NO.- 0002

FIRST GENERATION   SECOND GENERATION THIRD GENERATION   FOURTH GENERATION FIFTH GENERATION

```
                                                    0032* - SALLE JOSEPH SR - B. 3SEP1746
                                      0016 - SALLEE JOSEPH L - B. ?CA 1766
                                                    0033 - MAXEY JEMIMA - B.

                        0008 - SALLEE EDWARD MAXEY - B. ?CA 1807

                                                    0034 - PANKEY SAMUEL - B. CA 1758
                                      0017 - PANKEY JUDITH - B. CA 1767
                                                    0035 - BINFORD BETSEY KINSEY - B. CA 1739

          0004 - SALLEE EUSEBIUS MCCOY - B. JUL1835

                                                    0036 - MCCOY WILLIAM - B. 1754
                                      0018 - MCCOY ROYSE (RICE) - B. 16JUN1789
                                                    0037 - ROYSE ELIZABETH - B. 1758

                        0009 - MCCOY CHRISTIANA POUND - B. 21APR1814

                                                    0038 - POUND JOSEPH - B. 23NOV1770
                                      0019* - POUND MALINDA - B. 11APR1796
                                                    0039 - STARK ELIZABETH - B.

0002 - SALLEE CLAUDE HOWARD - B. MAR 1879

                                                    0040 - UNKNOWN - B. ????
                                      0020 - PIERSON JACOB - B. SEE NOTE
                                                    0041 - UNKNOWN - B. ????

                        0010 - PIERSON GOWAN B - B. CA 1834

                                                    0042 - UNKNOWN - B. ????
                                      0021 - PIERSON TERESA - B. 15JUL1812
                                                    0043 - UNKNOWN - B. ????

          0005 - PIERSON TERESA (POLLY) - B. JUN 1858

                                                    0044 - CHASTAIN BARNETT SR. - B. CA 1774
                                      0022 - CHASTAIN WILLIAM - B. 1797
                                                    0045 - HIXON SARA - B.

                        0011 - CHASTAIN CYNTHIA ANN - B. CA 1841

                                                    0046 - UNKNOWN - B. ????
                                      0023 - THORNTON POLLY - B. CA 1796
                                                    0047 - UNKNOWN - B. ????
```

```
PEDIGREE CHART FOR  SALLEE EDWARD MAXEY,  GEN.NO.- 0008

FIRST GENERATION  SECOND GENERATION  THIRD GENERATION  FOURTH GENERATION  FIFTH GENERATION


                                                      0128 - SALLE ABRAHAM - B. 22FEB1674
                                            0064 - SALLE PIERRE - B. OCT 1714
                                                      0129 - PERRAULT OLIVE - B. ?CA 1680

                                0032* - SALLE JOSEPH SR - B. 3SEP1746


                                                      0130 - BONDURANT JEAN PIERRE - B.
                                            0065 - BONDURANT FRANCOISE - B. CA 1715
                                                      0131 - UNKNOWN - B. ????

                    0016 - SALLEE JOSEPH L - B. ?CA 1766


                                                      0132 - MAXEY EDWARD SR. - B.
                                            0066 - MAXEY WILLIAM - B.
                                                      0133 - MAXEY SUSANNAH (?) - B.

                                0033 - MAXEY JEMIMA - B.


                                                      0134 - UNKNOWN - B. ????
                                            0067 - MAXEY MARY (SUBLETT?) - B.
                                                      0135 - UNKNOWN - B. ????

0008 - SALLEE EDWARD MAXEY - B. ?CA 1807


                                                      0136* - PANETIE JEAN PIERRE - B.
                                            0068 - PANKEY STEPHEN - B.
                                                      0137 - UNKNOWN - B. ????

                                0034 - PANKEY SAMUEL - B. CA 1758


                                                      0138 - UNKNOWN - B. ????
                                            0069 - UNKNOWN - B. ????
                                                      0139 - UNKNOWN - B. ????

                    0017 - PANKEY JUDITH - B. CA 1767


                                                      0140 - UNKNOWN - B. ????
                                            0070 - UNKNOWN - B. ????
                                                      0141 - UNKNOWN - B. ????

                                0035 - BINFORD BETSEY KINSEY - B. CA 1739


                                                      0142 - UNKNOWN - B. ????
                                            0071 - UNKNOWN - B. ????
                                                      0143 - UNKNOWN - B. ????
```

Plate 47. Genealog Software *Genealog II* Pedigree Chart

```
    PEDCHART :  #1
_____
_____


                                                              CONT
                                     16-SPENCER FAULKNER         16
                        8-GEORGE D FAULKNER
                                     17-SUSAN MCKINSEY           17

            4-JOHN S FAULKNER

                                     18-DANIEL VANLANDINGHAM     18
                        9-ADELIA VANLANDINGHAM
                                     19-ANN E NORTHCUTT          19

    2-GEORGE FAULKNER

                                     20-WILLIAM A SMITH          20
                       10-WILLIAM C SMITH
                                     21-MELISSA BELL             21

            5-FAWN FERN SMITH

                                     22-SAMUEL BRIERTON          22
                       11-ELIZABETH BRIERTON
                                     23-MARY MANN                23

1-VELMA FAULKNER

                                     24-PASQUAL CHIAPPETTI       24
                       12-FRANCESCO CHIAPPETTI
                                     25-ROSARIO COSENTINO        25

            6-PASQUALE CHIAPPETTE

                                     26-DOMENICO SCANGA          26
                       13-MARIA TERESA SCANGA
                                     27-CARMINO MUTO             27

    3-ASUNTA CHIAPPETTI

                                     28-                         28
                       14-MUSIO ABATE
                                     29-                         29

            7-FILOMENA ABATE

                                     30-                         30
                       15-ROSA MAZZOTTO
                                     31-                         31
SPOUSE: ARNO PROCHTER
```

Plate 48. Ancestors =*Ancestors*= Pedigree Chart

Person No. 1 on this chart
same as No. 8 on chart No. 1

Compiler Sandra Lee Ritzinger
7378 Zurawski Court
Custer WI 54423
06/02/84

16 DELISLE
Jacques
Born: 00 Jan 1800
( )
Marr: 21 Jan 1834
Died:
( )

8 DELISLE
Eugene   Joseph
Born: 15 Jan 1848
Ecureuil, Quebec
Marr: 00 Unk 18--
Died: 19 Dec 1905
Chippewa Falls, WI

17 LEVEILLE
Francoise
Born:
( )
Died:
( )

--------Spouse--------
VAUDREUIL
Evelyn
Born: 27 Mar 1859
Lotbiniere, Quebec
Died: 04 Nov 1950
Wauwatosa, WI

32 DELISLE
Jacques
Born: 30 Mar 1782
Ecureuil, Quebec
Marr: 10 Feb 1806
Died:
( )

33 PAGE
Madeleine
Born:
( )
Died:
( )

34 LEVEILLE
Jean   Baptiste
Born: 11 Aug 1771
Pte aux Treables, Quebec
Marr: 21 Jan 1800
Died:
( )

35 GERMAIN
Marie   Angelique
Born: 18 Sep 1776
Ecureuil, Quebec
Died:
( )

64 DELISLE
Jacques
Born: 20 Jun 1755
Marr: 23 Feb 1778
Died:
( )

65 FISET
Marie   Elisabeth
Born: 18 Jun 1757
Died: '
( )

66 PAGE
Jean   Baptiste
Born: 00 Unk 1753
Unknown
Marr: 23 Jul 1781
Died:
( )

67 DUSSAULT-TOUPIN
Clotilde
Born: 19 May 1764
Ecureuil, Quebec
Died:
( )

68 LEVEILLE
Jean
Born: 27 Dec 1738
Marr: 00 Unk 1769
Died:
( )

69 BERTRAND
Therese
Born: 11 Mar 1751
Cap Sante, Quebec
Died:
( )

70 GERMAIN
Pierre   Etienne
Born: 19 Dec 1743
Marr: 00 Unk 1769
Died:
( )

71 LANGLOIS
Angelique   Marie
Born:
( )
Died:
( )

128 DELISLE
Jacque
Born: 18 Mar 1718   Cont. on 128
Marr: 23 Nov 1750
Died:

129 PAGE
Angelique
Born: Cont. on ....
Died:

130 FISET
Jerome   Thierry
Born: 00 Unk 1725 Cont. on 130
Marr: 07 Feb 1752
Died:

131 PLEAU
Marie   Elisabeth
Born: 23 Feb 1730 Cont. on ....
Died:

132 PAGE
Joseph
Born: 24 Aug 1721 Cont. on 132
Marr: 19 Feb 1748
Died: 16 Feb 1776

133 TOUPIN-DUSSAULT
Madeleine
Born: 20 Nov 1729 Cont. on ....
Died: 08 Mar 1773

134 TOUPIN
Jean   Baptiste
Born: 00 Unk 1719 Cont. on 134
Marr: 11 Apr 1763
Died:

135 AIDE-CREQUY
Angelique   Marie
Born: 13 Oct 1740 Cont. on ....
Died:

136 LEVEILLE
Jean
Born: 08 Jan 1707 Cont. on ....
Marr: 03 Feb 1738
Died: 27 Feb 1779

137 GAUDIN
Marie   Catherine
Born: 24 May 1706 Cont. on ....
Died:

138 BERTRAND
Jean   Baptiste
Born: 13 Mar 1706 Cont. on 138
Marr: 21 Nov 1735
Died:

139 LETELLIER
Marie   Joseph
Born: 06 Apr 1713 Cont. on ....
Died:

140 GERMAIN
Jacque   Alexis
Born: 14 Apr 1713 Cont. on 140
Marr: 29 Oct 1738
Died:

141 BIGUET-NOBERT
Elisabeth
Born: 06 Apr 1722 Cont. on ....
Died:

142
Born: Cont. on ....
Marr:
Died:

143
Born: Cont. on ....
Died:

Plate 49. Software Solutions *Arbor-Aide* Pedigree Chart

Prepared by: JENNY LOUISE SMITH
Date: 09 SEP 1984

```
                                                                            :: EDWARD HARRISON_____
                                                                            ::                                 20
                                                  :: EDWIN LEWIS HARRISON_____ ::
                                                  :: 01 AUG 1859                    ::
                                                  :: BANGOR, PENOBSCOT, ME          :: SARAH NEWBERRY_____
                                                  :: 30 NOV 1890                    ::                          21
                          :: GILBERT DONALD HARRISON_____ :: 17 MAY 1904          ::
                          :: 28 APR 1887                      :: PARK CITY, SUMMIT, UT ::
                          :: EUREKA, JUAB, UT                 ::
                          :: 12 DEC 1900                      ::                        :: MARTIN FINDLEY_____
                          :: SALT LAKE CITY, SALT LAKE, UT    ::                        ::                        22
                          :: 8 FEB 1951                       :: MARY EVANNAH FINDLEY___ ::
                          :: SALT LAKE CITY, SALT LAKE, UT    :: 08 MAY 1861            ::
                          ::                                   :: SPANISH FORK, UT, UT   :: ELIZABETH HEAL_____
                          ::                                   :: 15 DEC 1949            ::                        23
                          ::                                   :: SALT LAKE CITY, SALT LAKE, UT ::
          :: JAMES PATRICK HARRISON_____
          :: 04 APR 1920
          :: SALT LAKE CITY, SALT LAKE, UT
          :: 12 DEC 1940
          :: SALT LAKE CITY, SALT LAKE, UT                      :: SWEN LARSON_____
          :: 12 SEP 1977                                        ::                          24
          :: PANAMA CITY, BAY, FLA          :: JOHN HOWELLS LARSON_____ ::
          ::                                 :: 24 DEC 1859                    ::
          ::                                 :: BALTIMORE, BALTIMORE, MD       :: INGRID ANDERSSON_____
          ::                                 :: 30 SEP 1880                    ::                          25
          ::              :: FRANCENE FAYE LARSON_____ :: SALT LAKE CITY, SALT LAKE, UT ::
          ::              :: 14 DEC 1891                 :: 17 NOV 1946                    ::
          ::              :: SILVER CITY, JUAB, UT       :: SALT LAKE CITY, SALT LAKE, UT  ::
          ::              :: 08 JUL 1975                 ::                               :: JOHN BARNEY_____
          ::              :: SALT LAKE CITY, SALT LAKE, UT ::                             ::                          26
          ::                                              :: RUTH ELIZABETH BARNEY_____ ::
          ::                                              :: 29 JUL 1866                    ::
          ::                                              :: SANTAQUIN, UTAH, UT            :: RUTH MC LEARY_____
          ::                                              :: 16 JUL 1936                    ::                          27
:: NANCY RUTH HARRISON_____                          :: SALT LAKE CITY, SALT LAKE, UT ::
:: 24 OCT 1941
:: SALT LAKE CITY, SALT LAKE, UT
                                                                            :: CHARLES PETERSON_____
                                                                            ::                          28
                                                  :: CHARLES SINCLAIR PETERSON_____ ::
                                                  :: 03 JUL 1865                    ::
:: JOHN EDWARD JONES_____                    :: MUSKEGON, MUSKEGON, MI         :: ELIZABETH LOWE_____
                                                  :: 04 JUL 1885                    ::                          29
                          :: ROBERT CALVIN PETERSON_____ :: 07 NOV 1946          ::
                          :: 30 APR 1892                     :: LOS ANGELES, LOS ANGELES, CA ::
                          :: LOS ANGELES, LOS ANGELES, CA    ::
                          :: 01 JAN 1918                     ::                        :: LUTHER BENNETT_____
                          :: SALT LAKE CITY, SALT LAKE, UT   ::                        ::                          30
                          :: 11 JAN 1955                     :: ETTA MAE BENNETT_____ ::
                          :: SALT LAKE CITY, SALT LAKE, UT   :: 08 MAR 1868            ::
                          ::                                  :: ELBA, WASHINGTON, OH   :: _____
                          ::                                  :: 06 JUL 1952            ::                          31
                          ::                                  :: SALT LAKE CITY, SALT LAKE, UT ::
          :: PATRICIA ANN PETERSON_____
          :: 28 NOV 1919
          :: SALT LAKE CITY, SALT LAKE, UT
                                                                            :: WILLIAM TYLER_____
                                                                            ::                          32
                                              :: WILLIAM ALFRED TYLER_____ ::
                                              :: 27 DEC 1861                    ::
                                              :: SALT LAKE CITY, SALT LAKE, UT  :: BESSY MILLS_____
                                              :: 23 JUN 1893                    ::                          33
                          :: MARY GRACE TYLER_____ :: SALT LAKE CITY, SALT LAKE, UT ::
                          :: 15 OCT 1895                    :: 09 NOV 1908                    ::
                          :: SALT LAKE CITY, SALT LAKE, UT  :: SALT LAKE CITY, SALT LAKE, UT  ::
                          :: 21 JUN 1974                    ::                               :: NOEL ADAMS GREENWOOD____
                          :: SALT LAKE CITY, SALT LAKE, UT  ::                               ::                          34
                                                            :: VILATE WHITNEY GREENWOOD_____ ::
                                                            :: 23 OCT 1867                    ::
                                                            :: SALT LAKE CITY, SALT LAKE, UT  :: SUSETTE CAROL MARTIN____
                                                            :: 16 JAN 1922                    ::                          35
                                                            :: SALT LAKE CITY, SALT LAKE, UT  ::
```

Plate 50. Array Systems *Treesearch* Pedigree Chart

COMMSOFT ROOTS/M   V1.02.02 PEDIGREE CHART
6 Aug 1981

No. 1 on this chart is the
same person as no.
on chart no.

Chart   1

Alistair Bright
```
16   CONTINUED ON CHART   2
```

Archibald Bright
```
8  BORN      11 Mar 813
*  WHERE     Moorhead
   DIED      8 Sep 851
   WHERE     Oxland
   MARRIED   4 Dec 829
```

Anne Pritkin
```
17   CONTINUED ON CHART   3
```

Sir Arthur Bright
```
4  BORN      1 Feb 830
*  WHERE     Regencia
   DIED      15 Nov 861
   WHERE     Oxland
   MARRIED   6 Sep 847
```

Gwendolyn Gibbon
```
9  BORN      16 Oct 810
   WHERE     Oxland
   DIED      1 Feb 882
   WHERE     Regencia
```

Alchemy Gibbon
```
18   CONTINUED ON CHART   4
```

Katherine Swamp
```
19   CONTINUED ON CHART   5
```

Arnold Bright
```
2  BORN      16 May 848
*  WHERE     Regencia
   DIED      22 Feb 880
   WHERE     Oxland
   MARRIED   10 Jun 868
```

George Cap
```
10  BORN      30 Jan 801
*   WHERE     Highcastle
    DIED      12 Jun 838
    WHERE     Regencia
    MARRIED   10 Mar 828
```

William Cap
```
20   CONTINUED ON CHART   6
```

Bonnie Halp
```
21   CONTINUED ON CHART   7
```

Helen Cap
```
5  BORN      8 May 832
   WHERE     Regencia
   DIED      17 Jul 857
   WHERE     Regencia
```

Marion Smith
```
11  BORN      12 May 812
    WHERE     Highcastle
    DIED      14 Sep 842
    WHERE     Regencia
```

Alan Smith
```
22   CONTINUED ON CHART   8
```

Frances Forge
```
23   CONTINUED ON CHART   9
```

Albert Bright
```
1  BORN      3 Jan 870
   WHERE     Regencia
   DIED
   WHERE
   MARRIED
```

NAME OF HUSBAND OR WIFE

George Griffen
```
12  BORN      15 Oct 814
*   WHERE     Regencia
    DIED      8 Jul 860
    WHERE     Regencia
    MARRIED   27 Jun 830
```

Henry Griffen
```
24   CONTINUED ON CHART   10
```

Ophelia Fairbanks
```
25   CONTINUED ON CHART   11
```

Harold Griffen
```
6  BORN      30 May 833
*  WHERE     Regencia
   DIED      23 Sep 853
   WHERE     Regencia
   MARRIED   5 Jun 849
```

Helen Randall
```
13  BORN      8 Feb 817
    WHERE     Headwater
    DIED      31 Dec 840
    WHERE     Regencia
```

Charles Randall
```
26   CONTINUED ON CHART   12
```

Genevieve Gorge
```
27   CONTINUED ON CHART   13
```

Elizabeth Griffen
```
3  BORN      20 Feb 850
   WHERE     Regencia
   DIED      18 Apr 885
   WHERE     Regencia
```

Jack Goode
```
14  BORN      12 May 810
*   WHERE     Regencia
    DIED      20 Mar 858
    WHERE     Oxland
    MARRIED   18 Sep 828
```

Samuel Goode
```
28   CONTINUED ON CHART   14
```

Glynn Waters
```
29   CONTINUED ON CHART   15
```

Sarah Goode
```
7  BORN      1 Jun 829
   WHERE     Regencia
   DIED      2 Jul 860
   WHERE     Regencia
```

Mary Belly
```
15  BORN      16 Aug 815
    WHERE     The Coast
    DIED      14 Aug 846
    WHERE     Regencia
```

William Belly
```
30   CONTINUED ON CHART   16
```

Winnifred Strong
```
31   CONTINUED ON CHART   17
```

Plate 51. Commsoft, Inc. *Roots/M* Pedigree Chart

Standard Five Generation Pedigree Chart
Prepared on: 01-05-1984

HARTER, John

HARTER, Benjamin F.

| 16   CONTINUED ON CHART   2

8   born 15 Sep 1828
Licking Twp, Licking Co Ohio
died 23 Nov 1882
Smith Twp., Whitley Co., Ind.
md. 16 Sep 1858

BOWER, Mary

17   CONTINUED ON CHART   3

JOHNSON, Benjamin Franklin

HARTER, Arlando Washington

4   born 23 Aug 1868
Whitley County, Indiana
died 07 Aug 1936
Smith Twp, Whitley Co., Ind.
md. 25 Dec 1901

JOHNSON, Elizabeth C.

| 18   CONTINUED ON CHART   4

9   born 05 Sep 1837
Knox County, Ohio
died 19 Dec 1900
Collins, Whitley County, Ind

ZOLMAN, Lydia

19   CONTINUED ON CHART   5

SOURS, Andrew

HARTER, Benjamin Isaac

2   born 16 Dec 1918
nr Collins, Whitley Co., Ind.
died st ill aliv

md. 24 Apr 1954

SOURS, Isaac

| 20   CONTINUED ON CHART   6

10 born 08 Aug 1828
Stark County, Ohio
died 06 Feb 1914
Clear Creek Twp., Huntington
md. 19 Feb 1857

WESTON, Hannah

21   CONTINUED ON CHART   7

HAYWARD, Charles

SOURS, Olive Mae

5   born 11 Oct 1875
Huntington County, Indiana
died 30 Jun 1951
Columbia City, Indiana

HAYWARD, Ann

| 22   CONTINUED ON CHART   8

11 born ?? ??? 1834
Chautauqua County, New York
died 19 Jan 1898
Clear Creek Twp., Huntington

COWAN, Anna

23   CONTINUED ON CHART   9

KIEFER, Adam

HARTER, Stuart Alan

1 born 20 Apr 1957
Columbia City, Indiana
died st ill aliv

md.

KIEFER, Jacob (Johann Jacob)

| 24   CONTINUED ON CHART 10

12 born 21 Jun 1849
Preble Twp., Adams Co., Ind.
died 03 Apr 1924
S. Whitley, Whitley Co, Ind.
md. 11 Jul 1872

?, Maria Elisabeth

25   CONTINUED ON CHART 11

SCHINBECKLER, Nynrod

NAME OF HUSBAND OR WIFE

KIEFER, Frank August Henry

6   born 13 Aug 1884
Whitley County, Indiana
died 04 Aug 1944
Columbia City, Indiana
md. 21 Aug 1913

SCHINBECKLER, Susan

| 26   CONTINUED ON CHART 12

13 born 26 Dec 1852
Jefferson Tp, Whitley Co Ind
died 28 Jan 1928
Whitley County, Indiana

AUER, Mary

27   CONTINUED ON CHART 13

LAHM, John

KIEFER, Velas Jean

3   born 13 Jan 1921
Columbia City, Indiana
died st ill aliv

LAHM, Lewis John

| 28   CONTINUED ON CHART 14

14 born 10 Feb 1861
Columbia Twp, Whitley Co Ind
died 13 Apr 1924
Whitley County, Indiana
md. 28 Oct 1885

BUSH, Amanda

29   CONTINUED ON CHART 15

FULLERTON, John Wesley

LAHM, Augusta Julia

7   born 30 Mar 1893
Whitley County, Indiana
died 29 Jan 1969
Smith Twp, Whitley Co., Ind.

FULLERTON, Mary Jane

| 30   CONTINUED ON CHART 16

15 born 31 Oct 1866
Whitley County, Indiana
died 15 Feb 1950
Whitley County, Indiana

HILDEBRAND, Martha Elizabeth

31   CONTINUED ON CHART 17

Prepared by:
CoapuGen Systems
P. O. Box 15604
Fort Wayne, IN 46885

Plate 52. CompuGen Systems *FamilyFile* Pedigree Chart

ANCESTOR CHART

```
                                                                    JOSEPH LUPTON            236
                                                                    :================================:
                                        JOSEPH LUPTON        228   : b. 11/08/1645   d.          :
                                        :================================: a. 06/06/1679              :
                                        : b.    / /1686           : ANN HALL                 236   :
                                        : bp YORKSHIRE CO., ENGLAND :--------------------------------:
                    WILLIAM LUPTON      98  : d. 08/09/1758           : b.    / /1654   d. 05/05/1737
                    :================================: dp FREDERICK CO., VIRGINIA
                    : b. 14/01/1714           : a. 10/07/1713           STEPHEN TWINING          237
                    : bp BUCKS CO., PENN.     : ap BUCKS CO., PENN.      :================================:
                    : d. 04/11/1783           : MERCY TWINING      228  : b. 06/02/1659   d.   /04/1720 :
                    : dp FREDERICK CO., VIRGINIA :--------------------------------: a. 13/01/1683              :
                    : a. 07/08/1745           : b. 08/09/1690           : ABIGAIL YOUNG            237   :
                    : ap                        bp EASTHAM, BARNSTABLE,MASS :--------------------------------:
WILLIAM LUPTON        75  :                     d. 25/05/1726           b.   /10/1660   d.   /11/1715
:================================:                     dp BUCKS CO., PENN.
b.  09/11/1754       :
bp FREDERICK CO., VIRGINIA :
d.  08/02/1811       :                       SAMUEL PICKERING    229  : b.              d.          :
dp FAIRFIELD,HIGHLAND,OHIO :                :================================: a.                         :
a.  04/11/1779       :                       : b.                      :                            :
ap SMITH'S CREEK,SHEN., VA. :               : bp                      :--------------------------------:
                    : GRACE PICKERING     98  : d. 10/01/1727           b.              d.
                    :--------------------------------: dp PENNSYLVANIA
                    : b. 24/08/1722           : a. 07/11/1712           JOHN SCARBOROUGH         286
                    : bp                      : ap PENNSYLVANIA         :================================:
                    : d.                      : MARY SCARBOROUGH   229  : b.    / /1667   d. 27/01/1727 :
                    : dp                      :--------------------------------: a.   /CA/1690              :
                                              b. 08/08/1695           : MARY (PROBILE)          286   :
                                              bp SOLEBURY, BUCKS CO.,PENN :--------------------------------:
    DAVID LUPTON       59  RUTH ADAMS        59  d.    / /1791           b.   /CA/1676   d. 23/01/1751
>>>>++++++++++++++++++++++++++++++++++++++++++++++++++++++++++++++ dp FREDERICK CO., VIRGINIA
    b.  11/01/1           21/04/1797                                    JOSEPH ALLEN             315
    bp    VIRGINIA          VIRGINIA                                    :================================:
    d.  18/10/1883         03/03/1874         REUBEN ALLEN        314  : b.   /CA/1642   d.   /09/1704 :
    dp UNIONVILLE, PUTNAM, MO.  UNIONVILLE, PUTNAM, MO. :================================: a.   /CA/1779              :
    a.  03/01/1816                            : b.    / /169?           : SARAH HULL              315   :
    ap SHENANDOAH CO., VIRGINIA               : bp                      :--------------------------------:
                    JACKSON ALLEN        99  : d.    / /1741           b.   /03/1650   d.   /CA/1705
                    :================================: dp ORANGE CO., VIRGINIA
                    : b.                      : a.    / /1720
                    : bp                      : ap CECIL CO., MARYLAND  :================================:
                    : d. 30/08/1786           : MARY (JACKSON)     314  : b.              d.          :
                    : dp SHENANDOAH CO., VIRGINIA :--------------------------------: a.                         :
                    : a.                       b.                      :                            :
                    : ap                       bp                      :--------------------------------:
BATHSHEBA ALLEN       75  :                   d.    / /1751           b.              d.
:--------------------------------:                   dp AUGUSTA CO., VIRGINIA
b.  04/10/1760       :
bp SMITH'S CREEK,SHEN., VA. :                 JOHN DAVIS          305  : b.              d.          :
d.  01/01/1847       :                        :================================: a.                         :
dp FAIRFIELD,HIGHLAND,OHIO :                  : b.                      :                            :
                    :                         : bp                      :--------------------------------:
                    : ELIZABETH DAVIS     99  : d. CA/06/1759           b.              d.
                    :--------------------------------: dp SPOTSYLVANIA CO., VA.
                    b.                        : a.
                    bp                        : ap                      :================================:
                    d. CA/02/1821             : ANN                305  : b.              d.          :
                    dp SHENANDOAH CO., VIRGINIA :--------------------------------: a.                         :
                                              b.                      :                            :
                                              bp                      :--------------------------------:
                                              d.                      b.              d.
    DATE: 10/30/84                            dp
```

Plate 53. Soft-Gene *Ancestry I/III* Pedigree Chart

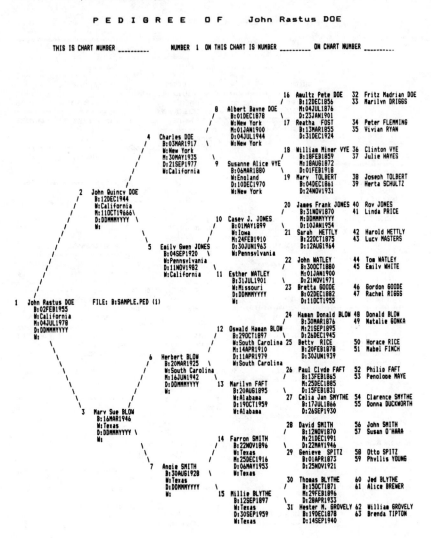

PEDIGREE   OF   John Rastus DOE

THIS IS CHART NUMBER _____   NUMBER 1 ON THIS CHART IS NUMBER _____ ON CHART NUMBER _____

```
                                                                16  Amultz Pete DOE    32  Fritz Madrian DOE
                                                                  / B:12DEC1856        33  Marilyn DRIGGS
                                                   8  Albert Bayne DOE M:04JUL1876
                                                    / B:01DEC1878    \ D:23JAN1901
                                                   /  M:New York     17  Reatha FOST     34  Peter FLEMMING
                                   4  Charles DOE  /   M:01JAN1900       B:13MAR1855     35  Vivian RYAN
                                    / B:03MAR1917 \    D:04JUL1944       D:31DEC1924
                                   /  M:New York   \   M:New York
                                   /  M:30MAY1935   \                18  William Miner VYE 36  Clinton VYE
                                   /  D:21SEP1977    \                 / B:18FEB1859     37  Julie HAYES
                                   /  M:California    9  Susanne Alice VYE M:18AUG1872
                  2  John Quincy DOE                  / B:06MAR1880    \ D:01FEB1918
                   / B:12DEC1944                     /  M:England      19  Mary TOLBERT   38  Joseph TOLBERT
                  /  M:California                   /   D:10DEC1970       B:04DEC1861    39  Herta SCHULTZ
                 /   M:11OCT1966\                  /    M:New York        D:24NOV1931
                /    D:DDMMMYYYY \                /
                /    M:          \               /                  20  James Frank JONES 40  Roy JONES
               /                  \             /                     / B:31NOV1870     41  Linda PRICE
              /                    \           10  Casey J. JONES      M:DDMMMYYYY
             /                      \           / B:01MAY1899         \ D:10JAN1954
            /                        \         /  M:Iowa             21  Sarah HETTLY    42  Harold HETTLY
           /                          5  Emily Gwen JONES M:24FEB1910    B:22OCT1875    43  Lucy MASTERS
          /                            / B:04SEP1920  \    D:30JUN1963     D:12AUG1964
         /                            /  M:Pennsylvania \   M:Pennsylvania
        /                            /   D:11NOV1982     \               22  John WATLEY   44  Tom WATLEY
       /                            /    M:California      \               / B:30OCT1880  45  Emily WHITE
      /                            /                  11  Esther WATLEY     M:01JAN1900
     /                            /                    / B:31JUL1901      \ D:21NOV1971
1  John Rastus DOE  FILE: B:SAMPLE.PED (1)            /  M:Missouri       23  Bretta GOODE  46  Gordon GOODE
   B:02FEB1955                                       /   D:DDMMMYYYY         B:02DEC1882   47  Rachel RIGGS
   M:California                                     /    M:                  D:11OCT1955
   M:04JUL1978                                      /
   D:DDMMMYYYY                                     /                    24  Haman Donald BLOW 48  Donald BLOW
   M:          \                                  /                       / B:30MAR1876   49  Natalie GONKA
    \                                  12  Oswald Haman BLOW M:21SEP1895
     \                                   / B:29OCT1897      \ D:26DEC1945
      \                                 /  M:South Carolina 25  Betty RICE    50  Horace RICE
       \                               /   M:14APR1910         B:20FEB1878   51  Mabel FINCH
        \                             /    D:11APR1979         D:30JUN1939
         \                           /     M:South Carolina
          6  Herbert BLOW           /                          26  Paul Clyde FAFT 52  Philip FAFT
           / B:20MAR1925           /                             / B:13FEB1865   53  Penolope MAYE
          /  M:South Carolina     /                              M:25DEC1885
         /   M:16JUN1942         /                             \ D:15FEB1831
        /    D:DDMMMYYYY        13  Marilyn FAFT                27  Celia Jan SMYTHE 54  Clarence SMYTHE
       /     M:          \       / B:20AUG1895                    / B:17JUL1866   55  Donna DUCKWORTH
      /                   \     /  M:Alabama                       D:26SEP1930
     /                     \   /   D:19OCT1959
  3  Mary Sue BLOW          \ /    M:Alabama                    28  David SMITH     56  John SMITH
     B:16MAR1946            /                                     / B:12NOV1870   57  Susan O'HARA
     M:Texas               /                                      M:21DEC1991
     D:DDMMMYYYY \        14  Farron SMITH                      \ D:22MAY1946
     M:          \         / B:22NOV1896                        29  Genieve SPITZ   58  Otto SPITZ
                  \       /  M:Texas                               B:01APR1873    59  Phyllis YOUNG
                   \     /   M:25DEC1916                           D:25NOV1921
                    \   /    D:06MAY1953
                  7  Angie SMITH  M:Texas                       30  Thomas BLYTHE   60  Jed BLYTHE
                    / B:30AUG1928                                 / B:15OCT1871   61  Alice BREWER
                   /  M:Texas                                     M:29FEB1896
                  /   D:DDMMMYYYY \                             \ D:28APR1933
                  /   M:          \                           15  Millie BLYTHE    31  Hester M. GROVELY 62  William GROVELY
                                    / B:12SEP1897                 B:19DEC1878    63  Brenda TIPTON
                                   /  M:Texas                     D:14SEP1940
                                      D:30SEP1959
                                      M:Texas
```

07-31-1984

Plate 54.   Personal Software *Family Reunion* Pedigree Chart

```
PEDIGREE OF GORDON PAYEN HILLMAN <# 10>
**************************************************************************
                                                 .

                                           ***HILLMAN,THOMAS(#45)
                               ***HILLMAN,THOMAS(# 29)
                    ***HILLMAN,PETER (# 21)   ***MITCHELL,SARAH(#46)
                    *    B. 28 DEC 1851       ***HAMPER,JOHN    (#47)
          ***HILLMAN,ERNEST(# 13)   ***HAMPER,ELIZABE(# 30)
          *    B. 10 MAR 1878       ***UNKNOWN,EMMA   (#48)
          *    M. 22 JUL 1901       ***NICHOLSON,JOHN(#49)
          *    D. 18 DEC 1950   ***NICHOLSON,NELS(# 31)
***HILLMAN,FRANK (# 11)   ***NICHOLSON,ESTH(# 22)   ***UNKNOWN,UNKNOW(#50)
*  B. 28 JUN 1902         B. 3 AUG 1855     ***HOTSTONE,WILLI(#51)
*  M. 20 JUN 1923                   ***HOTSTONE,MARY (# 32)
*  D. 12 NOV 1972              *        ***UNKNOWN,RHODA  (#52)
*                   *                   ***NICOLA,GIOVANN(#53)
*                   *        ***NICOLA,LUIGI P(# 33)
*                   ***NICOLA,FRANCES(# 23)   ***CAPRA,CATERINA(#54)
*                   *    B. 18 AUG 1839       ***UNKNOWN,UNKNOW(#75)
*         ***NICOLA,LEANORA(# 18)   ***PAGUENNE,GIULA(# 34)
*              B. 13 OCT 1879       ***UNKNOWN,UNKNOW(#75)
*              D. 9 FEB 1963        ***MORGAN ,JOHN   (#55)
*                   *        ***MORGAN,HENRY   (# 35)
*                   ***MORGAN,EMILY   (# 24)   ***BRAINE,ROSE   (#56)
HILLMAN,GORDON(# 10)        B. 25 SEP 1856    ***HAYWARD,JOSEPH(#57)
B. 1 DEC 1939                       ***HAYWARD,MARIA (# 36)
M. 21 JAN 1960                  *        ***UNKNOWN,HANNA  (#58)
D. ALIVE                   *        ***BOURNE,WILLIAM(#59)
                    ***BOURNE,WILLIAM(# 37)
SPOUSE: SABADOS,MARGAR(#9)  ***BOURNE,ALFRED (# 25)   ***UNKNWN,UNKNOWN(#75)
*              *    B. 27 MAR 1851       ***POND,JOHN     (#60)
*         ***BOURNE,CHARLES(# 19)   ***POND,SARAH    (# 38)
*         *    B. 5 JUL 1872       ***JACOB,SARAH   (#61)
*         *    M. 4 OCT 1892       ***COOPER,JACOB  (#62)
*         *    D. 11 MAY 1959   ***COOPER,DANIEL (# 39)
***BOURNE,EMMA    (# 12 )   ***COOPER,EMMA    (# 26)   ***UNKNOWN,ELIZAB(#63)
   B. 3 DEC 1899         B. 20 MAY 1849     ***UNKNOWN,UNKNOW(#75)
   D. 16 AUG 1975                   ***PIDGEN,MARY AN(# 40)
              *                   ***UNKNOWN,UNKNOW(#75)
              *                   ***SHARP,HARVEY   (#64)
              *        ***SHARP,JOHN      (# 41)
              ***SHARP,CHARLES (# 27)   ***UNKNOWN,AMY   (#65)
              *    B. 5 SEP 1840       ***ELLSWORTH,BENJ(#66)
         ***SHARP,RACHEL A(# 20)   ***ELLSWORTH,MARY(# 42)
              B. 23 AUG 1871       ***SHARP,ELIZABET(#67)
              D. 27 FEB 1953       ***UNKNOWN,UNKNOW(#75)
              *        ***UNKNOWN,UNKNOW(# 43)
              ***PURDY,LAVINA A(# 28)   ***UNKNOWN,UNKNOW(#75)
                   B. 1 MAR 1848       ***ELLSWORTH,BENJ(#70)
                   ***ELLSWORTH,ELIZ(# 44)
                        ***UNKNOWN,UNKNOW(#75)
```

Plate 55. Genealogy Software *Family Tree* Pedigree Chart

```
        PREDECESSORS OF HANS MATHENEY MINGER  (6) (ID=527)           03/07/1983


0      1      2      3      4      5      6      7      8      9     10     11     12     13     14     15
!      !      !      !      !      !      !      !      !      !      !      !      !      !      !      !
!      !      !      !      !      !PETER MINGER I (ID=667)
!      !      !      !      !      !
!      !      !      !      !HANS MINGER (2) (ID=666)
!      !      !      !      !      !
!      !      !      !      !      !ANA UNKNOWN I (ID=747)
!      !      !      !
!      !      !      !PETER MINGER (3) (ID=639)
!      !      !      !      !
!      !      !      !      !BARBI LINIGER (2) (ID=688)
!      !      !
!      !      !HANS MINGER (4) (ID=731)
!      !      !      !
!      !      !      !MADLENA KOPS (3) (ID=668)
!      !
!      !HANS MATHENEY MINGER (5) (ID=26)
!      !      !
!      !      !ANA LINIGER (4) (ID=683)
!
!HANS MATHENEY MINGER (6) (ID=527)
!      !      !      !      !      !
!      !      !      !      !      !PETER MINGER I (ID=667)
!      !      !      !      !
!      !      !      !      !ZACHARIAS MINGER (ID=589)
!      !      !      !      !      !
!      !      !      !      !      !ANA UNKNOWN I (ID=747)
!      !      !      !
!      !      !      !CHRISTIAN MINGER (ID=587)
!      !      !      !      !
!      !      !      !      !ELISABETH KAMEL (ID=590)
!      !      !
!      !      !HANS MINGER  (ID=583)
!      !      !      !
!      !      !      !ANNA HARMI (ID=588)
!      !
!      !ELIZABETH MINGER (5) (ID=600)
!      !      !
!      !      !STINA MERZ (ID=586)
```

Plate 56. Quinsept, Inc. *Family Roots* Predecessor Chart

PREDECESSORS OF EPPA HUNTON   (ID=408)   03/07/1983


```
                    GRAND-
PERSON    PARENTS    PARENTS
!          !          !
!          !          !WILLIAM HUNTON (ID=552)
!          !          !    B: CA 1725 @ LANCASTER CO VA
!          !          !    M: CA 1750 TO JUDITH KIRK (ID=553) @ FAUQUIER CO. VA
!          !          !    D: 12 Feb 1809 @ FAIRVIEW NEAR NEW BALTIMORE
!          !          !    (1: LEFT LANCASTER CO. VA 1750 TO FAUQUIER)
!          !          !    (2: WILL P. 398 RIXEY BOOK-2/12/1809)
!          !          !    9 Children
!          !
!          !JAMES HUNTON (ID=551)
!          !    B: 31 Jul 1763 @ FAIRVIEW FAUQUIER CO VA
!          !    2 Marriages
!          !    M: 06 Feb 1786 TO HANNAH LOGAN BROWN (ID=555) @ KING GEORGE CO. VA
!          !    RM: 01 May 1809 TO ELIZABETH MC NISH (ID=415)
!          !    OCC: FARMER
!          !    D: D @ THE VALLEY ADJOINING FAIRVIEW
!          !    8 Children
!          !          !
!          !          !JUDITH KIRK (ID=553)
!          !          !    B:  @ ?
!          !          !    M: CA 1750 TO WILLIAM HUNTON (ID=552)
!          !          !    D: D @ FAIRVIEW FAUQUIER CO VA
!          !          !    (1: FAIRVIEW FAMILY HOME NEAR NEW BALTIMORE)
!          !          !    11 Children
!
!EPPA HUNTON (ID=408)
!    B: 30 Jan 1789 @ FAIRVIEW FAUQUIER CO VA
!    M: 22 Jun 1811 TO ELIZABETH MARYE BRENT (ID=556) @ FAUQUIER CO VA
!    OCC: TAUGHT SCHOOL OFFICER WAR OF 1812
!    D: 08 Apr 1830 @ FAUQUIER CO VA
!    (1: VA LEGISLATURE)
!    11 Children
!          !
!          !HANNAH LOGAN BROWN (ID=555)
!          !    B: 11 Feb 1765 @ KING GEORGE CO.
!          !    M: 06 Feb 1786 TO JAMES HUNTON (ID=551) @ KING GEORGE CO. VA
!          !    D: 04 Mar 1806 @ ?
!          !    8 Children
```


Plate 57.   Quinsept, Inc. *Family Roots* Predecessor Chart

```
--------------------------------------------------------------------
            PREDECESSORS OF JOHN JAMES ARMSTRONG
--------------------------------------------------------------------

                                                    GREAT
                                           GREAT    GREAT
                                   GREAT   GREAT    GREAT
                           GRAND   GRAND   GRAND    GRAND
PERSON        PARENTS      PARENTS PARENTS PARENTS  PARENTS
 |             |            |       |       |        |
 |             |            |       |       |        |ROBERT ARMSTRONG (1778-1845)
 |             |            |       |       |DAVID SAMPSON ARMSTRONG (1814-1901)
 |             |            |       |       |        |MARY ELIZABETH MCCLAIN (ARMST
 |             |            |       |       |        |  RONG) (1776-1848)
 |             |            |       |JOHN YARGER ARMSTRONG (1845-1931)
 |             |            |       |       |        |JOHN YARGER (????-????)
 |             |            |       |       |MARY JANE YARGER (ARMSTRONG) (1827-1908
 |             |            |       |       |  )
 |             |            |       |       |        |MARGARET KELLY (YARGER) (????
 |             |            |       |       |        |  -????)
 |             |            |JAMES LEE ARMSTRONG (1873-1948)
 |             |            |       |       |        |DAVID ZIMMERMAN (????-????)
 |             |            |       |       |LEVI ZIMMERMAN (1822-1898)
 |             |            |       |       |        |MARY ???????? (ZIMMERMAN) (??
 |             |            |       |       |        |  ??-????)
 |             |            |       |SUZANNA ZIMMERMAN (ARMSTRONG) (1848-1929)
 |             |            |       |       |ELIZABETH WILGUS (ZIMMERMAN) (1822-1907
 |             |            |       |       |
 |             |DAVID CLINTON ARMSTRONG (1912-   )
 |             |            |       |       |WILLIAM HENRY LUCAS (????-1838)
 |             |            |       |CHARLES DAVID LUCAS (1843-1915)
 |             |            |       |       |???????? ???????? (LUCAS) (????-????)
 |             |            |EFFIE MAE LUCAS (ARMSTRONG) (1875-1956)
 |             |            |       |       |JOEL SMITH (????-????)
 |             |            |       |REBECCA SMITH (LUCAS) (1845-1917)
 |             |            |       |       |DAVID CONOLY (????-????)
 |             |            |       |       |MILDRED CONOLY (SMITH) (????-????)
JOHN JAMES ARMSTRONG (1949-   )
 |             |            |       |CARL JOHAN GORANSSON (1845-1900)
 |             |            |JOHAN WILHEM GORANSSON (1887-1978)
 |             |            |       |ANNA CHARLOTTA LARSSON (GORANSSON) (1845-????)
 |             |ANNA MARIE GORANSON (ARMSTRONG) (1920-   )
 |             |            |       |        |JOHANN TEMPLIN (1827-1899)
 |             |            |       |FREDERICK CHRISTIAN TEMPLIN (1865-1948)
 |             |            |       |        |MARIA MUELLER (TEMPLIN) (1828-1880)
 |             |            |SOPHIE TEMPLIN (GORANSON) (1895-1968)
 |             |            |       |REBEKKA EHLERS (TEMPLIN) (1873-1901)
--------------------------------------------------------------------
```

The above chart includes information as of 11 Feb 1981.
From the Family Book entitled: "ARMSTRONG-GORANSON GENEALOGY"
Compiled by: JOHN J. ARMSTRONG
Married names are in parentheses.
Years of birth and death follow each name.
Each person is flanked by their parents, if recorded. The father is above and
the mother is below. The paternal side of anyone in the chart is above and to
the right of that person and the maternal side is below and to the right.

Plate 58. Armstrong Genealogical Systems *Genealogy: Compiling*
Roots and Branches Predecessor Chart

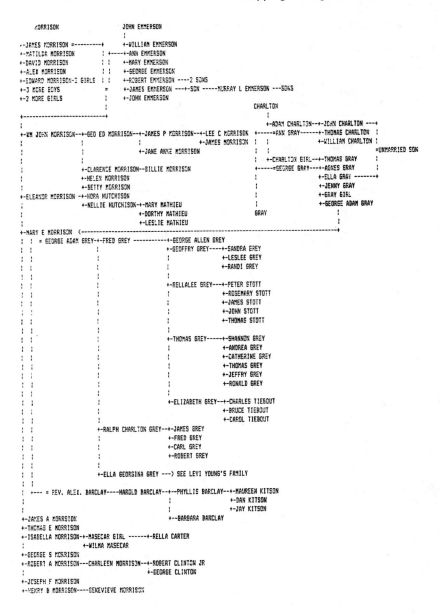

Plate 59. Team Approach Ltd. *Port for Genealogists* Descendant Chart

Records from B:SAMPLE.PED as of 07-31-1984, Descendants of Creanson   Rush   DOE   Born: 03DEC1798   Page: 1

```
M   74 Creanson    Rush      DOE              0    0
M   42 Fritz       Madrian   DOE             74   75
   M   26 Aaultz      Pete      DOE          42   43
      M   18 Albert     Bayne    DOE         26   27
         M   14 Charles    Aaultz    DOE        18   19
         M  148 Mack       Moses     DOE        18   19
            M   12 John       Quincy    DOE     14   15
            M  139 James      Wilcox    DOE     14   15
            F  141 Janette    Fry       DOE     14   15
            M  150 Haskell    Mack      DOE    148  149
               M   1 John       Rastus    DOE     12   13
               F   2 Bertha     Ann       DOE     12   13
               F   3 Diana                DOE     12   13
               M 143 James      William   DOE    139  140
               F 144 Sandra               DOE    139  140
               M 145 Kyle       Sam       DOE    139  140
               M 146 Bradley    Dana      QUINN  142  141
               M 147 Bryan      Curtis    QUINN  142  141
                  M 151 Ryan       Blow      DOE      1  152
```

Plate 60. Personal Software *Family Reunion* Descendant Chart

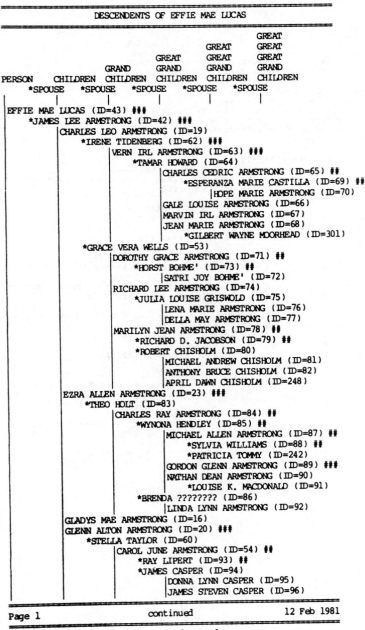

```
                        DESCENDENTS OF EFFIE MAE LUCAS

                                                            GREAT
                                                    GREAT   GREAT
                                            GREAT   GREAT   GREAT
                                    GRAND   GRAND   GRAND   GRAND
PERSON          CHILDREN   CHILDREN CHILDREN CHILDREN CHILDREN
    *SPOUSE     *SPOUSE    *SPOUSE  *SPOUSE  *SPOUSE
       |           |          |        |        |        |
EFFIE MAE LUCAS (ID=43) ###
    *JAMES LEE ARMSTRONG (ID=42) ###
        CHARLES LEO ARMSTRONG (ID=19)
            *IRENE TIDENBERG (ID=62) ###
                VERN IRL ARMSTRONG (ID=63) ###
                    *TAMAR HOWARD (ID=64)
                        CHARLES CEDRIC ARMSTRONG (ID=65) ##
                            *ESPERANZA MARIE CASTILLA (ID=69) ##
                                |HOPE MARIE ARMSTRONG (ID=70)
                        GALE LOUISE ARMSTRONG (ID=66)
                        MARVIN IRL ARMSTRONG (ID=67)
                        JEAN MARIE ARMSTRONG (ID=68)
                            *GILBERT WAYNE MOORHEAD (ID=301)
                *GRACE VERA WELLS (ID=53)
                    DOROTHY GRACE ARMSTRONG (ID=71) ##
                        *HORST BOHME' (ID=73) ##
                        |SATRI JOY BOHME' (ID=72)
                    RICHARD LEE ARMSTRONG (ID=74)
                        *JULIA LOUISE GRISWOLD (ID=75)
                        |LENA MARIE ARMSTRONG (ID=76)
                        |DELLA MAY ARMSTRONG (ID=77)
                    MARILYN JEAN ARMSTRONG (ID=78) ##
                        *RICHARD D. JACOBSON (ID=79) ##
                        *ROBERT CHISHOLM (ID=80)
                            MICHAEL ANDREW CHISHOLM (ID=81)
                            ANTHONY BRUCE CHISHOLM (ID=82)
                            APRIL DAWN CHISHOLM (ID=248)
        EZRA ALLEN ARMSTRONG (ID=23) ###
            *THEO HOLT (ID=83)
                CHARLES RAY ARMSTRONG (ID=84) ##
                    *WYNONA HENDLEY (ID=85) ##
                        MICHAEL ALLEN ARMSTRONG (ID=87) ##
                            *SYLVIA WILLIAMS (ID=88) ##
                            *PATRICIA TOMMY (ID=242)
                        GORDON GLENN ARMSTRONG (ID=89) ###
                        NATHAN DEAN ARMSTRONG (ID=90)
                            *LOUISE K. MACDONALD (ID=91)
                    *BRENDA ???????? (ID=86)
                        |LINDA LYNN ARMSTRONG (ID=92)
        GLADYS MAE ARMSTRONG (ID=16)
        GLENN ALTON ARMSTRONG (ID=20) ###
            *STELLA TAYLOR (ID=60)
                CAROL JUNE ARMSTRONG (ID=54) ##
                    *RAY LIPERT (ID=93) ##
                    *JAMES CASPER (ID=94)
                        DONNA LYNN CASPER (ID=95)
                        JAMES STEVEN CASPER (ID=96)

Page 1                     continued                  12 Feb 1981

* spouse      ## divorced      ### deceased
```

Plate 61. Armstrong Genealogical Systems *Genealogy: Compiling Roots and Branches* Descendant Chart

```
              DESCENDANTS OF WILLIAM HENRY BICE    (ID=16)
                 19 JAN 1984


                                              GREAT
                                   GREAT      GREAT
                         GRAND     GRAND      GRAND
PERSON       CHILDREN    CHILDREN  CHILDREN   CHILDREN
  !            !          !          !          !
!WILLIAM HENRY BICE (ID=16)
  !   B: 07 Apr 1860 @ KANSAS
  !   M: 29 Sep 1881 TO ELIZABETH YEAST (ID=15) @ YORK NEB
  !   D: 05 Oct 1886 @ SO.OF WILLIAMSBURG VA
  !   (1: DIED OF TYPHOID FEVER)
  !   4 Children
  !        !
  !        !LAURA BICE (ID=17)
  !        !    B: 03 Sep 1883 @ O'NEAL NEBRASKA
  !        !    M. 06 Jun 1916 TO ERNEST JACOB MAYER (ID=13) @
  !        !       KLAMMATH FALLS OREGON
  !        !    OCC: TEACHER
  !        !    D: 05 May 1970 @ LAS VEGAS NM
  !        !    (1: A.B. DEGREE 1933 NMNU)
  !        !    1 Child
  !        !    MOTHER: ELIZABETH YEAST (ID=15)
  !        !        !
  !        !        !ESTHER JOSEPHINE MAYER (ID=20)
  !        !        !    B: 17 Oct 1920 @ KLAMMATH FALLS ORE
  !        !        !    2 Marriages
  !        !        !    M: 20 Aug 1939 TO HARRY MATTHEW VORENBERG
  !        !        !       (ID=23) @ LAS VEGAS NM
  !        !        !    Widowed
  !        !        !    RM: 25 May 1979 TO HOWARD JONES (ID=24) @
  !        !        !        AMARILLO TX
  !        !        !    Living @ AMARILLO TX
  !        !        !    3 Children
  !        !        !    FATHER: ERNEST JACOB MAYER (ID=13)
  !        !        !        !
  !        !        !        !STEPHEN CARL VORENBERG (ID=1)
  !        !        !        !    B: 13 Mar 1943 @ LAS VEGAS NM
  !        !        !        !    M: 09 Jan 1969 TO PATRICIA JEAN
  !        !        !        !       MINGER (ID=2) @ NASHUA NH
  !        !        !        !    OCC: ENGINEER
  !        !        !        !    Living @ LEXINGTON MA 02173
  !        !        !        !    (1: CO-OWNER OF CHARTING COMPUTER)
  !        !        !        !    1 Child
  !        !        !        !    FATHER: HARRY MATTHEW
  !        !        !        !            VORENBERG (ID=23)
```

Plate 62.   Quinsept, Inc. *Family Roots* Descendant Chart

CHART OF MARY VIRGINIA (MOSS) RECTOR (ID=33), SCHAUMBERG ILLINOIS

1. MARY VIRGINIA (MOSS) RECTOR (ID=33) b 31 Aug 1897, ARKANSAS, liv SCHAUMBERG ILLINOIS, m 21 Jun 1921, FORT SMITH ARKANSAS.

2. ELIAS RECTOR (ID=39) b 13 Jun 1860, FORT SMITH ARK, d 18 Apr 1953, FORT SMITH ARKANSAS, m 10 Jan 1889, FORT SMITH ARKANSAS.

3. ANNA LUCILLE HORTON (ID=50) b 04 Nov 1866, VIRGINIA, d 31 Oct 1956, PARK RIDGE ILL, m 10 Jan 1889, FORT SMITH ARK.

4. ELIAS (MAJ) RECTOR (ID=53) b 28 Sep 1802, MAIDSTOWN VA FAUQUIER CO, d 22 Nov 1878, ARKANSAS, m 24 Nov 1835, FT SMITH ARK.

5. CATHERINE JAMIRA DUVAL (ID=54) b --/--/1818, WELLSBURG VA (NOW V.VA), d 18 Dec 1891, FT SMITH ARK., m 24 Nov 1835, FT SMITH ARK.

6. JOHN BRENT HORTON (ID=62) b 27 Sep 1821, FAUQUIER CO VA, d 30 Apr 1900, FT SMITH ARK, m 01 Oct 1861.

7. MARY MOSS (ID=63) b ?, FAIRFAX VA, d CA 1884, FT SMITH ARK, m 01 Oct 1861.

8. WHARTON RECTOR (ID=381) b 1772-3, VA, d ?, ?, m PRE 1806, VA.

9. MARY VANCE (ID=409) b NORTH CAROLINA, d PRE 1806, ?, m PRE 1806.

10. WILLIAM DUVAL (ID=73) b --/--/1784, FREDERICK CO. MD, d 30 Jun 1851, FT SMITH ARK, m PRE-1820, WELLSBURG DOONE CO. WVA.

11. HARRIET TABITHA DODDRIDGE (ID=74) b ??/??/1802, WELLSBURG V VA, d 15 Jun 1841, FORT SMITH ARK, m PRE-1820, WELLSBURG BOONE CO. WVA.

12. THOMAS E. HORTON GEN. (ID=534) b 06 Aug 1772, FAUQUIER CO VA., d 27 Oct 1826, VA. BURIED IN JOS. HORTON FAM. CEMETERY, m 20 Aug 1817, VA.

13. MATILDA BRENT (ID=610) b 15-Apr 1787, VA, d 19 Apr 1854, VA, m 20 Aug 1817, VA.

16. FREDERICK RECTOR (ID=376) b 16 Jul 1750, MAIDSTOWN VA, d 24 Oct 1811, OAK HILL KASKASKIA ILL TERR., m 07 Feb 1770.

17. ELIZABETH CONNOR (ID=380) b --/--/1755, NORFOLK VA, d 18 Sep 1811, KASKASKIA ILL TERRITORY, m 07 Feb 1770.

20. BENJAMIN DUVAL (3) (ID=671) b 05 Nov 1746, Q.ANNE PAR. PR. G. CO. MD, d 06 May 1820, MD, m ??/??/1772, MD.

21. JEMIMA TAYLOR (ID=724) b MIDDLE PLANTATION MD, d PRE1807, m ??/??/1772, MD.

22. JOSEPH DODDRIDGE (3) (ID=530) b 14 Oct 1769, V.VA/PA, d 09 Nov 1826, m PRE1795.

23. JEMIMA BUCKEY (BUKEY) (ID=602) b ??/??/1777, ?, d SEPT 1829, m PRE1795.

24. WILLIAM HORTON (ID=552) b CA 1725, LANCASTER CO VA, d 12 Feb 1809, FAIRVIEW NEAR NEW BALTIMORE, m CA 1750, FAUQUIER CO. VA.

Plate 63. Quinsept, Inc. *Family Roots* Ahnentafel

PEDIGREE OF

DANIEL, MARTIN HUGHES   FRN 25
DATE: AUGUST 01, 1984   PAGE 1
==

FRN	NAME	LIFE-SPAN	PAR.FRN

==

PARENTS

| 25 | HUGHES, PATRICK DAVID JOHN | 1938- | 35 |
| 25 | HARRISON, MADELINE CAROL | 1941- | 3 |

GRAND PARENTS

35	HUGHES, PATRICK JOSEPH	1910-	183
35	JOSS, MARY	1912-1984	182
3	HARRISON, MARTIN AMOS	1917-	5
3	GOLDSMITH, RUBY FLORENCE	1917-	1

1ST GREAT GRAND PARENTS

183	HUGHES, JAMES	-1910	
183	KANE, FRANCIS	-	184
182	JOSS, DANIEL	1888-1975	190
182	SHYMANSKI, ANNA	0000-1959	233
5	HARRISON, OSCAR WENTWORTH	1887-1960	28
5	SPENCER, JESSIE EDNA	1893-1967	6
1	GOLDSMITH, WILLIAM JOHN	1879-1941	2
1	BOYCE, FLORENCE	1883-1950	4

2ND GREAT GRAND PARENTS

184	KANE, JOHN	-	
184	????, EMILY	-	
190	JOSS, GRAMPA	-	
190		-	
233	SHYMANSKI, LEON	-	
233		-	
28	HARRISON, PETER LAVEE	1851-1927	109
28	MCNEILL, EVANGELINE	1859-1938	168
6	SPENCER, NELSON	1864-1952	204
6	HICKS, ELIZABETH	1867-1954	46
2	GOLDSMITH, JOHN NELSON	1851-1932	206
2	FINKLE, ESTER	1850-1918	250
4	BOYCE, ALBERT EDWARD	-	
4	WALL, ANN	-	

3RD GREAT GRAND PARENTS

109	HARRISON, JAMES EDWARD	1828-1892	
109	MINAKER, HANNAH	1830-1916	328
168	MCNEILL, PETER	-	
168	VARCOE, EMILY	-	315
204	SPENCER, EZRA	1817-1877	
204	ROSE, SARAH A	1822-	
46	HICKS, JOHN WELLINGTON	-1906	141
46	LANE, CELIA	-1901	

==

Plate 64.   M.A. Harrison *Roots and Relatives* Pedigree List

```
                 PEDIGREE  OF

DANIEL,  MARTIN  HUGHES              FRN  25
DATE: AUGUST 01, 1984                  PAGE 2
=====================================================
    FRN   NAME                     LIFE-SPAN   PAR.FRN
=====================================================
    206   GOLDSMITH, WILLIAM         -
    206   SHIBLEY, HARRIETT          1825-          207
    250   FINKLE, GEORGE             1817-1868
    250   SCHAMAHORN, SUSANNAH       1827-1904      249

4TH GREAT GRAND PARENTS


    328   MINAKER, PETER             -
    328                              -
    315   VARCO, RICHARD             -
    315   PARSONS, JENNIE            -


    141   HICKS, JOSEPH              1784-1866
    141   OUDERKIRK, MARIA           -1877          211
    207   SHIBLEY, JOHN              1786-1869      208
    207   FRALIK, CATHERINE          1781-1887
    249   SCHERMERHORN, HENRY        1793-1887      248
    249   REBECCA, SMITH             1797-1879

5TH GREAT GRAND PARENTS

    211   OUDERKIRK, PETER           1781-1847
    211                              -
    208   SHIBLEY, JOHN              1752-          209
    208   GORDANIER, ELLEN           1750-
    248   SCHERMERHORN, LEONARD      1758-1841
    248   DOTY, MARY (POLLY)         1760-1831      247

6TH GREAT GRAND PARENTS

    209   SHIBLEY, JOHN              -
    209   WERGMAN, ANN               -
    247   DOTY, JOSEPH               1708-1788      246
    247   DELONG, LUCRETIA           1722-

7TH GREAT GRAND PARENTS

    246   DOTY, JOSEPH               1680-1716      245
    246   CARPENTER, SARAH           -1745

8TH GREAT GRAND PARENTS

    245   DOTTY, ISAAC               1648-1728      244
    245   ENGLAND, ELIZABETH         1651-
```

Plate 65. M.A. Harrison *Roots and Relatives* Pedigree List

PEDIGREE OF

DANIEL, MARTIN HUGHES   FRN 25
DATE: AUGUST 01, 1984   PAGE 3
==
       FRN   NAME   LIFE-SPAN   PAR.FRN
==

9TH GREAT GRAND PARENTS

       244   DOTY, EDWARD   1599-1655
       244   CLARKE, FAITH   1619-1675

==

Plate 66.   M.A. Harrison *Roots and Relatives* Pedigree List

```
            DESCENDANTS OF
HARRISON, OSCAR WENTWORTH          FRN 5
DATE: AUGUST 01, 1984                        PAGE 1
================================================================
    FRN   NAME                   DATE OF BIRTH    FRN
================================================================
```

PARENTS

| | HARRISON, OSCAR WENTWORTH | JANUARY 18, 1887 | 5 |
| | SPENCER, JESSIE EDNA | JANUARY 27, 1893 | 5 |

CHILDREN

5	HARRISON, MARTIN AMOS	FEBRUARY 03, 1917	3
5	HARRISON, EARL BYRON	FEBRUARY 05, 1924	29
5	HARRISON, ALLEN LEROY	SEPTEMBER 27, 1928	22
5	HARRISON, DONNA ADELLA DOROTHY	FEBRUARY 17, 1931	24

GRAND CHILDREN

3	HARRISON, MADELINE CAROL	DECEMBER 11, 1941	25
3	HARRISON, BETTY JUNE	JUNE 05, 1945	26
3	HARRISON, WILLIAM GARTH	AUGUST 06, 1946	27
22	HARRISON, SARAH ANN(SALLY)	FEBRUARY 09, 1950	186
22	HARRISON, EDNA JUNE	OCTOBER 30, 1951	187
22	HARRISON, MILDRED ELAINE	SEPTEMBER 24, 1953	188
22	HARRISON, LAURA KATHLYN(CATHY)	MAY 19, 1957	189
24	SHILLINGTON, DOUGLAS WAYNE	APRIL 17, 1953	223
24	SHILLINGTON, MELVIN ALEXANDER	DECEMBER 24, 1954	
24	SHILLINGTON, MELVIN(DIED)	JANUARY 26, 1980	
24	SHILLINGTON, BEVERLY ANN	AUGUST 25, 1959	224
24	SHILLINGTON, JOSEPH ANTHONY	AUGUST 02, 1960	
24	SHILLINGTON, BRENDA LEE	AUGUST 27, 1966	

1ST GREAT GRAND CHILDREN

25	HUGHES, DANIEL MARTIN	OCTOBER 04, 1966	
25	HUGHES, MICHAEL DAVID JOSEPH	AUGUST 25, 1968	
25	HUGHES, BONNIE SHERISSE	NOVEMBER 18, 1969	
25	HUGHES, TRACY LEANNE	OCTOBER 18, 1976	
26	BROADHURST, VIVIAN MARGARET	FEBRUARY 02, 1972	
26	BROADHURST, RICHARD DOUGLAS HARRISON	MAY 27, 1974	
26	BROADHURST, VALERIE JUNE	JULY 09, 1977	
26	BROADHURST, MILES WILLIAM GARTH	MAY 03, 1980	
27	HARRISON, MARC WILLIAM(ADOPTED)	JULY 15, 1971	
27	HARRISON, KRISTA ANN(ADOPTED)	NOVEMBER 06, 1974	
186	GAUDET, LISA MARIE	JULY 27, 1971	
186	GAUDET, RAYMOND NEIL	SEPTEMBER 15, 1972	
187	KLEIN, CANDACE	00 00, 1970	
187	KLEIN, CATHRINE	00 00, 1972	
187	KLEIN, ELIZABETH	00 00, 1973	
187	KLEIN, BOBBY JEAN	00 00, 1977	
188	HENDERSON, GILLIAN DAWN	JANUARY 30, 1975	
188	HENDERSON, PAMELA TRACY	FEBRUARY 20, 1977	
188	HENDERSON, JEFFERY ALLEN	00 00, 1982	
189	GEISINGER, JENNY	00 00, 1977	

Plate 67. M.A. Harrison *Roots and Relatives* Pedigree List

DESCENDANTS OF

HARRISON, OSCAR WENTWORTH   FRN 5
DATE: AUGUST 01, 1984   PAGE 2
===

FRN	NAME	DATE OF BIRTH	FRN
189	GEISINGER, KERRI-ANN	AUGUST 04, 1978	
223	SHILLINGTON, DOUGLAS MELVIN	FEBRUARY 24, 1980	
223	SHILLINGTON, TERRA HAZE	OCTOBER 06, 1982	

===

Plate 68.   M.A. Harrison *Roots and Relatives* Pedigree List

DATE OF REPORT 04/19/82

PEDIGREE FOR PERSON # 4

PATRIARCHAL LINE:

NAME: Frank Herbert LERCHEN   (# 4)
BORN OR BAPTIZED: 18 JAN 1875
   WHERE: MUDDY STAGE STATION, COL
DIED OR BURIED: 07 AUG 1939
   WHERE: LOS ANGELES, CA DISTRICT 1901
FATHER: Charles W. LERCHEN   (# 8)
MOTHER: Jennie EAMES   (# 9)
MARRIED TO:
  (1) Susan Mary JONES
   DATE: 19 APR 1904
   PLACE: LOS ANGELES, CA

NAME: Charles W. LERCHEN   (# 8)
BORN OR BAPTIZED: 11 SEP 1839
   WHERE: QUEPEN, SAXON, GERMANY
DIED OR BURIED: @ 1930
   WHERE: DENVER, LITTLETON, COLORADO
FATHER: Charles W. LERCHEN   (# 16)
MOTHER: UNKNOWN   (# 17)
MARRIED TO:
  (1) Jennie EAMES
   DATE: 03 APR 1867
   PLACE: DENVER, ARAPAHOE, COLORADO

NAME: Charles W. LERCHEN   (# 16)
BORN OR BAPTIZED: UNKNOWN
   WHERE: UNKNOWN
DIED OR BURIED: UNKNOWN
   WHERE: UNKNOWN
FATHER: UNKNOWN   (# 32)
MOTHER: UNKNOWN   (# 33)
MARRIED TO:
  (1) UNKNOWN
   DATE: UNKNOWN
   PLACE: UNKNOWN

Plate 69. Frank Lerchen *Genealogy Program* Pedigree List

DATE OF REPORT 04/19/82

PEDIGREE FOR PERSON # 5

MATRIARCHAL LINE:

NAME: Susan Mary JONES   (# 5)
BORN OR BAPTIZED: 21 AUG 1872
    WHERE: BRIGHTON, IL
DIED OR BURIED: .23 FEB 1934
    WHERE: EAGLE ROCK CITY, CA (L.A.)
FATHER: William JONES   (# 10)
MOTHER: Margaret FORCE   (# 11)
MARRIED TO:
  (1) Alexander ROBERTSON
  DATE: 26 OCT 1892
  PLACE: UNKNOWN
MARRIED TO:
  (2) Frank Herbert LERCHEN
  DATE: 19 APR 1904
  PLACE: LOS ANGELES, CA

NAME: Margaret FORCE   (# 11)
BORN OR BAPTIZED: UNKNOWN
    WHERE: OHIO; OR BRIGHTON, ILLINOIS
DIED OR BURIED: UNKNOWN
    WHERE: UNKNOWN
FATHER: -- FORCE   (# 22)
MOTHER: UNKNOWN   (# 23)
MARRIED TO:
  (1) William JONES
  DATE: 02 NOV 1870
  PLACE: BRIGHTON, ILLINOIS

NAME: UNKNOWN   (# 23)
BORN OR BAPTIZED: UNKNOWN
    WHERE: UNKNOWN
DIED OR BURIED: UNKNOWN
    WHERE: UNKNOWN
FATHER: UNKNOWN   (# 46)
MOTHER: UNKNOWN   (# 47)
MARRIED TO:
  (1) -- FORCE
  DATE: UNKNOWN
  PLACE: UNKNOWN

Plate 70. Frank Lerchen *Genealogy Program* Pedigree List

```
                        Sandra Lee DeLisle Disk
  06/02/84                                                Page 2
                          *** Master Chart ***


--INDIVIDUAL--    -------PARENTS--------
ID NO.  MEMBER    FAMILY  FATHER  MOTHER    CHLDRN    CHART
  002     h1       004      1       1         05        2

Eugene      Daniel                      RELIGION:    Catholic
DeLisle                                 OCCUPATION:  Letter Carrier
615 Stanley St                          MILITARY:    US Army 1940-45
Chippewa Falls  WI   (chi)


          ----DATE----    ---------------LOCATION----------------

BIRTH:      30 Aug 1918  PLACE    St Joseph's Hospital (sjh)
                         CITY     Chippewa Falls (chi)
                         COUNTY   Chippewa
                         STATE    WI
                         COUNTRY  USA

CHRSND:     00 Sep 1918  PLACE    Notre Dame Church (ndc)
                         CITY     Chippewa Falls (chi)
                         COUNTY   Chippewa
                         STATE    WI
                         COUNTRY  USA

MARRIAGE:   04 Sep 1946  PLACE    St Patrick's Church (spc)
                         CITY     Eau Claire (eau)
                         COUNTY   Eau Claire
                         STATE    WI
                         COUNTRY  USA

DEATH:      16 Sep 1982  PLACE     (chi)
                         CITY     Chippewa Falls
                         COUNTY   Chippewa
                         STATE    WI
                         COUNTRY  USA

BURIED:     20 Sep 1982  PLACE    Forest Hill Cemetary (fhc)
                         CITY     Chippewa Falls (chi)
                         COUNTY   Chippewa
                         STATE    WI
                         COUNTRY  USA
```

Plate 71. Software Solutions *Arbor-Aide* Individual Record

```
                                                                RAY 1

-----------------------------------------------------------------------
Data Sheet:                   WILLIAM              RAY
-----------------------------------------------------------------------


Id No.  1    WILLIAM            RAY              Refs.   13    1    25
Born:    CA 1754    ENGLAND                              1    13
Married: APR 15 1778 OLD NECK  NARRAGUAGUS ME    To No. 2    25
Died:    JUN 1 1826  HARRINGTON MAINE                       25
MALE         DESCENDANT   Generation No. 1       Birth Order No. 1
Father:     0          RAY
Mother:     0
Ancestor No. 104              Other Ref Nos.  26   27   28   29   45   47

Spouse ( 1 ): RACHEL              STROUT          ID NO. 2


Children:
1   JOSEPH            RAY           b. 1779        ID NO.  3
2   JOHN              RAY           b. JAN 1781    ID NO.  5
3   JAMES             RAY           b. JAN 1785 ?  ID NO.  8
4   WILLIAM           RAY           b. CA. 1787    ID NO.  11
5   MARTHA            RAY           b. CA. 1788    ID NO.  13
6   BETSEY            RAY           b. CA 1790     ID NO.  14
7   DOLLY             RAY           b. 1792        ID NO.  15

-----------------------------------------------------------------------

Data File Identifier: RAY
                              DATE: 09-05-1984
```

File RAY0001. Captain William Ray   — Identity No. 1

William Ray was a sea captain. He lived his adult
life in Washington Co. Maine in what is now the Milbridge
area. He is said to have come from England as a young boy;
but it is not clear whether he came with his parents.

There was a William Ray living in the Falmouth
(Portland) Me., area in the 1760's. It is from that area
that many of the original settlers in the Milbridge area
came ; e.g., Dyers, Smalls, Collins', Strouts, etc.

According to some compilations, a William Ray married a Hannah Dyer (Miss or Mrs. unknown) in 1768 in Falmouth. A plausible hypothesis is that that William Ray was
Captain Ray's father, who, after his first wife died, married Hannah. Captain William Ray, while still young, may
have come to the Milbridge area with the Dyers, with or
without his father.

Plate 72. Joyce P. Davis *Ancestor File Program* Individual Record

JOHN BRENT HUNTON (ID=62)
   (Last Updated 30 Dec 1982)

BORN: 27 Sep 1821
  AT: FAUQUIER CO VA
NUMBER OF MARRIAGES: 2
MARRIED TO: ANN ELIZA RIXEY (ID=728)
        ON: 13 Apr 1842
        STATUS: Widowed
REMARRIED TO: MARY MOSS (ID=63)
        ON: 01 Oct 1861
        STATUS: Married
DIED ON: 30 Apr 1900
     AT: FT SMITH ARK
NUMBER OF CHILDREN: 12
    1) ANNA LUCILLE HUNTON (ID=50)
    2) ALFRED HUNTON (ID=258)
    3) CHARLIE HUNTON (ID=410)
    4) EVA HUNTON (ID=419)
    5) EDGAR HUNTON (ID=257)
    6) GEORGE B. HUNTON (ID=421)
    7) MAMIE HUNTON (ID=256)
    8) MATILDA HUNTON (ID=254)
    9) ROBERTA HUNTON (ID=422)
    10) JOHN W. HUNTON (ID=248)
    11) MOSS HUNTON (ID=432)
    12) MARTHA HUNTON (ID=433)
FATHER: THOMAS E. HUNTON GEN. (ID=534)
MOTHER: MATILDA BRENT (ID=610)
OCCUPATION: ENGLISH PROFESSOR
(1: MOVED TO FT SMITH 1882)
(2: WOOLEN MILLS TO SUPPLY SOLDIERS DURING CW)
(3: OPENED SCHOOL AT E RECTOR'S SEPT 1882)

Plate 73.   Quinsept, Inc. *Family Roots* Individual Record

```
                    FAMILY  RECORD

SPENCER,  CARL  NELSON                          FRN  12
=========================================================================
     2. FATHER:              SPENCER, CARL NELSON
     3. PARENT'S FRN:         6
     4. DATE BORN:           JUNE 08, 1890
     5. BORN AT:             CARNDUFF SASK
     6. DATE DIED:           OCTOBER 07, 1944
     7. BURIED AT:           CARNDUFF SASK
     8. OCCUPATION:          FARMER
     ------------------------------------------------------------------
     9. MOTHER:              CLEMENTS, IDA MILDRED
    10. PARENT'S FRN:
    11. DATE BORN:           SEPTEMBER 29, 1896
    12. BORN AT:
    13. DATE DIED:           JANUARY 26, 1924
    14. BURIED AT:           CARNDUFF SASK
    15. OCCUPATION:          HOUSEWIFE
     ------------------------------------------------------------------
    16. MARRIAGE DATE:       DECEMBER 13, 1916
    17. MARRIED AT:          COTTESLOE ONTARIO
    18. RELIGION:            PROTESTANT
=========================================================================
                        * * * CHILDREN * * *
     ------------------------------------------------------------------
        NAME                         BORN              FRN
     ------------------------------------------------------------------
    19.  HAROLD MAXWELL             NOVEMBER 06, 1917   99

    20.  LORNA IRENE                MAY 17, 1919        138

    21.  LESLIE GEORGE              JANUARY 13, 1921    142

    22.  CHARLES CLEMENT            NOVEMBER 05, 1923   134
     ------------------------------------------------------------------
    41. NOTES:

     CARL DIED IN ESTEVAN HOSPITAL




     DATE: AUGUST 09, 1984
=========================================================================
```

Plate 74. M.A. Harrison *Roots and Relatives* Family Group Sheet

ARMSTRONG-GORANSON GENEALOGY

```
==================================================================================
Page 81                          FAMILY BOOK                        19 Feb 1981
==================================================================================
FREDERICK CHRISTIAN TEMPLIN                    (ID=241)   revised: 14 Mar 1980
      father: JOHANN TEMPLIN                   (ID=575)
      mother: MARIA MUELLER (TEMPLIN)          (ID=576)
b.  24 Aug 1865 at HAMBURG,MINNESOTA
spouse:  REBEKKA EHLERS (TEMPLIN)       (ID=240)  m.  18 Apr 1891
m.  at ?                                       marital status: WIDOWED
2nd spouse: META MEYER (TEMPLIN)           (ID=420) rm. 19 Jan 1902
rm. at ?                                       2nd marital status: WIDOWED
d.  27 Dec 1948 at HAMBURG,MINNESOTA
number of children:  14
1.  AUGUST TEMPLIN              (ID=418) 9. ELSIE TEMPLIN (BIELKE)    (ID=267)
2.  MARY TEMPLIN (SCHULTE(SC*   (ID=262) 10. DELLA TEMPLIN (KELM)      (ID=268)
3.  SOPHIE TEMPLIN (GORANSON)   (ID=41)  11. WILLIAM TEMPLIN           (ID=269)
4.  ANNA TEMPLIN (WIETZKE)      (ID=263) 12. EWALD TEMPLIN             (ID=270)
5.  REBECCA TEMPLIN             (ID=419) 13. HERMAN TEMPLIN            (ID=271)
6.  HILDA TEMPLIN (LARSON)      (ID=264) 14. HERBERT TEMPLIN           (ID=272)
7.  FRED TEMPLIN                (ID=265)
8.  CLARA ANNA TEMPLIN (PERI*   (ID=266)
================= A shortened name is followed by an asterisk. =================
==================================================================================
PATRICIA TOMMY (ARMSTRONG)                     (ID=242)   revised: 31 Mar 1980
      father: ?
      mother: ?
b.  ?? ??  ???? at ?
spouse:  MICHAEL ALLEN ARMSTRONG        (ID=87)   m.   8 May 1979
m.  at AMARILLO,TEXAS                           marital status: SEPARATED


LIVING   at AMARILLO,TEXAS




==================================================================================
==================================================================================
ELMER WILLIAM LUCAS                            (ID=243)   revised: 15 May 1980
      father: GEORGE ALLEN LUCAS                (ID=343)  see footnote #    9
      mother: EMMA CHARLOTTE KOOPMAN (LUCAS)    (ID=344)
b.  19 Oct 1913 at GREAT BEND,KANSAS
spouse:  IRENE ELIZABETH GISICK (LUC*   (ID=408)  m.   5 Apr 1942
m.  at GREAT BEND,KANSAS                         marital status: WIDOWED


LIVING   at LARNED,KANSAS
number of children:  1
1. MARCIA LYNN LUCAS (MCPHA*    (ID=409)




================= A shortened name is followed by an asterisk. =================
```

Plate 75. Armstrong Genealogical Systems *Genealogy: Compilng
Roots and Branches* Family Group Sheet

```
                    PETER  HILLMAN
-----------------------------------------------------------------------

     NAME            :HILLMAN,PETER (# 21 )
     BIRTHDATE       :28 DEC 1851
     BIRTHPLACE      :SCAYNES HILL SUSSEX ENGLAND
     FATHER'S NAME   :HILLMAN,THOMAS (#29)
     MOTHER'S NAME   :HAMPER,ELIZABETH (#30)


     DEATH DATE      :29 NOV 1924
     DEATH PLACE     :BRIGHTON SUSSEX ENGLAND


     MARRIAGE# 1
     SPOUSE'S NAME   :NICHOLSON,ESTHER (#22)
     MARRIAGE DATE   :UNKNOWN
     MARRIAGE PLACE  :UNKNOWN


     CHILDREN:


             SURNAME              GIVEN NAMES        NUMBER
             -------              -----------        ------
      1      HILLMAN              ERNEST PETER         13
      2      HILLMAN              GEORGE HERBERT       14
      3      HILLMAN              LILLIAN MARY         15
      4      HILLMAN              BERTHA               16
      5      HILLMAN              ETHEL LINDA          17


     ----------------------
       COMMENTS RECORDS OF FRANK HILLMAN (G SON) AND ESTHER NICHOLSON (WIFE)
```

Plate 76.   Genealogy Software *Family Tree* Family Group Sheet

```
            FAMILY GROUP SHEET
              ┌┐ HUSBAND'S DATA:
              ▐▌ NAME:    DAVID LUPTON
              ▐▌ BIRTH:        VIRGINIA          11/01/1795
              ▐▌ DEATH:   UNIONVILLE, PUTNAM, MO. 18/10/1883
              ▐▌ FATHER:  WILLIAM LUPTON
              ▐▌ MOTHER:  BATHSHEBA ALLEN

              ┌┐ WIFE'S DATA:
              ▐▌ NAME:    RUTH ADAMS
              ▐▌ BIRTH:        VIRGINIA          21/04/1797
              ▐▌ DEATH:   UNIONVILLE, PUTNAM, MO. 03/03/1874
              ▐▌ FATHER:  JOSEPH ADAMS
              ▐▌ MOTHER:  MARY (WRIGHT)

              ┌┐ MARRIAGE DATA:
              ▐▌ DATE:    03/01/1816
              ▐▌ LOCAT:   SHENANDOAH CO., VIRGINIA
```

```
SEX   CHILDREN'S NAME        CHILDREN'S DATA              10/30/84
---   --------------         ---------------
F     MARIA LUPTON           BIRTH:      OHIO             18/09/1821
      THOMAS MCKAY           DEATH: UNIONVILLE, PUTNAM, MO. 02/01/1857
                             MARIG: HILLSBORO, HIGHLAND,OHIO 06/02/1842

M     ASA C. LUPTON          BIRTH:      OHIO             26/04/1824
      EMILINE HARGRAVE       DEATH: UNIONVILLE, PUTNAM CO.MO 13/05/1897
                             MARIG:

F     LOUISA E. LUPTON       BIRTH:      OHIO               /  /1840
                             DEATH:
                             MARIG:

M     DAVID E. LUPTON        BIRTH:      OHIO               /  /1842
      JOSEPHINE              DEATH:
                             MARIG:

F     MARGARET LUPTON        BIRTH:      OHIO               /  /1834
                             DEATH: UNIONVILLE, PUTNAM CO.MO 04/11/1855
                             MARIG:

F     DAUGHTER               BIRTH:                        /CA/1818
                             DEATH:
                             MARIG:

M     JOSEPH LUPTON          BIRTH:      OHIO              /CA/1823
                             DEATH:
                             MARIG:

F     RACHEL LUPTON          BIRTH:      OHIO              /CA/1827
      GEORGE W. PHILLIPS     DEATH:
                             MARIG:

F     DAUGHTER               BIRTH:                        /CA/1828
                             DEATH:
                             MARIG:

F     SYDNEY LUPTON          BIRTH:      OHIO              /CA/1833
      ALFRED POPE            DEATH:
                             MARIG:
```

Plate 77. Soft-Gene *Ancestry I/III* Family Group Sheet

Family Record No.: HR16

HUSBAND: HARTER, Jacob Dove   KEY NO.: HR16
BIRTH DATE: 05-Apr-1792 PLACE: Rockingham County, Virginia
MARR. DATE: 13-Nov-1813 PLACE: Falmouth, Pendleton County, Kentucky
DEATH DATE: 25-Sep-1874 PLACE: Elizabeth Twp., Miami County, Ohio
                  BURIAL PLACE: Rose Hill Cemetery, Troy, Ohio
FATHER: HARTER, Henry   MOTHER: DOVE, Catharine

WIFE: SMISER, Elizabeth   KEY NO.:
BIRTH DATE: 20-Jan-1792 PLACE: Harrison County, Kentucky
DEATH DATE: 12-Mar-1871 PLACE: Miami County, Ohio
                  BURIAL PLACE: Rose Hill Cemetery, Troy, Ohio
FATHER: SMISER, George   MOTHER: LAIR, Catherine

----

 1) HARTER, Darius S.   HR161   md. MCCULLOUGH, Isabella
 2) HARTER, Dr. Milton G.   HR162   md. STATLER, Hannah W.
 3) HARTER, Bennett Jasper   HR163   md. GREEN, Nancy
 4) HARTER, Dr. Matthias L.   HR164   md. ABBOTT, Jane F.
 5) HARTER, Samuel Kyle   HR165   md. MEREDITH, Olivia
 6) HARTER, Melinda A.   HR166   md. LILLY, John D.
 7) HARTER, Martha   HR167   died as a child
 8) HARTER, Catharine S.   HR168   md. RANDOLPH, John W.
 9) HARTER, Newton Jasper   HR169   md. DYE, Lizzie Jane
10) HARTER, Sabin D.   HR16A   never married
11) HARTER, William Franklin   HR16B   md. SENIOUR, Clara Maria

----

He moved to Harrison County, Kentucky in 1795 with his parents. He was a
hatter and served in the War of 1812 in Captain Sim's Company of Kentucky
volunteers and was in Dudley's defeat when the Kentucky troops were nearly
all destroyed by the British and Indians.
     Her father, George Smizer, was born in Virginia 30 Dec. 1778 and removed
to Kentucky in 1798.
     They moved to Miami County, Ohio in 1820 and settled in Elizabeth township
which was then an almost unbroken wilderness. There he supplied woolen hats
to the settlers for miles around.

1820 census: Elizabeth Twp., Miami County, Ohio - 3 males < 10; 1 male 10-16
             1 male 18-26; 1 male 26-45; 1 female 16-26 and two people were
             engaged in manufacture.
1830 census:
1840 census:
1850 census: Elizabeth Twp., Miami County, Ohio (#182-182)
1860 census: Troy, Concord Twp., Miami County, Ohio (#22-22)
1870 census: Troy, Concord Twp., Miami County, Ohio (#275-296)

references: BIOGRAPHICAL CYCLOPEDIA AND SKETCHES, STATE OF OHIO by J F Brenn
            GENEALOGICAL INDEX OF PIONEERS IN THE MIAMI VALLEY by L M Brien
            A HARTER JOURNAL by Byron E. Harter p. 361-362
            correspondence with Susan George, Phoenix, AZ

LAST REVISION DATE: 04-Nov-1983   Prepared by: CompuGen Systems
                                                 P. O. Box 15604
                                                 Fort Wayne, IN 46885

Plate 78. CompuGen *FamilyFile* Family Group Sheet

COMMSOFT ROOTS/M   V1.02.02 FAMILY GROUP SHEET   6 Aug 1981

HUSBAND: Arnold Bright _____ *
  BORN: 16 May 848   PLACE: Regencia
  MARR: 10 Jun 868   PLACE: Regencia
  DIED: 22 Feb 880   PLACE: Oxland
  FATHER: Sir Arthur Bright *
  MOTHER: Helen Cap
  HUSBAND'S OTHER WIVES:

WIFE: Elizabeth Griffen _____
  BORN: 20 Feb 850   PLACE: Regencia
  DIED: 18 Apr 885   PLACE: Regencia
  FATHER: Harold Griffen *
  MOTHER: Sarah Goode
  WIFE'S OTHER HUSBANDS:

CHILDREN

  1. Albert Bright _____
  M BORN: 3 Jan 870   PLACE: Regencia
     FIRST MARRIED: DIED:
       TO:
  2. _____
     BORN: PLACE:
     FIRST MARRIED: DIED:
       TO:
  3. _____
     BORN: PLACE:
     FIRST MARRIED: DIED:
       TO:
  4. _____
     BORN: PLACE:
     FIRST MARRIED: DIED:
       TO:
  5. _____
     BORN: PLACE:
     FIRST MARRIED: DIED:
       TO:
  6. _____
     BORN: PLACE:
     FIRST MARRIED: DIED:
       TO:
  7. _____
     BORN: PLACE:
     FIRST MARRIED: DIED:
       TO:
  8. _____
     BORN: PLACE:
     FIRST MARRIED: DIED:
       TO:
  9. _____
     BORN: PLACE:
     FIRST MARRIED: DIED:
       TO:
 10. _____
     BORN: PLACE:
     FIRST MARRIED: DIED:
       TO:

Plate 79. Commsoft, Inc. *Roots/M* Family Group Sheet

```
HUSBAND:  JAMES PATRICK HARRISON
      Born:  04 APR 1920                  Place:  SALT LAKE CITY, SALT LAKE, UT
      Chr :                               Place:
      Mar :  12 DEC 1940                  Place:  SALT LAKE CITY, SALT LAKE, UT
      Died:  12 SEP 1977                  Place:  PANAMA CITY, BAY, FLA
      Bur :                               Place:  SALT LAKE CITY, SALT LAKE, UT
      Father:  GILBERT DONALD HARRISON
      Mother:  FRANCENE FAYE LARSON
      Other wives:
WIFE:  PATRICIA ANN PETERSON
      Born:  28 NOV 1919                  Place:  SALT LAKE CITY, SALT LAKE, UT
      Chr :                               Place:
      Died:                               Place:
      Bur :                               Place:
      Father:  ROBERT CALVIN PETERSON
      Mother:  MARY GRACE TYLER
      Other husbands:
CHILDREN:
NANCY RUTH HARRISON
      Born:  24 OCT 1941                  Place:  SALT LAKE CITY, SALT LAKE, UT
      1st mar:          (JOHN EDWARD JONES)
      Died:                               Place:
EARL ROBERT HARRISON
      Born:  1 JUN 1943                   Place:  SALT LAKE CITY, SALT LAKE, UT
      1st mar:
      Died:                               Place:
PAULA HARRISON
      Born:  19 DEC 1943                  Place:  SALT LAKE CITY, SL, UT
      1st mar:
      Died:                               Place:
PENNY LYNN HARRISON
      Born:  08 MAR 1945                  Place:  PROVO, UTAH, UT
      1st mar:
      Died:                               Place:
EDWIN LEWIS HARRISON
      Born:  23 DEC 1946                  Place:  LEHI, UTAH, UT
      1st mar:
      Died:                               Place:
BRADLEY HARRISON
      Born:  27 JUL 1947                  Place:  SALT LAKE CITY, SL, UT
      1st mar:
      Died:                               Place:
KATHLEEN HARRISON
      Born:  25 JUN 1950                  Place:  MURRAY, SALT LAKE, UT
      1st mar:
      Died:                               Place:
PATRICIA ANN HARRISON
      Born:  26 MAR 1954                  Place:  SALT LAKE CITY, SALT LAKE, UT
      1st mar:
      Died:                               Place:
ELLIE LOUISE HARRISON
      Born:  13 JUL 1959                  Place:  SALT LAKE CITY, SALT LAKE, UT
      1st mar:  01 AUG 1970   (SCOTT CARPENTER)
      Died:  03 AUG 1962                  Place:  SALT LAKE CITY, SALT LAKE, UT
```

Prepared by: JENNY LOUISE SMITH
Date: 11 SEP 1984

Plate 80. Array Systems *Treesearch* Family Group Sheet

```
    FAMGROUP  SHEET:  16
```


NAME: SPENCER FAULKNER   TITLE: NONE

BIRTH: C1811 ORAN CO,VA   DATA: KENT CO,KY CENSUS 1850

DEATH: 6 APR 1877 KENT CO,KY   DATA: INV BK6 P417/8 KENT CO
                                 CEMETERY: PRIVATE ON LAND

OCCUPATION: FARMER
MILITARY: NONE

FATHER: GEORGE FAULCONER   MOTHER: NANCY COLEMAN

MARRIAGE: 9 JAN 1838 CAMP CO,KY DATA: MRBK 1826/46 #111

WIFE'S NAME: SUSAN MCKINSEY
BIRTH: C1812   DATA: KENT CO,KY CENSUS 1850

DEATH: 25 APR 1880 KENT CO,KY   DATA: DAR MORT SCHED 1880

FATHER: DAVID MCKINSEY   MOTHER: ANN REESE

CHILDREN IN BIRTH ORDER

CHILD 1   CHILD 6

NAME: JOHN W   NAME: SPENCER F
BIRTH: CA 1839 KENT CO,KY   BIRTH: CA 1849 KENT CO,KY
DEATH: CA 1881 GRAN CO,KY   DEATH:
SPOUSE: ALICE VANLANDINGHAM   SPOUSE: SUSAN E FAULCONER

CHILD 2   CHILD 7

NAME: MARY   NAME: SUSAN FRANCES
BIRTH: CA 1841 KENT CO,KY   BIRTH: CA 1852 KENT CO,KY
DEATH: DEATH:
SPOUSE: GEORGE DOWD   SPOUSE: CHARLES J RILEY

CHILD 3   CHILD 8

NAME: GEORGE DAVID   NAME: EMMA JANE
BIRTH: 24 OCT 1842 KENT CO,KY   BIRTH: 8 APR 1856 KENT CO,KY
DEATH: 5 MAY 1884 PEND CO,KY   DEATH:
SPOUSE: ADELIA VANLANDINGHAM   SPOUSE: JASPER RIGGS

CHILD 4   CHILD 9

NAME: JAMES R   NAME:
BIRTH: CA 1845 KENT CO,KY   BIRTH:
DEATH: DEATH:
SPOUSE: LAURA LANCASTER   SPOUSE:

CHILD 5   CHILD 10

NAME: RICHARD MCKINSEY   NAME:
BIRTH: CA 1847 KENT CO,KY   BIRTH:
DEATH: 18 NOV 1878 KENT CO,KY   DEATH:
SPOUSE: NONE   SPOUSE:
```

**Plate 81.** Ancestors =*Ancestors*= Family Group Sheet
```

```
(1)   GEN. NO. -    0032*
(2)   SUBJECT-     SALLE JOSEPH SR
(3)   FATHER-      0064
(4)   MOTHER-      0065
(5)   BIRTH DATE-  3SEP1746
(6)   PLACE-       KING WM PARISH VA
(7)   RESIDED-     VA KY
(8)   DATE OF DEATH-  1815
(9)   PLACE-       JESSAMINE CTY KY
(10)  CAUSE DEATH-
(11)  CEMETERY-
(12)  CHURCH-
(13)  EDUCATION-
(14)  MILITARY-
(15)  OCCUPATION-  FARMER
(16)  MARRIAGE NO. -  1*
(17)  SPOUSE-      MAXEY JEMIMA 0033
(18)  MARRIAGE DATE-  CA 1770
(19)  PLACE-       VA
(20)  SPOUSE'S FATHER-   0066
(21)  SPOUSE'S MOTHER-   0067
(22)  CHILDREN-    JOSEPH 0016/JOHN 0032B/JUDITH 0032C/FRANCES 0032D/MARYANNE 0032
              E
(23)  FOOTNOTES-   IS LISTED AS PATRIOT BY DAR FOR CONTRIBUTIONS OF FOOD AND DONA
      TING MONEY TO HIRE SUBSTITUTE. HIS MIDDLE NAME MAY HAVE BEEN ADOLPHUS.
```

Plate 82.   Genealog Software *Genealog II* Family Group Sheet

```
FAMILY  GROUP  SHEET

                          ByteWare

Compiled by   (Your Name)
_____

HUSBAND:JOHN DOE                        OCCUPATION:FARMER
 BORN:1 JAN 1900               WHERE:ROSEVILLE IL
 BAP.:3 FEB '00                WHERE:WALNUT GROVE IL
 MARR.:22 APR '23              WHERE:ROSEVILLE IL
 DIED:3 AUG '75                WHERE:AMES IA
 CHURCH AFFIL.:PRESBY.         BUR.:WALNUT GROVE IL
 MILITARY SERV.:US ARMY - AUG 1918 TO MAR 1921
 FATHER:JACK C. DOE            MOTHER:JANE SMITH
 OTHER WIVES:NONE
_____


 WIFE:_____
  BORN:_____
  BAP.:_____         WHERE:_____
  DIED:_____         WHERE:_____
  CHURCH AFFIL.:_____    WHERE:_____
  FATHER:_____        BUR.:_____
  OTHER HUSBANDS:_____  MOTHER:_____
_____

                        CHILDREN


 1 :JOE DOE            BORN:1 JAN 1925   MARR.:6 AUG '50  DIED:3 AUG '82
                       ROSEVILLE IL      CHICAGO IL       TOPEKA KA
                       SEX:M   SPOUSE:HAZEL NUTT      BUR.:TOPEKA
 - - - - - - - - - - - - - - - - - - - - - - - - - - - - - - - -

 2 :_____       BORN:_____  MARR.:_____ DIED:_____

                       _____        _____       _____
                       SEX:_  SPOUSE:_____     BUR.:_____
 - - - - - - - - - - - - - - - - - - - - - - - - - - - - - - - -

ADDITIONAL REMARKS:
|HIS FAMILY GROUP SHEET WAS PREPARED USING FGS 2.5 TO SHOW BOTH A COMPLETED AND
A BLANK WORK SHEET APPEAR. PREPARED 3 AUG 1984
```

Plate 83. Byteware *FGS* Family Group Sheet

HERLACHE
FAMILY GROUP SHEET

Individual: ID: 1-8 is HERLACHE, August
My ID: 1 (-3)
Date of birth: 12 Oct. 1848 (?)
Place of birth: Ceroux-Mousty, Brabant, Belgium
Date of death: 02 Feb. 1929
Place of death: Green Bay, Brown Co., Wisconsin
Cause of death:

Alternate birth date: 4 August 1848.   Buried in Allouez, Wisconsin.   Reinterred at
    St. Francis Xavier Cemetery, Brussels, Wisconsin.   Sources for birth dates: Death
    Records (Brown County) for 4 August 1848, informant, Desire Herlache.   Funeral
    Home Mass Card for 16 October 1848.   Informant??   Marriage to Marceline BAUDHUIN:
    Charles I. Martin's History of Door County, 1881, p. 88. Marriage to Euphrasie
    MACCAUX/MACCO: Marriage Registration (Kewaunee County).   Death: Death Records
    (Brown County) and Funeral Home Mass Card.
Father: ID 1-0 Name: HERLACHE, Jean-Baptiste
Mother: ID 1-1 Name: DESTREE/DETRY, Marie-Therese

Marriage: ?? ???? 1874 at Door Co., Wisconsin

Spouse: ID: 1-9 is BAUDHUIN, Marceline
My ID: 1 (-3)
Date of birth: ?? ???? 1855
Place of birth: Belgium
Date of death: ?? ???? 1884
Place of death: Wisconsin
Cause of death:

May be buried in Namur, Wisc.

Father: Unknown.
Mother: Unknown.

   Children:

   ID 1-14: HERLACHE, Vital Joseph
   Born 27 Apr. 1875 at Gardner, Door Co., Wisc.
   Died 12 Feb. 1952 at Gardner, Door Co., Wisc.

   ID 1-10: HERLACHE, Zeno
   Born 09 Oct. 1877 (?) at Gardner Township, Door Co., Wisconsin
   Died 29 Apr. 1905 at Gardner Township, Door Co., Wisconsin

   ID 1-21: HERLACHE, Ralph
   Born 31 Jan. 1880 at Gardner Township, Door Co., Wisconsin
   Died 07 Mar. 1942 at Sturgeon Bay, Door Co., Wisconsin

   ID 1-22: HERLACHE, Desire Joseph
   Born 22 June 1881 at Gardner Township, Door Co., Wisconsin
   Died 13 Nov. 1965 at Green Bay, Brown Co., Wisconsin

Marriage: 22 Nov. 1887 at Grandlez-Lincoln, Kewaunee Co., Wisconsin

Spouse: ID: 1-16 is MACCAUX/MACCO, Euphrasie/Frasie
Date of birth: 26 Feb. 1859
Place of birth: Grandlez-Lincoln, Kewaunee Co., Wisconsin
Date of death: 27 Feb. 1932
Place of death: Rio Creek, Kewaunee Co., Wisconsin

Page 1

Plate 84.   Mark Peters *My Roots* Family Group Sheet

                              HERLACHE
                         FAMILY GROUP SHEET

Cause of death:

Buried at St. Peter's Cemetery, Lincoln.   Sources: Marriage registration, Kewaunee
   County;   Death record, Kewaunee County;   Obituary, Algoma Record Herald, 4 March
   1932.

Father: ID 1-23 Name: MACCAUX/MACCO, Jean-Baptiste
Mother: ID 1-24 Name: QUINARD/KINNARD, Eufrazie

   Children:

   ID 1-17: HERLACHE, Sylvester
   Born 03 July 1889 at Town of Gardner, Door Co., Wisconsin
   Died 19 May 1961 at Algoma, Kewaunee Co., Wisconsin
   Marriage to ID 1-18 JUNIO, Mary on 29 Jan. 1912 at Lincoln, Kewaunee Co.,
     Wisconsin

Plate 85.   Mark Peters *My Roots* Family Group Sheet

```
                          FAMILY GROUP SHEET
Roderick H. Payne Family                           Roderick Herman PAYNE
100 Villa Avenue                                   Pamela Rose SURFACE
Buffalo, New York 14216                            Printed 12-06-1983
(716) 877-2534


HUSBAND   Roderick Herman PAYNE                    Baptized 26MAY1962
  Born 27JAN1954 Miami, Dade, Florida              Endowded 17APR1974
  Died _____ _____
  Father John Alphus PAYNE      Mother Ethel May WALTA
  Married 18APR1974 Provo, Utah, Utah              Sealed   18APR1974


WIFE      Pamela Rose SURFACE                      Baptized 26MAY1962
  Born 27FEB1953 Indianapolis, Marion, Indiana     Endowded 17APR1974
  Died _____ _____
  Father Willard Jacob SURFACE   Mother Carolyn Joyce PATTON
```

SEX	CHILD'S NAME	BORN	DIED	MARRIED	BAPTIZED	ENDOWED	SEALED
M	John Jacob PAYNE	23MAY1975 Provo, Utah, Utah			29MAY1983		BIC
X F	Amy Dawn PAYNE	30MAY1976 Provo, Utah, Utah					BIC
M	Robert Andrew PAYNE	04MAR1978 Provo, Utah, Utah					BIC
M	David Joseph PAYNE	22FEB1980 Buffalo, Erie, New York					BIC
M	Adam Scott PAYNE	08JUL1982 Buffalo, Erie, New York					BIC

Plate 86.   Roderick H. Payne *Genealogical Records Program*
Family Group Sheet

```
        Family Group No. 002
                                    Husband: DeLisle                    Eugene      Daniel
    ---------- Sources / Notes -----------
    _____                         City, Town, Or Place   County or Province   State/Country
                                    Birth:      30 Aug 1918  Chippewa Falls         Chippewa             WI  USA
    _____  Chr'nd:   00 Sep 1918  Chippewa Falls         Chippewa             WI  USA
    _____  Marriage: 04 Sep 1946  Eau Claire             Eau Claire           WI  USA
                                    Death:      16 Sep 1982  Chippewa Falls         Chippewa             WI  USA
    _____  Burial:   20 Sep 1982  Chippewa Falls         Chippewa             WI  USA
                                    Residence:  615 Stanley St        Chippewa Falls       WI  USA
    _____  Occupation: Letter Carrier      Rel: Catholic    Military: US Army 1940-45
                                    Father:     DeLisle                        Peter      Eugene
    _____  Mother:   Pearson                        Edith      Sara


    _____
                                    Wife:    Trimbell                      Mary      Jane

    _____                         City, Town, Or Place   County or Province   State/Country
                                    Birth:      19 Jun 1924  Eau Claire             Eau Claire           WI  USA
    _____  Chr'nd:   00 Jun 1924  Eau Claire             Eau Claire           WI  USA
        Compiled by:                Death:
        Sandra Lee Ritzinger        Burial:
        7378 Zurawski Court         Residence:  615 Stanley St        Chippewa Falls       WI  USA
        Custer, WI  54423           Occupation: Housewife            Rel: Catholic    Military:
        06/02/84                    Father:     Trimbell                       Henry      Wilfred
                                    Mother:     Missman                        Hattie


    ------------------------------------------------------- Children --------------------------------------------------
        Child/Spouse                ---------Dates---------   City, Town, Or Place   County or Province   State/Country

    1  Daniel     Eugene            Birth:    01 May 1947  Chippewa Falls         Chippewa             WI  USA
                                    Marriage: 14 Oct 1972  Eau Claire             Eau Claire           WI  USA
       Blaeser                      Death:
       Jane                         Burial:

       McNamara                     Marriage: 00 Nov 1969  Jim Falls              Chippewa             WI  USA
       Judith     Faye

    2  Sandra     Lee               Birth:    21 May 1951  Chippewa Falls         Chippewa             WI  USA
                                    Marriage: 20 Jun 1970  Chippewa Falls         Chippewa             WI  USA
                                    Death:
                                    Burial:

    3  Diane      Marie             Birth:    06 Dec 1955  Chippewa Falls         Chippewa             WI  USA
                                    Marriage:
                                    Death:
                                    Burial:

    4  Deborah    Mary              Birth:    07 Oct 1959  Chippewa Falls         Chippewa             WI  USA
                                    Marriage:
                                    Death:
                                    Burial:

    5  Julie      Ann               Birth:    05 Jun 1961  Chippewa Falls         Chippewa             WI  USA
                                    Marriage:
                                    Death:
                                    Burial:
```

Plate 87. Software Solutions *Arbor-Aide* Family Group Sheet

```
------------------------------------------------------------------
      Family of  WILLIAM      and  MARY       FICKETT       RAY
------------------------------------------------------------------


Husband:
Id No.   19    WILLIAM      COLLINS    RAY               Refs.    64
Born:    CA 1806      HARRINGTON  MAINE                            64
Married: NOV 1 1824  HARRINGTON MAINE ?        To No. 20          64
Died:    1859         MILLBRIDGE ME (EVERGREEN)                    64
MALE         DESCENDANT    Generation No. 3        Birth Order No. 2
Father:    3   JOSEPH    RAY
Mother:    4   BETHIA COLLINS
                        Other Ref Nos.    64


Wife:
Id No.   20    MARY                  FICKETT       Refs.    64
Born:    OCT 15 1805 GORHAM NH / CHERRYFIELD ME
Married: NOV 1 1824  HARRINGTON  MAINE          To No. 19    64
         NOV 22 1860 MILLBRIDGE ME             To No. 21
Died:    SEP 12 1903 MILLBRIDGE ME (EVERGREEN)
FEMALE       DESCENDANT'S SPOUSE  Generation No. 3
Father:    239  MOSES    FICKETT
Mother:    240  SARAH WARREN
                        Other Ref Nos.


------------------------------------------------------------------
                            Children
------------------------------------------------------------------

1   WARREN              RAY                        ID NO.   97
        Born: CA 1826    MILLBRIDGE MAINE
        Died: AFTER 1872 NY OR NJ ?
        Married: CA 1855         CAROLINE      JOHNSON ?   ID NO. 98
                                    BORN:
                                    DIED:

2   MARTHA     ANN      RAY                        ID NO.   99
        Born: CA 1830    MILLBRIDGE ME
        Died: 1834       MILLBRIDGE ME
                               Unmarried

3   MARY       JANE     RAY                        ID NO.  100
        Born: SEP 25 1832 MILLBRIDGE ME
        Died: NOV 21 1915 NEW YORK
        Married ( 1)  CA 1855        J.         JOHNSON     ID NO. 101
                                    BORN:        WEST INDIES
                                    DIED: BEF 1883
        Married ( 2)  JUL 29 1883  NEW YORK NY   HENRY    ANDREW   JACKSON   ID NO. 87
                                    BORN:
                                    DIED:        NEW ROCHELLE NY


                                             --------------------
                                             Continued on Pg  2
                                             --------------------
```

Continued on Pg 2

Plate 88.   Joyce P. Davis *Ancestor File Program*
Family Group Sheet

```
Family of  WILLIAM      and  MARY      FICKETT        RAY          Pg  2
```

4   ELMIRA   J.   RAY   ID NO. 102
        Born: AUG 2 1835   MILLBRIDGE ME
        Died: MAY 29 1914 NEW YORK NY
        Married: JAN 29 1854 MAINE   JOSEPH   L.   WALLACE   ID NO. 103
                                          BORN: 1834   MAINE
                                          DIED:

5   MARTHA   F.   RAY   ID NO. 104
        Born: 1834   MILLBRIDGE ME
        Died: OCT 11 1838 MILLBRIDGE ME
                                        Unmarried

6   MARTHA   ANN   RAY   ID NO. 105
        Born: APR 19 1839 MILLBRIDGE ME
        Died: JAN 21 1856 MILLBRIDGE ME
                                        Unmarried

7   CAROLINE   L.   RAY   ID NO. 106
        Born: DEC 6 1844   MILLBRIDGE ME
        Died: MAR 28 1872 MILLBRIDGE ME
        Married: SEP 28 1867 MAINE   DANIEL   F.   STROUT   ID NO. 107
                                          BORN: JUN 26 1843 MILBRIDGE MAINE
                                          DIED: MAR 26 1917

8   SARAH   E.   RAY   ID NO. 108
        Born: CA 1846   MILLBRIDGE ME
        Died: AFTER 1914
        Married: SEP 8 1866 MAINE   FREDERICK L.   NASH   ID NO. 109
                                          BORN: 1842   HARRINGTON MAINE
                                          DIED:

Data File Identifier: RAY

Prepared by J. P. DAVIS   Date: 09-05-1984
             10650 HICKORY RIDGE ROAD
             COLUMBIA MARYLAND 21044

Plate 89. Joyce P. Davis *Ancestor File Program*
Family Group Sheet

HUSBAND: JAMES HUNTON (ID=351)
Born 31 Jul 1763   Place FAIRVIEW FAUQUIER CO VA
Marr 06 Feb 1786   Place KING GEORGE CO. VA
Died D   Place THE VALLEY ADJOINING FAIRVIEW
Bur.   Place
HUSBAND'S   HUSBAND'S
FATHER: WILLIAM HUNTON (ID=352)   MOTHER: JUDITH KIRK (ID=353)
HUSBAND'S
OTHER WIVES: ELIZABETH MC NISH (ID=415)

WIFE: HANNAH LOGAN BROWN (ID=355)
Born 11 Feb 1765   Place KING GEORGE CO.
Died 04 Mar 1806   Place ?
Bur.   Place
WIFE'S   WIFE'S
FATHER: MOTHER:
WIFE'S
OTHER HUSBANDS:

M/F	CHILDREN	WHEN BORN	WHERE BORN	FIRST MARRIAGE	WHEN DIED
1 M	CHARLES HUNTON (ID=404)	04 Jan 1787	VA		1856
2 M	EPPA HUNTON (ID=408)	30 Jan 1789	FAIRVIEW FAUQUIER CO VA	22 Jun 1811 08 Apr 1830 ELIZABETH MARYE BRENT (ID=556)	
3 M	THOMAS LOGAN HUNTON (ID=405)	23 Apr 1802	VA	ANN D. D. MOXLEY (NO ID)	
4 F	MARGARET L HUNTON (ID=416)	01 Mar 1805		ARTHUR BLACKWELL (NO ID)	
5	SILAS B 10/23/1794 (NO ID)				
6	JAMES B 7/1/1791 D 6/19/1791 (NO ID)				

SOURCES OF INFORMATION   OTHER MARRIAGES

                                                4--JOHN BROWN (NO ID)

Plate 90.   Quinsept, Inc. *Family Roots* Family Group Sheet

FOOTNOTES

1. Noel C. Stevenson, *Genealogical Evidence, A Guide to the Standard of Proof Relating to Pedigrees, Ancestry, Heirship and Family History* (Laguna Hills, Calif.: Aegean Park Press, 1979), p. 147.

2. *Is That Lineage Right?* (Washington, DC: National Daughters of the American Revolution, 1982), p. 1.

3. Val D. Greenwood, *The Researcher's Guide to American Genealogy* (Baltimore: Genealogical Publishing Company, Inc., 1973), p. 69.

4. Richard W. Price, William Thorndale, and Arlene H. Eakle, "Introduction to Genealogical Research and Techniques," in Arlene H. Eakle and Johni Cerny, eds., *The Source: A Guidebook of American Genealogy* (Salt Lake City: Ancestry Publishing, 1984), p. 21.

CHAPTER 8

Variations in Genealogy Software

J ust as there are variations in genealogy practice (kinology, family history, genealogy, local history, and so on), there are bound to be variations in the kinds of things genealogy programs do. Each vendor should make full disclosure of what his programs do and don't do. Some genealogy programs have interesting capabilities that illustrate how computers will be able to do more and more things genealogists want to do. But before we look at genealogy program variants, let's look at the two major variations in genealogy itself.

Ethel Williams says:

> There are two methods of compiling ancestral history; one is by ascendants and the other is by descendants. The end results are quite different. A family history is a compilation of the ascendants of one individual. A family genealogy is a compilation of descendants of an immigrant ancestor or ancestors. One should first undertake the preparation of his family history before attempting the more complicated task of doing a family genealogy. To do a family history, one starts with oneself and works back (by ascent), from generation to generation, to the immigrant ancestor, if possible. The end result is the complete lineage of one individual. The family genealogy starts with the immigrant ancestor, or ancestors . . . and traces down, (by descent), generation to generation, all of their descendants, to the present generation. This is an arduous, complicated task, involving many individuals, which requires widespread research and voluminous correspondence, but when completed, it is a great achievement, if well done.[1]

CONSANGUINITY DETERMINING

Computerized family files usually carry "pointers" in the individual records of family members. The pointer "points" to the records of father, mother, spouse(s), and children of a given subject. This enables the computer program to go to another record in the computer file and get it next. This is how a computerized genealogy file handles the linkages between a family member and any other family member (through bloodline or marriage links).

It follows that any two persons in a computerized file can be selected by a genealogist and (if the genealogy software is programmed for it) the relationship between those two people can be ascertained. *Roots/M,* by Commsoft, Inc., is one genealogy program which can handle consanguinity or relationship determination. The *Roots/M* user manual says that if you wish to determine the relationship of two or more individuals, you can press the appropriate numeric keys. With such a relationship-finding routine, you can learn that person A and person B are second cousins twice removed or that you have a grand aunt that you have always thought was "grandpa's sister." Computerizing family records usually produces capabilities that can be achieved in manually kept records systems only by extraordinary human effort (and usually only by expending more time than the information is worth).

THE VERY DIFFERENT PROGRAM

Some genealogy programs do not purport to handle family data or research note files. So long as they are clearly and honestly advertised, they have a place in the spectrum of genealogy applications programs. Even if software *only* processes names and creates Soundex code translations of them, it has a place in genealogical computing. Or if some other genealogy task is the single goal of the programmer, the price and advertising are reasonable *if* the limits of the software are described clearly.

An example of such special-task software is *Calendar G/J* by Edward R. Swart. This is what Swart says of his unique program: "Calendar G/J is a computer program specifically created for genealogists in order to facilitate the conversion of Julian dates to Gregorian dates and vice versa. In addition it supplies other useful information including the day of the week associated with a given date, the phases of the moon, the date of Easter and the times of occurrence of the solstices and equinoxes."

As you can see, this is a specialized tool (and one that takes advantage of a computer's unique abilities to aid us in complicated conversions). It is honestly presented. There ought to be some differentiated way of classifying "genealogy programs" so that such a program doesn't fall in a deceptive listing among other "full feature" genealogy programs.

Another "very different" type of genealogy program is represented by *Treesearch* (sold by Array Systems Inc. and written by Marie Irvine and Nancy Carpenter). What is different about this software is that it emphasizes the *event* rather than the *person* as a research-file basis. We wish we had space to put the program description here.

To see a truly different approach, examine *Treesearch* before buying genealogy software. We might sum up the difference between this program and other genealogy programs this way: Most genealogy programs are an effort to translate genealogists' manual systems to computerized versions. *Treesearch's* programmers feel that genealogists should manage research findings differently than most do; their program is an attempt to show what their unique system has to offer genealogists and to show how a computer can help do it even if manually kept record systems cannot totally adopt this records management system.

Genealogist Val Greenwood says:

> There are many different systems of keeping research notes in current use, which is all very well because what pleases us may be distasteful to you. We each have our own ideas about what is best. Any system is good which gets the job done with a proper balance between completeness and simplicity. An imbalance in either direction is serious. It is as bad to spend too much time and effort on over-elaborate notes as it is to be too brief. No system is good if the note keeping takes more time than research. Some persons become so involved with keeping notes and setting up filing systems that they forget their real purpose – the proper determination of family relationships.[2]

There are more than fifty genealogy programs currently sold. They run on a variety of computers and we've listed them all in this book. Unfortunately, there is not space to describe them all for you. We regret skipping past some truly different and excellent programs. *Roots II* is probably the most "state of the art" in programming. You can even put pictures and maps in your genealogical computer files with it! And *Patriarch I* is written especially to accomodate Jewish families. Write to the publishers of these and other genealogy programs listed in this book to get descriptions, to buy user manuals, and to apply our scale questions. One of them may exactly suit your needs.

One genealogy package showing a different approach is *FamilyFile* by CompuGen Systems. Its difference lies in the patriarch's descendants approach to family records. The following extract is from a description of *FamilyFile* by Karen Cavanaugh:

> *FamilyFile* uses the descendant approach to organizing family data (i.e., beginning with the oldest ancestor in a line and coming forward). The original ancestor is assigned a key number by the user which can consist of up to 15 characters. Usually this takes the form of two letters, such as HR for the surname Harter, and subsequent numbers for each generation. An example is HR15. The original ancestor is assigned the key number HR and HR15 is the fifth child of the first child of the original ancestor, HR. Should a new ancestor or descendant be discovered, the resequencing feature allows any key number to be reassigned to any person or persons in the data base as we will

see later. The ancestor numbering system is meaningful (i.e., you can see how one ancestor is related to another) and the automatic assignment of numbers speeds entry of data and assures accurate numbering . . . .

ENTER FAMILY RECORDS – Husband, wife, and children information is entered at one time with this option. A blank family group sheet, a familiar form to all genealogists, appears on the screen. The user then types in the information as the cursor moves from field to field. After a family record is entered, the user is given the option of entering documentation text at that time. When data entry is completed, the data is written to disk . . . .

UPDATE FAMILY RECORDS – After entering family data it may be necessary to add, delete, or change some information. The user responds to the on-screen prompt for the key number and the previously entered family record is displayed on the screen for modification. By choosing this option you can keep your family data error-free.

DISPLAY FAMILY RECORDS – This feature is used to display on screen any family group record.

ENTER-UPDATE DOCUMENTATION – *FamilyFile* allows up to 24 lines of documentation or comments within each family record. The text is entered on screen to provide footnotes, bibliographic citations, or interesting facts about the family. This information is then printed on the family group sheet, providing a great research aid . . . .

After footnoting the information on the family group sheet and entering those footnotes in the documentation area, the user can assign folder numbers for copies of the documents, such as a birth certificate or census record. In addition, correspondents can quickly see the sources for the information on the family group sheet.

PRINT FAMILY GROUP SHEETS and PEDIGREE CHARTS – The user can choose any person in the database to print both family group sheets and pedigree charts. The user is prompted for the key number of the individual for which the record will be printed . . . .

PRINT DESCENDANT LISTING – This option prints a descendant listing of the ancestor of your choice, with each generation indented from the left margin. Also included are the birth and death dates, comments on the children from the family group sheet, and key numbers of each descendant listed. It allows a one-line, user-defined title for each listing, such as "Descendants of John and Jane Doe." At the end of each listing a statistical list showing the number of descendants for each generation and the total number of descendants is presented.

SEARCH FAMILY RECORDS – This function allows the genealogist to specify any field or number of fields to locate a record. For example, if the user is looking for an ancestor born between 1820 and 1830, who died in Maryland, these specifications can be entered. The program will display in family group sheet form any records matching these specifications . . . .

A powerful report generator (user-defined) will be available this summer. This new feature will allow you to print out lists of the data contained in your family records, such as an alphabetical listing of persons and key numbers, or a listing of those born at a certain location, etc.

FamilyFile maintains family data on a data diskette in six data files. One file contains the husband and wife information, a second file maintains the children information, and a third contains the documentation data. Each of these three files has a corresponding index file which allows the *FamilyFile* program to access the data quickly.

These six files on a data diskette are normal ASCII files which can be viewed with the DOS TYPE command. These files may be read or updated with any BASIC program that accesses them as random-access files of fixed length.

The *FamilyFile* programs contained on the program diskette are executable versions of compiled BASIC programs. Source code is not provided for these programs; therefore the programs may not be modified. *FamilyFile* users can write their own programs for special functions since they may access the data files.[3]

SOPHISTICATION IN SOFTWARE

Commsoft, Inc., is probably the one vendor of genealogy software which approximates the software companies found in "big-time microcomputing" (where *Lotus 1-2-3*, *WordStar*, *MULTIPLAN*, and other mass-market software is sold). Starting with *Roots/89* for Heath/Zenith computers, following with *Roots/M* for CP/M computers, and then coming up with *Roots/II* in the summer of 1984, this company has treated genealogy as a subject worthy of more than pastime programming and marketing. Almost all other genealogy software comes out of the labors of love and sideline businesses that genealogists (who can program) create. Publication of genealogy software and genealogical computing periodicals is cottage industry, so far, because of the very thin market an emerging field presents. But Commsoft, Inc., is applying itself vigorously to that marketplace, risking this attention (and necessary capital investment) in the belief that computer use will be a very normal genealogy practice shortly. We concur, of course.

The latest version of Commsoft, Inc. genealogy software is bound to elevate the level of sophistication in programming for genealogists. It is founded in the experience with and feedback from users of the *Roots/89* and *Roots/M* packages. We think you ought to see what the latest in genealogy software is like:

Howard Nurse, president of Commsoft, Inc., says this of *Roots II*:

> *Roots II* is a data processing system specifically designed for genea-
> logical record keeping. It starts where *Roots/M* leaves off by provid-
> ing expanded storage capabilities, new data fields, improved search
> and data retrieval routines, additional and more flexible print func-
> tions, and the capability to store unlimited biographical text, source
> documentation, and user defined "private" files. In addition to stor-
> ing text, *Roots II* will also store and retrieve pictures—maps, plot plans,
> coats of arms, and even pictures of people! In short, *Roots II* is a major
> rewrite of *Roots/M*, taking into account all that we have learned from
> users of *Roots/M* . . . .

The program will run on a single disk drive computer, with only one
floppy disk required for the maximum size database. To illustrate, a *Roots
II* disk running on the PCjr will hold the entire program, a full database,
and the complete back-up file for the database. This disk storage efficiency
is made possible because the program is written in machine language
which is very compact, and the database itself is highly compressed. Rather
than storing the name "Smith" each time it is used, the program only stores
the name Smith once, and then reuses that name over and over . . . .

The major new *Roots II* subject fields include spaces for occupation,
christening, and three user defined date/place fields. Marriage records now
include two additional date/place fields, one of which is user defined.
Reference flags are available for each line of data entry so you can footnote individual entries. There are also many new single character fields,
such as marriage status, and birth information.

The link to text and picture files is provided by a "reference" field which
can be defined for each record. *Roots II* looks for files having this reference name, and allows you to display them when they are found. The
files may be created with most word processing programs in any format
you wish. The length of the files does not diminish the *Roots II* memory
space, and disks other than your main disk may be used.

Picture files may be created with many IBM graphics programs. One
useful graphics tool is the Versawriter by Versa Computing, Inc. The Versawriter is similar to a graphics tablet for it allows you to trace, then color
and label, your own pictures. Maps of countries, states, and counties may
be traced and then labelled with landmarks or special locations that you
wish to document. Once the picture is prepared, it can be stored on a
Roots II disk, and displayed from within *Roots II*.

The procedure for entering data into the *Roots II* database is similar
to that used for *Roots/M*. All data are entered via a full screen editor, of
which there are two. One screen allows the subject data to be entered,
while a second is for marriage data. Data for each individual are only
entered once.

When the time comes to record your recently entered data, *Roots II* checks your entries for logical consistency. All fixed format dates are checked to make certain that marriages, births, christenings, and deaths occur with natural time relationships. If there is a question, or you have forgotten to enter data that would make a record complete (such as the marriage date for parents of a subject), the program will ask you to make the correction or addition . . . .

One of the important improvements to *Roots II* is the ability to specify which name in a subject's name-string is the surname. Once you have specified the surname, the program will use that information elsewhere in other routines.

There are a number of ways to retrieve information once you have entered it into the database. The LIST routine lets you search by name or occupation. A partial name (one or more letters) can be entered, and all matches will be listed on the screen. You may also conduct a Soundex search of all surnames, or specify a Soundex number for the search.

The PLACES routine allows you to conduct the same kind of search as the LIST routine, except that place names are used for the search.

The ANNIVERSARY routine searches the calendar day by day to look for all anniversaries that occurred on a single day. With this routine you might find why someone was named Valentine, or who was born on Christmas day.

The SEARCH routine allows you to specify a number of conditions that must be met in order to produce a report. For example, you may want a list of all male relatives who are still alive and were born between 1900 and 1910.

Because the database is always in the computer, finding information you have specified is lightning fast. With a database containing several thousand records, it is possible to isolate a single record in a few seconds without the need to switch disks.

Once you have searched for records you wish to display, *Roots II* provides a number of options. TRACE is similar to the routine of the same name provided with *Roots/M*. At the top of the screen is the subject you have specified, with fathers to the left and down, and mothers to the right and down. Six generations of this "vertical pedigree chart" are displayed on the screen at one time, and the display window may be moved down 99 generations. As you move the cursor on the chart, all of the data associated with the person specified by the cursor position are presented in the middle of the screen. If you wish to move a name from the chart into the fetch table, it is simply a matter of specifying the line on the table you wish to use.

FAMILY is similar to a family group sheet in that it displays the parents and all children of those parents. If there is a second spouse for an individual, that spouse and any resulting children are also listed. In the

FAMILY routine the program looks for text and picture files that are associated with the top person on the chart. If the files are found, it is possible to display the text or pictures, and then return to the FAMILY screen. Using FAMILY you can move forward and backward in time to look at later and earlier generations.

RELATIONSHIP computes the relationship between any two people, as long as they are related by blood within eleven generations. The Ahnentafel relationship between the two selected persons is shown, along with canon and civil consanguinity numbers. A reverse Ahnentafel search is conducted by specifying an Ahnentafel number while displaying a selected subject, and *Roots II* will search for the ancestor's name based on the number you entered.

Printed copies of *Roots II* records can be obtained in two ways. At any time you may obtain a listing of the contents of the screen by using the IBM PrtSc key. But where *Roots II* really shines is in the formal print routines.

Roots II will let you print a book from start to finish, keeping track of page numbers, adding text and footnotes, and then printing a complete index for you, all automatically! For example, you may start out with an Ahnentafel chart which takes four pages, followed by a Pedigree Chart which takes another 45, then a collection of Family Group Sheets which takes 257 pages (including biographies), and finally an alphabetized index that gives up to ten page references for each name in your book. If you wish to have a custom book for a third cousin, choose that person as the starting point and in several hours you will have a completed book.

Since *Roots II* keeps track of double-dating conventions, events which fall in the user defined double dating range will be printed in the correct format by the program. For example, a birthdate occurring on January 24, 1714 (old calendar) would be printed as 24 Jan 1714/15.

It is possible to send the print data to one of three selectable printers, or to a disk file. If you choose a disk file, the data is saved as an expanded ASCII text file that can be used by any other program (especially word processing programs) which can read text files.[4]

COTTON-CANDY GENEALOGY PROGRAMS

There are genealogy programs sold that simply create blank pedigree charts and/or family group sheets. It occurs to us that it would be cheaper to buy such items from any of the many sources for blank genealogy forms, or to use the word processor program to draw the forms on the computer screen and save them as text files for form-printing as needed. To turn a computer into a printing press for blank forms just doesn't seem its best use. Worse, the existence of such "genealogy programs" amid *real* (and excellent) genealogy programs makes a confusing subject more confused.

There are other "cotton candy" genealogy programs. They do more than print blank forms, but less than we think is genealogically adequate. They would fare poorly on the scale of adequacy we have created.

An interesting example of a low-cost, low-performance program is *Your Family Tree* by Chuck Acree, translated for IBM PC by Andrew Bartorillo, sold by Acorn Software Products. From the software jacket: "Your Family Tree stores and organizes any genealogy with tremendous speed, efficiency and flexibility . . . . Updates are convenient, customized summaries a breeze, corrections are easy and reviews quick . . . . THE PROFESSIONAL QUALITY GENEALOGY THAT OFFERS EFFICIENCY, FLEXIBILITY AND SPEED . . . . MACHINE REQUIREMENTS: IBM PC with 128K and one disk drive. Your Family Tree runs on both monochrome and color monitors . . . . $29.95 . . . . A sophisticated data base of relations that charts your geographic and familial roots."

The words sound good and the novice genealogist might be persuaded that he is looking at a bargain in software. Is it? This kind of genealogy software has its use and its place. It is packaged attractively, priced inexpensively, and cataloged with the many games programs and education programs sold by Acorn Software Products. If only the manual and cover information did not make claims of genealogical adequacy and usefulness not backed by the software, this program would be fine as is. The real market (and the one the vendor really advertises for), is the personal computer owner who has tired of games, is looking for some practical and nontrivial use of his computer, and might find genealogy an interesting new avocation. It's a two-way street. If genealogists are "getting into" computing, why not computerists "getting into" genealogy? So long as there is no misrepresentation involved, the world needs a good set of training wheels for genealogy and a program that seductively leads nongenealogists to the "game of genealogy." There are board games (in the style of Monopoly) for future genealogists; why not computer games?

Your Family Tree presents an example in which the price is descriptive of the power of the program. Mass marketing and narrow profit margins will make it a success and introduce many to genealogy. But promoting the product by advertising it as something that would rate highly on our adequacy scale should be ended or radically changed in future production runs of this software.

THE IMPORT-EXPORT UTILITY PROGRAM

You will recall that you cannot automatically slip a floppy disk made on your computer into some other genealogist's computer and expect it to run. It is likely that the data recording formats will differ between computers of different brands and models. There may be a problem of incompatibility even if the two computers are exactly alike in all respects: the genealogy software used by you and the other computing genealogist may not be creating family files of the same content, layout, or data expression style. This kind of incompatibility will frustrate us all if not overcome.

The solution is for each genealogy software publisher to create a "utility program." Such a program isn't directly used for data entry or data manipulation, but in conjunction with files created by programs that were used in data entry and manipulation. The utility program we all need is an "import-export utility." To date, there is no such utility program – but that may change by the time this book is published.

Genealogy software authors are looking at a common family file format to which they can change their software format on the occasion of "exporting" data files to other computers using other file formats. The reciprocal program is to be written, too: an "import" utility would allow reading files in a universal family file format and rewriting them into the author's own file format. The big question: what will this "medium of exchange" file format be? Once that neutral family file format has been defined, tested for suitability, and adopted by *all* software vendors, work can begin on these export-import utilities.

The fact is, the genealogical computing experts who work on the *Ancestral File* and *Personal Ancestoral File* projects of the Church of Jesus Christ of Latter-day Saints have gone far in defining that medium-of-exchange file format. They call it GEDCOM. Once GEDCOM is ready, we will no longer worry about finding *the* genealogy software or computer; our entered files can be "exported" to the GEDCOM format and then "imported" to work under *different* genealogy software and/or a different computer. No reentering of family data will be required!

GEnealogical Data COMmunications (GEDCOM) format is quickly shaping up. The genealogist who uses a computer really doesn't have to know anything about GEDCOM; it is to be "transparent to the user." This means your software programmer needs to know about GEDCOM but you do not. (It is the same as saying your garage mechanic needs to know about timing your car's engine but you do not need to know how he does it or why he must do it.)

We assumed (as did the software vendors who were paying attention to file-transfer problems) that the Mormons would use some variant of their *Personal Ancestral File*'s data files as the standard for file transfers. It was a logical assumption because that software was probably written to accommodate the ultimate need to transfer the individual's computer holdings to a central ancestral file's database. Now that GEDCOM's nature is emerging, it is both surprising and gratifying that the assumption was wrong. PAF (*Personal Ancestral File*) files are just as much "third party" as is *any* family data file created by any genealogy program on the market! GEDCOM caters to no particular program vendor's file shapes and accommodates them all. It is a unique and wisely chosen format.

Readers who are good programmers already will want to know more than "it is transparent – leave it to the software programmers to understand." For them, we add this glimpse into the GEDCOM style:

GEDCOM (GEnealogical Data COMmunications format) was introduced in the July 1984 issue of *Genealogical Computing* (page 1). If you can run a special program that generates a GEDCOM version of your computerized genealogy, you can "export" your family data to another computer even if it runs very different genealogy software. Conversely, if you can run a program that converts a GEDCOM-format family file to the format your own computer and genealogy software uses, you can receive family data from other computers.

While GEDCOM is both a standard and file transfer system being devised by the LDS Church software development team, the future of genealogical computing is at stake and ideas and comments submitted *now* (to the Genealogical Library in Salt Lake City) may make the implementation smoother and all of us more comfortable with this file exchanging standard.

It appears that the only concession to PAF that has been made is ensuring that the data fields managed by PAF are among the data "elements" accounted for in first-round GEDCOM design. But even the most exotic data field (Health or Military Honors, for example) could be included in a GEDCOM file. By contacting the clearinghouse to be used in GEDCOM management, anyone (especially a commercial genealogy program publisher) can have a field of information "defined in the GEDCOM dictionary." A field such as Health might be assigned "HL" as its "data-type tag," and Military Honors might be given "MH" as its tag. Any one who, thereafter, puts such fields in GEDCOM-using files would use HL and MH as the official designators of the type of data being expressed. You do not have to have such an assigned tag, really. There are data-element tags that mean "miscellaneous" in GEDCOM, so that you can put in a "funny field" that will eventually be assigned a data-type tag – or left as not assigned. When such a tag is seen by a computer as it reads a GEDCOM-format file, the computer rejects the data field but prints out the tag and data element so that you can see and manually deal with the "odd-type" information-element.

GEDCOM will express *any* family file in hierarchy-of-data terms and will data-type tags. The hierarchical system uses ten numbers (0 through 9) just as you would use numbers and letters in outlines familiar to us all.

Do you see the GEDCOM manner of expressing the indentations and level indication in the following diagram? As in other hierarchical expressions, a GEDCOM level indicator is relative to the next-highest information in the hierarchy. A "2" refers to something subordinate to the last "1" seen (even if another "2" exists and refers to the same "1"). This is really not so complex as you might think.

OUTLINE	GEDCOM
I	0
A	1
1	2
2	2
3	2
B	1
C	1
1	2
a	3
(1)	4
(2)	4
b	3
c	3
(1)	4
(a)	5
(b)	5
(2)	4
D	1
1	2
2	2
E	1

Suppose a person in your family represents the highest level of information in a family record: DOE, John Henry would be the information element receiving a "0-level" GEDCOM level indicator. All else about his record would be between "1" and "9" in level and would all refer back to element "0" (his name). Perhaps showing a specimen of a GEDCOM-like file will make things a bit clearer. in the preceding illustration (which is *not* a true GEDCOM file's image) you can see how each information element is a subfact of the element one level higher in the outline. Every data element is allotted a maximum of 255 characters (less 4 characters needed for level indicator, tag for data type, and the terminating carriage return). Sex can be expressed with one of two letters: M or F. That the gender is male (M) or female (F) does not stand alone; we need to know *who* this male or female is. That is determined by going back up the hierarchy one or more levels to get to the name of the person whose gender is being expressed.

By now it should be coming clear: GEDCOM files break up databases and the records in them so that every information element (or data field, if you prefer that term) stands free of all else. The information element might be a birthdate, birthplace, name, research note, footnote, comment, biographical note, deathplace, address, occupation, cross-reference, and so forth.

Four pieces are part of each GEDCOM element:

1. *Level Indicator* (from 0 through 9 – ten "outline" places to indicate association and subordination of data elements).
2. *Data-Type Tag* (two letters that designate the nature of the information element – is it a birthdate? footnote?)
3. *Data-Element* (the text of the field's information –"16 Dec 1928" or "M" or some longer words, phrases, or codes.)
4. *Terminator* (a carriage return).

When the level, data-type tag, data-element information, and terminator are put together, they form a single "string." One character for level, two characters for a tag, a variable number of characters expressing the information of the element, and a carriage return terminator are included, with the string's total number of characters not exceeding 255.

In some cases, such a string may be a cross-reference to another record. For example, if you had an identification number for your father in your record, it would enable associating all the information in your father's record with that in your record. That number is the "pointer" which tells where to look for linking information. Pointers for spouses, parents, and children can be placed as data elements in a person's record so that climbing the family tree can be computer handled.

The general scheme of GEDCOM seems to be pretty well defined already and is much as we have tried to describe (although we take the blame for any inaccuracies our simplifications and illustrations have introduced). A "dictionary" of GEDCOM data-type codes has been circulated for comments from parties who might raise new ideas or divergent views. We expect the two-letter codes to be settled soon. What seems clear enough is that ten levels (0 through 9) will associate data elements within a record, and any element could be of any format or length of expression up to 255 characters (including level-tag-element-terminator). That's great! You can express data in your own way and otherwise be unique, eccentric, or innovative in your own genealogy file format.

With databases being broken down to data elements, there will be no advantaged genealogy software and no need for you to worry about using "standard software." The future is left to the future genealogists and programmers! It would have been a great disappointment to many of us if the chance to create better or different family file systems had been stifled by early regimentation of how we must computerize family files in order to swap computerized data. We want to raise a cheer for the folks out in Salt Lake City who avoided foisting any one computer or type of genealogy software as *the way* we must file our families. The GEDCOM scheme seems the one way out of the predictable and endless argument over whose software should be the "standard software" for genealogists. We can keep our records any way we want, on any computer we want, with any software we want to buy or write. Terrific! GEDCOM is coming along nicely and it is good.

The following Microsoft BASIC listing allows you to create a printout of a GEDCOM-like hierarchy of data. By doing so, you can become familiar with the hierarchy concept used in GEDCOM file formats. Following the listing is a specimen created by the program.

```
10 REM          GEDCOM/BAS 11/3/84
10 REM          by Paul Andereck, Editor
                GENEALOGICAL COMPUTING
30 ELPAD$#       " "
40 CLS
50 PRINT
60 REM          SOLICIT THREE-PART
                DATA ELEMENT ENTRY.
70 LINE         INPUT"1. LEVEL (0-9)            ♂";
                LVL$:LVL#VAL(LVL$):LVL#LVL*3
80 ELPAD$#      STRING$(LVL," ")
90 LINE         INPUT"2. TAG (2 LETTERS)         ♂";
                TAG$
100 LINE        INPUT"3. INFO (251 CHARS MAX)    ♂";
                INFO$
110 INFO#       LEN(INFO$):IF INFO ♂ 251 THEN PRINT
                "TOO LONG!":GOTO 100
120 REM            PRINT OUT LEVELS-INDENTED
                   GEDCOM ELEMENT.
130 LPRINT      ELPAD$;LVL$;"–";TAG$;" :";:
                LPRINT" ";INFO$
140             RUN 50
        — — — — — — — — — — — — — — — — — —-
```

0 – II: Paul*Arthur/Andereck/

    1 – X0 : 1
    1 – GN : M
    1 – BD : S19281216
       2 – NT :   Delivered by midwife at the home of his paternal grandparents.
    1 – BP :   Overland, St. Louis County, Missouri, USA
       2 – NT :   Birth Certificate ffl03452 – St. Louis County Courthouse, Clayton, Missouri.

3 – NT :   Name on birth certificate was spelled wrong by
           the midwife.
1 – FA :   Chester*Harold/Andereck/
1 – MO :   Catherine*Augusta/Hawn

MORMON CHURCH IMPACT
ON GENEALOGICAL SOFTWARE

Perhaps we have put the cart before the horse; at least we put the utility program before the program to which it is a related utility. The *Personal Ancestral File* is a genealogy software system that gave genealogical computing respectability in much the same way that IBM gave personal computers respectability by its entry into that market.

Several factors make *Personal Ancestral File* software one of the most significant genealogy software now being marketed. For one thing, it will set record-format standards. In the first few months after its May 1984 introduction, this software sold as many copies as had all other software in the several years since the genealogy program first appeared on the market. The influence of the The Church of Jesus Christ of Latter-day Saints on genealogy is tremendous, and that influence will carry over to genealogy programs. How the LDS program handles family information will be the de facto standard.

Another factor in *PAF*'s favor is that it is inexpensive. If any software producer other than the LDS Church tries to compete pricewise, it won't make a profit. This is going to make genealogy software *better* because being better will be the only price justification others will have.

With such special advantages, *PAF* is going to affect genealogical computing enormously – and to the field's great advantage.

The following is excerpted from *Genealogical Computing*'s May and July 1984 issues. It was written by Paul Andereck.

Personal Ancestral File is copyrighted by Corporation of the President of The Church of Jesus Christ of Latter-day Saints. All rights reserved. Direct inquiries to: The Genealogical Department, Ancestral File Operations Unit, 50 East North Temple Street, Salt Lake City, UT 84150, 801-531-2584. The following has been reviewed by the office for public information of the LDS Church and is presented with permission. The current software runs on IBM-PC and IBM-PC/XT personal computers. This six-disk system and users manual are available for $35 (catalog #PBGS 1019) from Salt Lake Distribution Center, 1999 West 1700 South, Salt Lake City, UT 84104.

Two distinct (and totally separate) computer systems comprise the *Personal Ancestral File* genealogy system . . . the *Lineage-Linked* system and the *Data Sort Utility* . . . .

The *Lineage-Linked* system is used for all operations related to records and notes on individuals and family groups. Generating printed family group sheets, pedigree charts, sorted indexes, documentation notes, and ordinance work notations are tasks performed by the *Lineage-Linked* system.

MAXIMUM LENGTH OF FIELDS (in characters);

Address lines (all) 40
Dates (birth, christening, death, burial, marriage)
    Day 2
    Month 9
    Year 9
Dates (LDS ordinance)
    Day 2
    Month 9
    Year 4
Divorced 1
FGR print 1
Given names (all) 16
History note 1
History note text 60
Levels (all) 16
Note type 1
Patron name 40
Relation to father/mother 1
Sex 1
Stake 25
Stake unit number 7
Surname 16
Telephone number 25
Temple code 5
Title * 16
User volume label 79

The use of these information fields of the *Lineage-Linked* system:

ADDRESS LINES — Upon initializing data diskettes to hold family files, the *Personal Ancestral File* user will give the patron's first, middle, and last names (which print on pedigree charts, family group records, and entry forms created by *Personal Ancestral Ffile*); a maximum of 40 characters can be used for patron-name. Up to three lines and a maximum of 40 characters can be used to give the patron's (*Personal Ancestral File* user's) address. The patron's home telephone number (including area code) can occupy another 25 characters. The stake number (which appears on temple recommends) of the patron (7 digits) and stake name (25 characters) are part of the initializing entries. The name of the diskette (up to 79 letters or numbers) is entered to name the primary line or lines on the diskette; it will appear as the title on all sorted lists.

DATES—The three parts of a date (day, month, and year) are separate information fields (an ENTER-key action is required after each field to indicate it is completed or skipped).

DAY—one or two digits can be used (e.g., '5' or '05' and '16' are day expressions possible).

MONTH—You can spell the month out, fully, use the first three letters of a month name as an abbreviation, or use a numeral for a month's number. Regardless of which way you enter a month, it ends up as a three-letter English abbreviation when printed or displayed on screens.

YEAR—Four digits are used to express year (e.g., "1984"). To record a dual date, you can follow one year with a second by using a slash and one to four digits after the slash. Use no spaces. Examples of year expression: "1984," "1983/4," "1983/84," "1983/1984."

Several alternative uses of the MONTH field allow handling of expressions of date uncertainties (or special notations): "ABT" or "ABOUT," "BEF" or "BEFORE," "AFT" or "AFTER," "INF" or "INFANT," "STI" or "STILLBORN," "SUB" or "SUBMITTED," "CLE" or "CLEARED," "UNC" or "UNCLEARED," "COM" or "COMPLETED," "CAN" or "CANCELLED," and "DNS" or "DNS/CAN" are the kinds of expressions you can put in the MONTH field to give date-expressing flexibility. (Some of the illustrations apply only to LDS church usage.)

DIVORCED—A one-character code indicates a divorce; prints out "(DIV)" wherever marriage date printing occurs if you use "Y" in response to prompt.

FGR PRINT—A one-character code is used to indicate whether or not a line of "history notes" should print when family group sheets are printed. This allows records to contain informal research notes (e.g., "check the county of birth with John") or other "hidden lines" available only by deliberate choice.

GIVEN NAMES (ALL)—Three given names are accommodated as information fields. Each can be 16 characters long. The *Personal Ancestral File* automatically locks in all upper-case before accepting person names. (Historical notes can be upper/lower case.)

Each part of a name and each part of a location specifier is a separate information field (surname, given 1, given 2, given 3; and level 1, level 2, level 3, level 4 locators—to be explained later). When name or place information entries are made, the program requires repeating the entry. This is a spelling-verification step. Once you have twice-entered the same spelling, you aren't required to do this double-entry step thereafter (as long as you are working with the same diskette's family data file). A name file (not accessible to the *Personal Ancestral File* user) is created each time a new person or place name is entered/verified. This functions as a spelling-verification dictionary once a name has been double-entered. (If you have to put "Kosciusko" repeatedly as place name or person name, the program watches that you spell it right. If you deliberately give a variant spelling sometime, you must repeat the new version so it can be added to the name file too.) The *Personal Ancestral File* user manual shows how you can prebuild a name file for often-used person or place names; the file then keeps an eye on how you spell entries therein without getting in your way (except when you goof or deliberately spell something differently).

HISTORY NOTE—An indicator you can set to show presence of historical notes.

HISTORY NOTE TEXT—Though you are allowed only 60 characters and spaces in a given "history note," you can have an unlimited number of such notes. Each note (consider it a line) gets two special one-character "flags" (aside from the HISTORY NOTE-extant flag). One indicates whether or not you wish to have the note print when making family group sheets (see FGR PRINT, above) and the other is a self-decided code to tell what kind of note you have just written. You can use "S" as a code to denote it as a source-documentation kind of note (line), "E" to indicate it is an extension of the preceding line's note (continuance of a note longer than 60 characters), or other codes useful to the *Personal Ancestral File* user.

History notes are tied to individuals rather than to events or family groups (though the notes of individuals within a family group can be printed as part of the family group's record). These notes can be upper/lower case.

These notes can be added after records are created; changed with the use of an editor function that allows inserts, deletes, and moves; or extended to include new information. The manual suggests that the HISTORY NOTES file be kept on the same data diskette as the *lineage linking* file (they are distinctly separate data files) for speedy access to both files while adding or modifying records. However, when the files begin to grow, the manual suggests you move the HISTORY NOTES file to a separate data diskette to allow growth of both data files to the diskettes' maximum available space. Note this file nature: While an unlimited number of records and historical notes can be accommodated by this genealogy system, the indexes are by-disk and it is a good idea to use separate data diskettes not only for lineage-linked individual and family group records and historical notes pertaining thereto, but also to create a "library" of data diskettes for each surname line or some other logical breakout of "clans" of the family. This leaves room on every data diskette (family records or historical notes diskettes) for growth of the files.

LEVELS (ALL)–The term "level" is given to the four locality designations allowed to express place information. LEVEL 1, LEVEL 2, LEVEL 3, and LEVEL 4 should be used to show the most-local to most-broad political jurisdiction named. (City, county, state, and nation are such levels.) The manual suggests you skip "USA" as the fourth level place name. Apparently, LEVEL 4 always prints out and then levels 1 thru 3 are printed as space allows (with the priority being given in this order: LEVEL 1, LEVEL 2, and then LEVEL 3). Each level can have 16 characters of place-name information. The manual shows how you can use the four available level fields in a variety of ways. One of the illustrations puts state name in the LEVEL 4 position and skips use of LEVEL 3 at all (it would be the one "lost" in printouts). Nowhere does the *Personal Ancestral File* manual say you lose (by truncation) any level's information; only printout-space is said to be a limiting factor (this comes up only in chart printing with *Personal Ancestral File* printout formats being program-controlled).

NOTE TYPE–see HISTORY NOTE TEXT.

PATRON NAME–see ADDRESS LINES.

RELATION TO FATHER/MOTHER–The one-digit code allows user-designation of how to express the manner by which a person is related to a parent. Suggestions include "N" for natural, "A" for adopted, etc.

SEX–Either "M" or "F" (or leaving it blank) is permissible in this one-character field.

STAKE–see ADDRESS LINES.

STAKE UNIT NUMBER–see ADDRESS LINES.

SURNAME–Up to 16 characters can be used to indicate a subject's surname. See also GIVEN NAMES (ALL).

TELEPHONE NUMBER–see ADDRESS LINES.

TEMPLE CODE–Part of the data entry fields about an individual, the TEMPLE CODE (5 characters) is one of several fields available for recording data of ordinances done in The Church of Jesus Christ of Latter-day Saints.

TITLE–Titles (e.g., "Sr.," "Jr.," "Duke," "Lady," or "Dr.") are up to 16 characters long. You are expected to enter occupations as history notes.

USER VOLUME LABEL—see ADDRESS LINES.

The *Lineage-Linked* subsystem uses the above fields for management purposes (e.g., the ADDRESS LINES information), individual subject records, family groups, and historical notations (including documentation of sources of data). In the process of using *Personal Ancestral File* the user is supplied two identification numbers automatically:

The RIN (Record Identification Number) is computer-supplied and appears on the screen and on listings of individuals in the database. The MRIN (Marriage Record Identification Number) can be thought of as a family group record number.

You enter information into *Personal Ancestral File* by selecting menu-displayed options. From the master menu you can choose the operation you wish to perform, and this gives you another menu (of options available in the selected operation). When data-entry or data-modification operations are involved, you are guided from field to field as you enter data. You can "override" the cursor-moves controlled by the program and make the cursor go back to a field you want to change. When modifications are involved, you can call up a record to be changed and then move the cursor to the field to be modified (by corrections or newfound information).

The RIN is the identifier used to most quickly get a wanted record on the screen. If it is the family group record (showing the marriage, parent, and children information as well as the subject's own data record) which is to be retrieved, the MRIN is used. The *Personal Ancestral File* program generates printed lists arranged in RIN and MRIN order. It also creates by-disk alphabetically ordered lists by names of individuals in the database. Such a list can supply the RIN needed for calling up a specific person. Once individuals have been represented by records in the system, they can be linked with parents, spouses, and children in a family group entry process. Those in the family group are called up by RIN and the relationship is specified by the user. At this point you may enter an individual's data as part of the family group entry process. The resulting family group record gets the machine-generated MRIN number. If a person is part of several family groups (via multiple marriages), that person has several family group records (for each spouse and the children of each marriage). When a marriage is dissolved, the *Personal Ancestral File* permits "breaking up the marriage" (as a record) without removing the individual records of those who were part of the dissolved family group. Up to 30 children per marriage can be accommodated and an unlimited number of marriages of an individual person can be entered.

While the RIN and MRIN are the "call numbers" which most quickly retrieve a given individual or family group for display, change, or printout, the *Personal Ancestral File* user can identify and retrieve persons by using search terms (which identify one person or group of candidates sharing the search terms as information fields). The search option lets you fill out a screen of field names with the search terms: You move the cursor to the fields in which the terms are found and enter a term in a field (e.g., "1917" in a year of birth field, and/or "Bradley" in a first given-name field) as necessary. Only person names, birthdates, or birthdate range are usable search terms. When you have given sufficient specificity to your search term(s), you use a function key to cause the search to begin. You are asked if the selected candidate is the one you want, and if it is not, the search presents the next terms-matching candidate.

The *Personal Ancestral File*-built database starts with data entry of information about individuals (after which family groups are defined, with marriage and children entries creating the lineage links of the immediate and extended family) . . . .

ENTERING DATA ABOUT AN INDIVIDUAL

When the ENTER-key is pressed, the cursor steps to the next information field (which you can record or skip by hitting ENTER again). This is the field sequence of *Personal Ancestral File*:

SEX; SURNAME; GIVEN 1; GIVEN 2; GIVEN 3; (at least one name must be supplied for the record to be stored); TITLE; BIRTH DAY; BIRTH MONTH; BIRTH YEAR; BIRTHPLACE LEVEL 1; BIRTHPLACE LEVEL 2; BIRTHPLACE LEVEL 3; BIRTHPLACE LEVEL 4; CHRISTENING (same date and place fields as BIRTH); DEATH (same date and place fields as BIRTH); BURIAL (same date and place fields as BIRTH); and these LDS-Church oriented fields: BAPTISM, ENDOWMENT, and SEAL to PAR (Sealed to Parents) dates (expressed as other dates are except that only one four-digit year is used); TEMPLE CODE (in which ordinance work was done; if the person was baptized for himself you may use "LIVE," "LVG," another meaningful code, or nothing; this code will have to be verified).

The opportunity to move the cursor back to a field and delete it (using the delete key) and reenter it is available. When satisfied with the record you can push the "F1" key (a control key) to cause the options to appear: store the data, change the data, or kill the record and return to the main menu.

ENTERING DATA ABOUT A FAMILY

First, you identify the HUSBAND (by RIN or search technique to get the correct individual record). If the husband is unknown, you skip this step. (You can add the husband's record at this point.) By answering "Y" to confirm that you have the correct husband, you have automatically entered him into the family record. Next, you identify the WIFE (the same way as husband).

Marriage information is entered next:

> DAY, MONTH, and YEAR of MARRIAGE; PLACE OF MARRIAGE; LDS WIFE-TO-HUSBAND SEALING DATE; CODE FOR TEMPLE IN WHICH SEALED; DIVORCE;

and then "F1" is used to bring up the same options as noted under individual-record entry.

Adding children requires use of the CHILD MENU. They are entered by order of birth, with a maximum of 30 children for each set of parents. You can add or change the order of children later (by using the MODIFY DATA option at the main menu, you delete and then reenter a child to change the order).

The *Personal Ancestral File* programs are "menu-driven." A master menu is the primary one from which the user chooses options that call up other menus. In turn, options chosen on the "submenus" may bring menus of prompts that pertain to the chosen topic. Answering these prompts with keyed-in data is the process of building the family ancestral file.

THE MAIN MENU:
1. DATA ENTRY
2. MODIFY DATA
3. DELETE DATA
4. LINEAGE-LINKED SEARCH
5. HISTORY NOTE FILE
6. PRINT FORMS AND REPORTS
7. SYSTEM UTILITIES
8. EXIT TO DOS

DATA ENTRY MENU:
1. MODIFY INDIVIDUAL INFORMATION
2. MODIFY MARRIAGE INFORMATION
3. MODIFY FAMILY STRUCTURE
4. RETURN TO MAIN MENU

MODIFY DATA MENU:
1. MODIFY INDIVIDUAL INFORMATION
2. MODIFY MARRIAGE INFORMATION
3. MODIFY FAMILY STRUCTURE
4. RETURN TO MAIN MENU

DELETE DATA MENU:
1. INDIVIDUAL
2. FAMILY
3. RETURN TO MAIN MENU

SEARCH OPTIONS MENU:
1. INDIVIDUAL INFORMATION
2. FATHER
3. MOTHER
4. SPOUSE
5. CHILD
6. OTHER MARRIAGE
7. SEARCH CANDIDATE LIST
8. LINEAGE-LINKED SEARCH
9. RETURN TO MAIN MENU

HISTORY NOTE FILE MENU:
1. ADD/MODIFY/DELETE NOTES
2. REORDER NOTES
3. PRINT NOTES
4. DISPLAY NOTES
5. PRINT/DISPLAY HISTORY DISKETTE DIRECTORY
6. MOVE NOTES TO ANOTHER DISKETTE
7. LOCATE ANOTHER INDIVIDUAL
8. RETURN TO MAIN MENU

PRINT FORMS AND REPORTS MENU:
1. PEDIGREE CHART
2. FAMILY GROUP RECORD
3. INDIVIDUAL ENTRY FORM
4. MARRIAGE ENTRY FORM
5. INDIVIDUAL SUMMARY
6. SORTED LISTS
7. RETURN TO MAIN MENU

SYSTEM UTILITIES MENU:
1. LINEAGE-LINKED DISKETTE INITIALIZATION
2. HISTORY DISKETTE INITIALIZATION
3. CHANGE/DISPLAY PATRON NAME AND ADDRESS
4. CHANGE/DISPLAY USER VOLUME LABEL
5. MOVE LINEAGE-LINKED OR HISTORY DATA
6. PRINTER SET-UP
7. RETURN TO MAIN MENU

Personal Ancestral File comes on six minifloppy diskettes. The user manual gives instructions for single-sided, double-sided, and hard-disk management of the programs and data files. A lot of disk swaps are necessary to move various programs and data diskettes in and out of the computer's disk drives; necessary moves are prompted by screen-displayed messages.

Five of the six diskettes contain programs and files related to the *Lineage-Linked* subsystem. The sixth diskette contains the DATA-SORT UTILITY subsystem's programs and files. The programs can be copied, backed up, listed, and modified (if you have need and have the ability) . . . . While the *Personal Ancestral File* makes use of the function keys, delete key, insert key, and control keys of the IBM PC . . . it would be easy to run 90 percent or more of the software on various IBM-workalikes . . . .

An experienced programmer should be able to create modifications which make *Personal Ancestral File* run on many Microsoft BASIC-using machines. Remember that these programs are copyrighted . . . . Development of variations to run on other computers would be welcomed but the copyright will be used to insure that standardization established by the *Personal Ancestral File* will be maintained in variations permitted . . . .

Operating system components that consume RAM will need to be slimmed to barest bones to accommodate some of the program module sizes (the manual tells how to set up the system disk and how to handle the program disks). Anyone thinking about adapting *Personal Ancestral File* to run on a skinny-RAM machine would be better off figuring out how to buy a fat-RAM instead.

No direct linkage exists between files created by DATA SORT UTILITY and *Lineage-Linked* files. You will necessarily keyboard data twice if it is common to both subsystems' files. This seeming hardship is appropriate once you see the differences in the two subsystems.

DATA SORT UTILITY helps you keep track of (1) your documents, and, (2) research data (which are contained in the documents).

DATA SORT UTILITY files-massaging permits you to distill data, squeezing it down to the essence—the data references you will put in the files made with *lineage-linked subsystem.* This doesn't mean that DATA SORT UTILITY must be used first and its program outputs then used as the source for information going into *Personal Ancestral File*'s other files. (Doing that is a fine idea, though.) This free-standing nature of the two subsystems of *Personal Ancestral File* software makes it possible to buy the *PAF* package, use DATA SORT UTILITY, and use some genealogy software other than the *lineage-linked subsystem of PAF* (my suggestion to those who use any of the several other IBM PC genealogy programs already).

The two-part *PAF* package . . . handles two different aspects of genealogy: Records management is the forte of *lineage-linked subsystem.* Research-notes handling is the specialty of DATA SORT UTILITY.

Two classes of data are handled by this subsystem. The first involves data about the document which contains family data. Document-describing data tells where your family data comes from. Each document (a will, deed, or other data-source item, either formal or informal) is given an identification number. This number allows associating the document data with each of the family data references found therein (without having to repeat your source citation in full for every unit of family data you enter). The second class of data handled is family data (or research notes). Describing the courthouse, book, and page where the will or deed is found is the kind of information-load that document data carries. Within the will or deed are references to several different family members. Those are the data which can be entered as excerpts, narratives, or verbatim. They are the family data units which carry the identification number to link data to document.

DATA SORT UTILITY is not easily described because it is flexible and adaptable to various kinds of ordinary or irregular data sources and data kinds we use in genealogy. To more fully know why this utility is important and how flexibly it can be used, the *Genealogical Computing* reader can order a copy of the cassette tape made of the excellent presentation by Marie Irvine and Nancy Carpenter at the May 1984 conference of the National Genealogical Society. (TRIAD Professional Productions, 700 S. Fifth St., Pekin, IL 61554 ; $4 each ; T-3 is the tape number.) *Genealogical Computing* will not try to cover what Irvine and Carpenter do so well or the user manual covers so thoroughly.

The *Personal Ancestral File* manual cautions you: "This program will force you to adopt some way of organizing your notes." You will continue to have paper files and manual systems, but the software helps you find data once it forces you to organize it. Once your notes are computer-entered, you will discover computer aid is more than family record information management, people indexing, and pedigree chart printing. You will be able to find quickly all information in your notes and documents that refer to a certain person name, date, location, relationship, birth, residence, marriage, death, or military service. Quick file searches for these kinds of things are within the utility's capability.

To search for file entries having a "combined term" (e.g., all John Smiths who are/were associated with the location of Lancaster, Pennsylvania but only those whose vital statistic dates fall in the eighteenth century), you let the utility program select all "John Smith" persons and then you save a computer-managed file of them. Then you use that file as the only data references to be searched for the place reference. You can save a new file of this reduced number of applicable references and use it as the next search's data source for matching candidates to the specified date information. This is not "Boolean logic" (using an "and" between each of several search terms to make one pass at selecting data references that meet the multiterm search criteria). But this selection process is functionally the same, and it has an advantage over Boolean search methods: It lets you know the also-hit references as you find matches in each search round of a multiround, narrowing search. (Boolean searching gives you only the multiterm matches between your query and your file contents—which is often nothing.) For genealogical purposes, this is a better search system than Boolean-Search. DATA SORT UTILITY leaves to the human that which the human does best: deciding what is important rather than what is a letter-for-letter match of terms.

If you look at the "MAP OF THE SYSTEM" in the manual, you will see why we go no further in describing DATA SORT UTILITY. It's a marvelous computing jungle out there in the software's mapped operations. Split screen usage, function-key callup of different operations, and a lot of other sophisticated user helps are described in the user manual.

Each of these operations is clearly covered in the user manual: changing active screens; getting new files from disk; saving new files on disk; locating by name or number; searching any field; sorting any field; restoring preaction condition to files; making new entries; making changes; deleting entries; copying entries from one file to another; printing files; and producing cross-referenced data and document outputs.

There is good genealogy software available *now* for a variety of good and reasonably priced personal computers. If you found this chapter to be tedious, you are of the right frame of mind for genealogical computing; computerizing family records *is* tedious. Learning what this chapter covered is the *other* expense associated with computer genealogy. (The first was several thousand dollars for hardware and software suitable for genealogy application.)

FOOTNOTES

1. Ethel W. Williams, *Know Your Ancestors, A Guide to Genealogical Research* (Rutland, Vt: Charles E. Tuttle Company, 1976), p. 138.
2. Val D. Greenwood, *The Researcher's Guide to American Genealogy* (Baltimore: Genealogical Publishing Company, Inc., 1973), p. 70.
3. Karen B. Cavanaugh, "FamilyFile—A Description," *Genealogical Computing* 4, no. 1 (July 1984): 27.
4. Howard L. Nurse, "Roots II, A Second-Generation Genealogical Database Program," *Genealogical Computing* 3, no. 6 (May 1984): 18.

CHAPTER 9

Looking at the Future of Computer Genealogy

S uppose you and many other genealogists have transformed your manually kept records and research notes to computerized files. What do you do besides that, and what's next?

While you are choosing, buying, and using a computer for genealogy, you can depend on great strides in telecommunications to take place. Telecommunications are simply communications by telephone. We communicate by phone every day, of course, but in computer context the term means *computers* talking to each other and, usually, each remembering what the other computer "said."

For the present, telecommunications is the most untapped area of microcomputing, and because so few are involved in modeming, the area is relatively undeveloped. No part of computing is so disorganized as is telecommunications. It seems that vendors of communications software and hardware assume that no one would buy telecommunications products for his computer unless he was the most advanced of microcomputerists. Manuals for modem operating or communications software invariably are written by people who assume far too much experience on the part of the buyer. With no tutorials and little organization to the explanations, the manuals jump right into protocols and parity checks without so much as a bow to a logical or psychological approach to the subject. No wonder there are so few modem users among so many computerists.

No matter. There aren't many genealogists yet who have computerized their records and are ready to swap data. Nor are there any grand family records databases available for you to call from your computer. Tomorrow is the time for telecommunicating; today is for computerizing your own records and using your computer for "in-house" records management and research-notes organization.

DATABASES AND THE GENEALOGIST

The linking of family members together within your own computer files is confined to the limits of your own interest in family lines. Naturally, the point where you choose to leave off (or must leave off for lack of further family links in a given family line) defines the maximum scope of your personal genealogy database. There are, of course, more people who can be linked to each of your dangling ancestral lines. Fellow genealogists are working on similarly limited databases, and more than a few of them will have information holdings (even computerized ones) of great interest to you.

It occurs to every family researcher who begins computerizing records that this marvelous new management tool could allow links between databases. Quickly, one becomes enthused at the prospects of some near-future capability to put *all* our computerized records in some mainframe computer and then share the aggregated and linked holdings for the grand mutual benefit of all contributors and users.

The grand central genealogical database is not yet available, and its existence will depend heavily on the contribution of individual computing-genealogists to create it. There are already commercial family databases, both large and small, and you can find most of them advertised in *The Genealogical Helper* in every issue. But the ideal central database would be one that we all put together from our own computerized holdings.

Because the experienced genealogist (who is a novice in computing) will want to know about the prospects of such a future research facility, we are giving our version of the future and the current pathways to it. Remember, the future is completely unpredictable and is likely to swerve from reasonable projections because technological, commercial, financial, and other forces lean on its trajectory.

An experienced genealogist will have noted that Salt Lake City is to genealogy what Hollywood is to movies, Washington is to politics, and Silicon Valley is to microcomputers. The extraordinary concentration of genealogy services there is, of course, related to Salt Lake City being the headquarters of The Church of Jesus Christ of Latter-day Saints. The million-plus rolls of microfilmed records in the Genealogical Library of the LDS Church illustrate the energies put into family research by members of that church. Why this extraordinary genealogical activity occurs may not be known by the casual genealogist and bears explaining:

> All Mormon families are encouraged to gather genealogical data about their ancestors in order to perform certain ceremonies they believe necessary to bind families together in eternity. Before these ceremonies can be done, individual ancestors within the families must be identified as to names, dates, places, and relationships. These ceremonies, among others, are then performed by living proxies in LDS temples throughout the country. It is, therefore, not out of mere curiosity or scholarly enthusiasm that Mormons have been pursuing genealogical research for almost a century. Indeed, they feel that each family has a mission to seek out its ancestors and perform these rites

and ceremonies for them so that their entire clan can be saved and exalted. One might ask whether this mandate means that Mormon genealogists pursue family studies only out of religious devotion. Despite this calling, many Mormons possess a genuine fervor for ancestral research.[1]

Fortunately, most of the genealogical research facilities and materials of the central genealogy library and more than 400 branch libraries are available to genealogists whether or not they are LDS members. Non-Mormons contribute to and draw from the vast LDS holdings of family records. Occasionally, a novice family historian will say, "Why should I look in the Mormon records? My family wasn't Mormon." This kind of thinking ignores the fact that for each generation you go back in any family line, you are more likely to share common ancestry with a Mormon (or a Catholic or a person of any other faith). Thus, the "Mormon families" are *your* families, too. The LDS Church generously and pragmatically shares its library (and its personal computer software for genealogy) with people outside its own membership. After all, the research you do may give a leg up in ancestor finding to some LDS member someday, and the reciprocity in sharing research findings makes us a "family of man."

The microfilm, a long roll of individual film frames, is the smallest unit of record in a microfilm-based database. It is not likely that the death of a person whose record is included in one of the frames on a microfilm roll will warrant reshooting the record, creating a new frame, and editing it into the roll in the place of the now-obsolete frame. Microfilm is the best method for storing past records; it is *not* the best method for condensed storage of dynamic (ever-changing) information. Computer indexing of microfilmed records was one of the first moves to genealogical computing made by the LDS Church. Microfiche (the squares of film one moves around under the lens of a fiche reader to see frames of information) is the current form of computer output most genealogists will see in the Genealogical Library. The computer-alphabetized lists of names, events, places, and dates in fiche form are the functional doorway to the rooms of microfilm rolls on which the indexed records reside.

Other microfilmed records (besides family group sheets) are in this huge collection, but our immediate interest is in family records. The IGI (International Genealogical Index) is the computer-generated searchable list (grouped by state or country) of completed LDS ordinances such as births and marriages in LDS Church records. While living persons' records are not ordinarily accessible due to the rights of privacy, the eighty million plus records found in the IGI microfiche files are worth exploration.

When you find an event listed for a person of interest to you, you note the batch number and serial sheet that accompanies the event description. This number can then be converted to a call number, and even if you are hundreds of miles from where that microfilm is stored (but happen to be near a branch of the Genealogical Library) you can order the film roll on which the original entry containing this event resides. For a nominal fee and with only a short waiting period, you can be cranking through that microfilm roll and reading the original entry from which the indexed event was abstracted. You can "go to Salt Lake City" without going far from home if you use an LDS branch library. The record was submitted by someone – a church member. Who was that submitter? This is the next most important piece of information (the most important being the genealogical facts on the filmed form). You can often make contact with these submitters who are researching the same persons and lines that you are. Think again if you have shrugged off the idea that Mormon records would have little value for you. And, there is no better place to have your own findings archived than in that genealogical library. If you want posterity to find what you have researched about your family, heirs are most likely to find your gleanings if they are in this foremost of all research collections in the world.

When this microfilming of family records was begun, the LDS Church could not afford computerizing the records any more than you could have afforded your own computer for genealogy. Microfilm was the practical "state of the art" technology which was affordable as well as useful. However, its greatest virtue is in compressing records to the smallest practical size. As we said, changing any information in a filmed record is impractical once the record has been filmed along with all the other records along the film's length. It was the computer which made searching these films practical. Genealogical computing, as it becomes more affordable and powerful and widespread, is going to be as spectacular in LDS family records management as is the microfilm collection of that church.

The *Ancestral File* is the name given to the computer technology system which will contain (rather than merely index) the contents of family records in the Genealogical Library. This project is likely to result in the first publicly accessible family records database in the world. And it is a project that aspires to linking all the family of man! What follows are the author's observations and speculations concerning central family records databases, and not necessarily an accurate description of what is now going on in the LDS Genealogical Library.

"System analysts" are people who study the jobs being done, the problems in doing those jobs, and the ways of improving the efficiency and cost of job performance. Once a better way is found, there must be planning for implementation of that way as well as transition from the old way to the new. Presumably, the computer way is the new way in family records management – superseding microfilming at least in part.

Mere transferring of records from paper or film to computerized files would be possible, but there are things we ought to be able to do with a computer that we've never been able to do before. What are they? Which of these things are worth doing? One would begin the "system design" phase with more than just a conversion task in mind.

If you were to convert a massive family records system to a computerized version, you would take considerable time in planning and testing the new way. Your personal ancestral file is bound to be a small scale model of the "mainframe system" which must contain the holdings and serve the records-management and research requirements of many genealogists. It is a difference in scale rather than kind that distinguishes the LDS *Ancestral File* project from your personal ancestral file project. (The fact that *Personal Ancestral File* – a trademark of the LDS Church – is the name of the Mormon-published genealogy software is not just a coincidence.)

Many considerations would surely have to be taken into account in any massive conversion of records to computerized versions. If your genealogy club has hundreds of family group sheets or pedigree charts, they can *now* be computerized on some club member's computer (or the club's own computer). They should be. In the future, club members ought to be able to submit already computerized versions of these sheets and charts; it would save volunteers a lot of keyboarding time and would assure that no mistakes were introduced in the computer-entry process. Maybe this is the real value of personal computer genealogy software in the LDS records-management plan. Surely the *Personal Ancestral File* software now being sold is the alternative to funnelling most of the old (and all of the new?) family records into the Genealogical Library's computers. The *Ancestral File* surely will be the depository for, and dispenser, of the accumulation of family data and family linkages of tomorrow. Personal databases can be passed through a "black box" to transform them from the data-file images handled by personal computers into the data-file images necessary for merging into the *Ancestral File*. This seems most logical and tremendously foresighted! (There's already a name for transfer-file standards: GEDCOM, or GEnealogical Data COMmunications format.)

How far off is "tomorrow"? Tomorrow has already dawned. The *Ancestral File* project is already several years old and should be deeply into the data-entry stage by now. Planning, investigating alternatives, designing the system, and testing the system should have occurred before the programmers could decide what the *Personal Ancestral File* software needed to be in order to contribute to a central ancestral file. Check the status of this project with the LDS Genealogical Library if you want more than speculation.

As each of us performs the conversion of our own research findings to our own computerized files, we are building pieces that can contribute to the whole of a true linking-us-all-together database. Sending our diskettes of data to some processing station will allow quick entry (automatic entry) of great segments of family groups into a central database of family information. The keyboarding was done by us on our own computers. "Batch processing" will allow quick and error-free transfer from microcomputer storage media to mainframe computer storage media. Those things we can do on our own computers can be done by large computers—quicker, with more data involved, and by routines not feasible on little computers like ours.

ONE SCENARIO FOR SEARCHING A CENTRAL GENEALOGY DATABASE

Suppose that it is five years from now. You and thousands of other genealogists have finished transferring your manually kept family records to your computers and have arrived at the other side of a mountain of family records that you have computerized in your own machine. Equipped with a phone-coupling device that allows you to call up a distant computer, you run its search and retrieval routines from your own keyboard. That computer contains all of the family records you and other genealogists have submitted for file merging. This is the legendary family-of-man database.

In this scenario—tomorrow's genealogical research style—you can access public records (such as census records, courthouse records, old newspaper files, ship lists, land records, and military records) and many private records (the genealogy holdings of other genealogists). The utopian condition for genealogical research finally has been realized and here you are, ready to make your first database query on the opening day of public-access to this new file system.

You load your communications program into your computer, set the communications parameters to match your computer to that distant computer, and dial up the "host computer" phone number. You get a connection:

WELCOME TO THE ANCESTRAL FILE—THE TIME AND DATE IS 10:20:05 MST 16/06/1990

PLEASE ENTER YOUR ACCOUNT NUMBER >

you supply "0049231"

YOU ARE—JOHN WILLIAM SCHROCK—CONFIRM (Y/N) >

you affirm "Y"

So goes the overture to a marvelous experience. You choose from a menu of functions the one you want. It is a search for the birthdate and birthplace of William Schrock who died in Romney, West Virginia. The computer sends you little blipping displays to remind you it is still searching and then spills out the wanted information. Then the computer (actually, the program in the computer) asks you:

EXTEND SEARCH (Y/N) > you answer "Y"

FAMILY RECORD ONLY (Y/N) > you answer "N"

LINKED SEARCH OF ALL RELATED INFORMATION (Y/N) > you say "Y" with one stroke

And the computer begins spilling the information in a chain reaction to your response. William's father, mother, children (and all their associated data in a family record) and then the information associated with the father, and then the mother, and then . . . .

Will your little computer's disk drives really hold all that can be triggered by an extended search that may run through family links to fantastic lengths?

If you limit your search to only the question of immediate concern (the wanted information about William Schrock's birth), you will have gained one increment of new information for your files. Do you have but one blank in your information fields? Wouldn't you love to have that full-run search of as many ascending and descending links as there may be for William Schrock? Can you afford the phone bill even if you can absorb the information in your computer by swapping disks when each gets filled?

Most people who have used computer databases have been looking for a very limited information domain. If the database searcher was a student working on a research paper, the query might be a literature search that finds all periodicals and books covered by the database in which there is a reference to RABIES and SKUNKS and URBAN or SUBURBAN settings published since 1970. Such a search may cost the searcher twenty-five dollars for computer time and phone line charges—at commercial rates of database services. Happy with the citations and abstracts describing books or articles about rabies in skunks in urban or suburban areas, the researcher is finished with the database and begins finding the cited books and journals in a library. That is how a typical database use works. Another kind of database user will call in daily to get a computer's update on the price of four stocks on the New York Exchange or the price of tea in China. Notice that these are as narrow as rifle shots, as queries go. If that student asks for everything on RABIES, everything on SKUNKS, everything on URBAN areas or SUBURBAN areas, and only that which was published since 1970, he has used a shotgun approach. The stock watcher who says give me *all* the stock prices of today, or the market watcher who says give me all commodities including rice on all markets, are also using a shotgun. Such searching will cost them far more than twenty-five dollars, to be sure.

Using a database requires some training. To get what you want but no more than you want from the huge amount of computerized information on the other end of the phone line takes a bit of planning and practice. Using search terms in an efficient pattern can make database searching economical and fully satisfying of requirements the database can fill. Searching can not be approached lightly.

Genealogists will have to get acquainted with the powerful tool of database accessing. And we are going to have to use the tool in a unique way because we are not interested in finding the answer to only one research question. What is that unique way?

This is a different scenario for tomorrow's genealogical searches of a huge family record database. It is but a logical thought and is not really a plan borrowed from any "real world" database builder. (What other database would have *linked* information, where one thing leads to another — one person linked to another — except a genealogy database?)

You mail backup copies of your disk files (after having passed them through a utility program that converts the layout of your records to the exchange format) to a service unit. That unit will have a staff who will pass your data through a "black box" to make the data format conform to that of the central database layout. In the process, every blank information field in your records will have "**???**" put in it (or some equivalent code for missing data). Then your whole linked-family database will be treated as an electronic version of a jigsaw puzzle piece.

Imagine a huge jigsaw puzzle that is partially complete — little segments that have been fitted together already which await some additional puzzle pieces to complete the picture. Your own database would be a group of linked pieces that may duplicate some of the pieces already fitted together, or fit into the edges of those solved parts of the master jigsaw puzzle. By "sliding around" your whole database (functionally treated as pieced-together puzzle pieces) "atop" the great puzzle being solved (the linked data in the database), data elements will be tested for fit or match.

Once your own small database is linked into the master database, each gives a "transfusion of data" to the other. Where your database had "**???**" instead of data, the data cells of the master database are copied into those missing-data fields, replacing the missing-data marker. And, your own data will be copied into any "**???**" cells in the master database. (Data quality control is another subject and must be attended to, of course.) When the two databases are separated, each has been enriched with data supplied by the other. Easier said than done! But this is a far more logical and economical scenario than the one-question-at-a-time kind of approach.

You had William SCHROCK as a parent of Perez Drue SCHROCK, and five or six other relevant facts well documented in your file. As those names and other facts are found in the master database, the linkage can be confirmed. This kind of procedure can be automated and automatic. Perfecting the details of such a scheme will take work and time and testing, of course.

If you need instant answers, on-line database searching may be the best pathway to the answers. But the beginning genealogist who knows little about his or her family will be better off with the off-line procedure described. Once each of us has used this "transfusion process" to enrich both personal and central database files, additional queries might be on-line and affordable. Identifiable costs incurred in behalf of a given genealogist would be passed on to that genealogist. Perhaps there might be some kind of pricing structure that accounts for the benefit derived by both parties to the transfusion: If 80,000 bytes of information flowed to your own database and 40,000 bytes to the central database in the exchange of data, you would owe for the difference of 40,000 bytes. If you already have decades of research, the exchange may end with the central database owing you for two megabytes of data that you supplied to fill information voids in the master file. Computers can keep track of this debit-credit situation automatically. Humans will have to decide what kinds of billing or usage rates should be applied.

No matter how they are accomplished, there *will* be transfusions of data among genealogists and between genealogists and centralized family research databases in the future. Beginning now, we all are building a better tomorrow for data exchange and fact finding. Before we are faced with them, we should begin learning about database services and how they are used.

GENEALOGICAL COMPUTING'S POTENTIAL

Technology and interest in family origins and relationships are the engine and fuel which will drive family research to new levels of popularity, adequacy, accuracy, and importance. But it is involvement with personal computers which will make each of millions of genealogists advocates of better documentation, greater standardization, more adequate access to existing (but hidden) information, and more sharing of unpublished data.

Massive numbers of people involved in microcomputing will quickly produce a society as familiar with technology as you are familiar with genealogical research methods. The marriage of technology and genealogical methodology is ripe and most promising. The potential for involving genealogists in computing is awesome. Many family researchers are being introduced to computers at their work places, through their children who are receiving computer-assisted educations, and from another hobbyist interested in computers. The realization is dawning on us that genealogical computing is a new, affordable, and powerful tool for research and records management or book production.

A lot of selfless people have been indexing the unindexed books, recording old cemeteries, and publishing the obscure holdings of newspapers, Bibles, and probate records. But such compilation and organization is labor-intense and requires a dedication to unrewarded labors. Alphabetizing endless lists has been done the hard way; sifting dry book matter for names, places, and dates has been heroic and unglamorous. What we now have for research facilities is far better than what was available just ten or twenty years ago, but it is far from a magical in-home tube that can be commanded to display any deed, any tombstone, any book page, or any marriage certificate we need to find. Between a utopian research world and nothing lies what we now have. Some say the millions of microfilm rolls in the National Archives or the LDS Genealogical Library represent a kind of mecca for family researchers. Others say the obvious: What we have is relatively puny facilities for fact finding. Granted, there are marvelous libraries and we have the automobile to get to these caches of information. But, despite our efforts to date, there is far more information available to each of us than we have knowledge of or access to. Until what we *might* find is what we *have* found, we'll never know how full a family history resides in the niches of recorded lives.

On the theory that every member can contribute to the improvement of family research facilities, DAR members across the country pack their lunches and pull on their boots and head for cemeteries with yellow pads and a supply of pencils in their tote bags. This is involvement. This is massive participation in the process of surfacing the buried information which someone, somewhere is going to want. Predictably, personal computing involvement is going to change the methodologies, release the unpublished holdings, organize, *and deliver to our homes* the identified ore for our backyard smelters of genealogy. In China, the collective efforts of tiny backyard iron-producers added up to a significant national production of that useful metal. An industrial nation would view such pathetic, heroic, piecemeal efforts at iron making with a patronizing smile. They did what they could and had to do in the only way it could be done. That sounds like genealogy to date.

If a DAR member could carry a battery-operated computer to a graveyard and collect the inscriptions in "machine-readable" form by copying the data on a typewriter-like keyboard, that little mobile computer could "dump" its contents into a central computer via phone lines. The information could be sorted, formatted, organized, annotated, and merged with the collections from other such gathering computers. The processed end product could be quickly accessed in distant places by would-be consumers.

If genealogy society volunteers went to local libraries and operated scanning machines that could read all the words in all the books (like scanners read bar codes at a supermarket checkout counter now), the computerized data could be sifted and organized into indexes. Like the cemetery-inscriptions gatherer, these in-library volunteers could be "siphoning" books for their unindexed names, dates, and places in a manner similar to the microfilming processes. The computerized, organized distillation of each book could be merged with other books, and new genealogy databases and indexes could be quickly compiled and readily accessed from our own homes by telephone links between personally owned equipment and the large, shared computers that hold such information.

Nothing quite so promising has been available to us before (1975 being the demarcation between computerless genealogists and genealogical use of computers). Nothing we can afford and can imagine is likely to be as practical a tool of genealogical research, holdings sharing, records management, or family history book production as is a personal computer. Individually and collectively we can now realize many of our dreams and technological fantasies.

What is possible and how it is possible is known to the relatively small population of genealogists who have begun using their own computers in their genealogy work. What personal computers can do today is the first new knowledge you need to acquire if you are to be among the computing genealogists. Concentrate on learning enough about personal computers and their genealogy uses so that you can make your own records and your own research work more manageable and better managed.

FOOTNOTES

1. Linwood E. Rich, "Ancestral Research and the Genealogical Library," *Ancestry Newsletter* 2, no. 4 (July/August 1984): 1.

CHAPTER 10

Where You Can Get Help in Getting Started

COMPUTER GENEALOGY
BOOKS AND PERIODICALS

There are genealogy periodicals and books, computer periodicals and books, and *now* genealogical computing periodicals and books. Computer genealogy books are few, and generally more booklet than book (aside from the one you have in your hands). *Tracing Your Roots by Computer* by Joanna W. Posey ($39.95 – Posey International, P.O. Box 338, Orem, Utah 84057) is another recently published overview and introduction to genealogical computer use.

There are several computer genealogy periodicals that serve this new field. (A periodical is able to catch the new and changing developments in its field of focus and complements a good book.) Here is the field from which you can choose regular reading matter:

Genealogical Computing, published by Data Transfer Associates, Inc., P.O. Box 2367, Fairfax, VA 22032; publisher, Sara Andereck; editor, Paul Andereck.

The Genealogical Computer Pioneer, published by Posey Enterprises, P.O. Box 338, Orem, Utah 84057; publisher, Joanna W. Posey; editor, Pat Woodbury.

The Computer/Genealogist, published by National Society of Computer/Genealogists, 1512 Womack Road, Atlanta, GA 30338; publisher and editor, Diane Dieterle.

Slakt-Forskar-Nytt (Family-Researchers-News), published by Foreningen for Datorhjalp i Slaktforskningen (DIS) (The Association for Computer-help in Family-Research/Genealogy), DIS c/o P.O. Bergman, Hjortronvagen 89, S-59054 Sturefors, Sweden.

Computers in Genealogy, published by The Society of Genealogists, c/o David Hawgood, 26 Cloister Road, London W3 0DE, England; editor, David Hawgood.

Genealogie & Computer van de Vlaamse Vereniging voor Familiekunde (VVF-afd. Antwerpen), c/o Pieter Donche, Britse Lei 4/16, B-2000 Antwerpen, Belgium.

GENS DATA, published by Netherlands Genealogical Society (Computerservice Department), c/o Anton J. van Reeken, Pastoriepad 2, 5046 DG Tilburg, Netherlands.

The above are the known national/international computer genealogy periodicals to date. Contact each for subscription rates, frequency of publication, editorial content, and intended purposes. The Swedish periodical was the first; *Genealogical Computing* was the first in America—followed by the British periodical. The others are newer (with the Netherlands group publishing its second issue in October 1984). All are young (none predate 1980) and each is small. Do not expect a magazine of the proportions you find on newsstands. Bimonthlies and quarterlies are usual, advertising revenues are slim, and subscription prices are high (a function of small circulation and little or no advertising income). But these periodicals represent genealogists who are becoming acquainted with computers and who share what they have learned with those who follow. Pooled experience, shared advice, startup helps, and how-to tips are common fare in each issue of these small periodicals. Consider that a subscription to any of them will be worth the cost to you, helping you get more from the computer, and keep up with the evolving field of genealogical computing most reliably. Your subscription helps them to help you and other genealogists master a most exciting technological tool.

COMPUTER INTEREST GROUPS FOR GENEALOGISTS

Although the writings of genealogists who have computing experience can be well worth the cost of special periodicals in which they are contained, these advice sources are not "interactive." The editors and article submitters cannot handle the inquiries of readers who number in the thousands. Unless a publisher specifically solicits "consulting business" (for which you should expect to pay a fee), the genealogist must read for useful help rather than ask for it.

A new kind of "club" has emerged alongside the personal computer sales industry. CIGs, or Computer Interest Groups, are formed by owners (or would-be owners) of computers. Usually the common bond among members is the shared interest in a specific brand of computer. For every kind of computer (Apple, Radio Shack, IBM, Kaypro, Commodore, and so on) there seems to be a CIG in every medium-to large-sized city. Although these groups are computer-centered (rather than genealogy-centered), they represent the best source of unpaid advice you can find. Members of these groups range from grass-green novices to true computer professionals. This disparity in computer experience provides a "ladder" of help. No matter which ladder-rung is your station, as a CIG member you can always find someone higher up who will help you and someone on a lower rung that you can assist. This is the way of mutual help which has educated most nonprofessional computerists in America and elsewhere.

As genealogical computing grew, the "Genealogy CIG" also grew. These groups are either subsets of computer CIGs (the computerists who share genealogy as a hobby) or they are subsets of genealogical societies (the genealogists who are computer users). *Genealogical Computing* publishes a directory to these special interest groups in each of its issues. Following is a sample of groups listed in a recent issue.

COMPUTER INTEREST GROUPS
DIRECTORY – SEPTEMBER 1984

This directory includes (a) computer interest groups that are allied with genealogy organizations; (b) genealogy interest groups allied with computer clubs; and (c) genealogy software user groups.

AUSTRALIA

Genealogical Society of Victoria, Computer Users Group. Contact Mr. A. F. Clark, CI-Genealogical Society of Victoria, 1st Floor, 98 Elizabeth, Melbourne, Australia 3000, 03-789-1699. Has ninety members as of May 1984. Open to members of the Genealogical Society of Victoria. The group meets monthly and has been organized since February 1984. Chairperson is Bruce Fullarton. Their purpose is to provide members with help and guidance in buying and using hardware and software, to help users get maximum genealogical benefit from their systems, and to help develop Australian standards for handling genealogical data.

NEW ZEALAND

New Zealand Society of Genealogists, New Zealand Genealogical Computing Group. Contact Paul Alpe, 8 Lupin Terrace, Linden, Wellington, New Zealand. Has twenty-five members as of July 1984. Membership is international with no restrictions, and dues are $3 per year with meetings by arrangement. They organized in May 1984 and publish a newsletter quarterly. Their purpose is to provide members with help and guidance in using computers as a tool for genealogical research and related projects.

UNITED STATES (NATIONAL)

National Genealogical Society, National Genealogical Society Computer Interest Group (NGS/CIG). Contact William Johnson, 7304 Mariposa, Manassas, VA 22111 (703) 791-5175. Membership as of June 1984 is 450. They offer international membership. *NGS/CIG Digest*, is published quarterly. Subscription rate is $5 per year. They were organized in April 1982, and were established as a committee-level organization to provide a forum for investigating, developing, and coordinating the use of computer techniques to support genealogical efforts and related tasks.

Kaypro Users Group, KUGIG: Kaypro Users Genealogy Interest Group. Contact Alice W. Peterson, 3010 Regency, Apt. 40, Ames, IA 50010 (515)

232-8276. Membership as of May 1984 is 117, with international membership for genealogists using CP/M or MS-DOS machines. Dues are $35 per year, $5 extra for double-sided disks. An additional $5 is needed if outside North America. Demo disk and trial membership offered for $5. They publish *KUGIG Newsletter disks* (February, May, August, November) and *KUGIG Newsletter Paper* (April, July, October) which are included in the membership fee. They were organized in January 1983 to offer genealogy uses and applications of *Wordstar, Infostar, dBASE II, Superfile,Smartkey,* and *Perfect Software,* on CP/M and MS-DOS computers. Program buying at user group rates.

Roots Users' Groups (RUG). Contact William Johnson, 7304 Mariposa, Manassas, VA 22111 (703) 791-5175. Membership in June 1984 was 200. Membership is open to *Roots* users and those interested in *Roots* software. *RUG* is offered for $12 per year for ten issues published quarterly. They have been organized since January 1982. Formed to promote interest in, and understanding and effective utilization of, the various *Roots* programs and utilities. Shared common interests: genealogy, computers, and *Roots* software.

Quinsept User Group. Contact Bob Mitchell, 5855 Santa Teresa, San Jose, CA 95123 (408) 226-9007. Membership as of June 1984 is 450. Organized in August 1983 the group offers membership to *Lineages* and *Family Roots* users and those interested in Quinsept Inc.'s software at a cost of $15 per year. They publish *Quinsept Users Group Newsletter* bimonthly at no additional cost. Their focus is on updates, future software additions or improvements, user probems, questions and answers, and user ideas related to the *Lineages* and *Family Roots* software.

CALIFORNIA

San Diego Genealogy Society, SDGS Computer Interest Group. Contact W. A. Shirer, 9350 Carmichael Drive, LaMesa, CA 92041 (619) 466-3578. Membership in May 1984 was twenty. Organized in May 1983, the group's objective is to help members get started in genealogical computing.

COLORADO

Pikes Peak Genealogy Society and Pikes Peak Computer Application Society, Genealogy Computer Study Group. Contact Mid Kolstad, 429 East San Rafael, Colorado Springs, CO 80903, (303) 633-8839. Membership in May 1984 was thirty. Must have membership in PPGS or PPCompAS to join. Dues are $5 per year for PPGS and $12 per year for PPCompAS; no dues for GCStudy Group. They publish a newsletter as needed. They were organized in November 1982; chairperson is Jim Ashenhurst. They offer demonstrations of genealogy programs used by the host(ess). Computers of various brands are thereby reviewed. Programs (including member-written) are studied.

Colorado Genealogical Society, CGS Computer Group. Contact Ruth and Ralph Gilbert, 1700 S. Monaco, Denver, CO 80224 (303) 757-3622. Membership in May 1984 was fifty-eight. Membership ($5 per (year) is open to anyone interested in genealogy. Meetings are every two months. They were organized in the spring of 1982. A planning committee identifies fields of interest (such as hardware, software, publications, and so on) that have not been covered, and plans programs to fill the gaps.

DISTRICT OF COLUMBIA AREA
Capital Heath Users Group, Genealogy Special Interest Group. Contact Phil Depauk, 2832 Andiron, Vienna, VA 22180, (703) 560-8006. Their organization was formed in June 1984 with no restrictions on membership. CHUG dues are $12 per year; meetings precede CHUG monthly meetings. They explore genealogical applications of interest to the group.

TEXAS
Apple Corps of Dallas, Apple Corps Genealogy SIG. Contact Minnie Champ, P.O. Box 821103, Dallas, TX 75231. Membership is required in parent organization with dues of $15 per year. SIG meets second Saturdays after parent group's meeting. Organized for genealogists and those newly interested in genealogy who have computers.

CP/M Houston and The Houston Genealogical Forum, Micro-Genealogy. Contact Jim Younglove, 4614 Rockwood Drive, Houston, TX 77004 (713) 747-6403. Membership in July 1984 was fifty-five. Meetings are held the second Friday of each month. They publish an occasional newsletter. They were organized in the spring of 1983 to provide a source of information and help for persons wishing to use micros in genealogical record keeping.

WASHINGTON
Seattle Genealogical Society, Computer Interest Group of Seattle Genealogical Society. Contact Ida Skarson McCormick, C/O SGS, P.O. Box 549, Seattle, WA 98111, (206) 682-1410 or (206) 633-5147. Membership in June 1984 was fifty. No restrictions on membership but membership in the parent society is encouraged. Dues are $10 per person per year or $12.50 per household for parent society membership. Meetings are held second Saturday of each month except July and August. Quarterly bulletins and newsletters of parent society contain CIG news. The group organized in March 1981 to offer sharing and speakers at meetings for members of diverse interests. Chairperson is Margaret Jenks. They participate in NWCS annual Personal Computer Fair.

Joining a computer interest group or genealogical computing interest group doesn't require you to attend meetings. The most useful kind of participation many experience is the one-on-one contacts made at the meetings they attend. Being able to invite a CIG member over to your house is a good way to establish such relationships. You can call on the phone (and, eventually, answer the phone) for "what do I do now?" kinds of quick questions. In addition, CIGs sponsor classes in using certain kinds of software or beginning or advanced courses in computer programming.

As more local, county, and state genealogical societies spawn CIGs for their members' benefit, the genealogy CIG will become the most valuable of all sources of instruction, information, and advice in this field.

Special Words You May Want to Know

The vocabulary of computing is, of course, specialized. So is that of genealogy in some cases. The average person does not need to know special fields and their special words. We give you a little help in knowing what computer words mean, but you really do not *need* to know ninety percent of them. Here is your translation dictionary. Reach for it when a computer salesman begins to speak a foreign language.

ALPHANUMERIC: Letters and numbers (alphabetic and numeric characters).

ASCII: Standardized code serving as the American Standard Code for Information Interchange.

ASSEMBLY LANGUAGE: A relatively simplified language permitting program writing in machine language without having to write in true binary.

BACKUP: A duplicate copy of programs and data files created for safety or archival purposes.

BASIC: (Beginners All-purpose Symbolic Instruction Code): A programming language most personal computer owners use if they program.

BAUD RATE: The term used to express the speed with which data is transmitted via telecommunications.

BINARY: A two number system of counting (0 and 1 being the two).

BIT: (BInary DigiT) The smallest information unit used in computing (0 or 1).

BOOLEAN LOGIC: A search logic system invented by George Boole which employs *and, or,* and *not* as operation instructions in a multiterm search.

BOOT: Startup procedure used after turning on the computer's power.

BUBBLE MEMORY: A chip-based memory system that is RAM-like and stores data in magnetic bubbles.

BUFFER: A temporary holding place for data or programs being processed.

BUG: An error in a program that causes a malfunction to occur.

265

BYTE: A group of eight *bits* of binary information representing a single letter, number, special character, or space in data.

CHARACTER: A letter, number, punctuation, etc.

CHIP: A silicon (sand) wafer on which a miniaturized integrated circuit is printed.

CMOS: (Complementary Metal Oxide Semiconductor): Chip technology using low power and useful in battery-operated computers.

COMMAND: An order to the computer to execute instructions.

COMPILER: A special program for converting programs written in a high-level language to the machine language used by the computer.

COMPUTER: A device having input, output, storage, arithmetic, logic, and control components used to apply prescribed processes to data.

COPROCESSOR: An auxiliary microprocessor chip that permits running another kind of disk operating system.

COPY PROTECTED: Software designed by the maker to prevent users from making copies.

CP/M: (Control Program for Microcomputers): Digital Research Corporation's disk operating system.

CPU: (Central Processing Unit) The unit that resides on a chip and provides the controlling and interpreting instructions to all other parts of the computer and its attached devices.

CRT: (Cathode Ray Tube): The televisionlike display used in a computer.

CURSOR: The square on the video display screen that shows where you are currently working.

DAISY-WHEEL: The printer type-font device equivalent to the print-ball on an IBM electric typewriter.

DATA: Information processed by the computer.

DATABASE: Any collection of information.

DEBUGGING: The process of eliminating program errors (bugs).

DEFAULT: The programmer's instruction, which is used if you do not choose an optional instruction in a menu of options.

DIGITAL: Binary-coded information.

DIRECTORY: A list of data and program files on a disk.

DISK: Magnetic media in a round platter form used for storing data and programs.

DISK DRIVE: A device having a motor, read/write heads, and electronics for spinning a disk and recording or reading data magnetically stored.

DISKETTE: Same as a disk (usually applied to 5 1/4 inch disks).

DISK OPERATING SYSTEM (DOS): A group of programs that manage the computer in the use of the CPU, disk drives, and other components of the computer's hardware/software system.

DOCUMENTATION: The instruction manual and description of software or hardware.

DOS: *See* Disk Operating System.

DOT MATRIX: Rows and columns of dots that form individual characters on paper or the video display screen which appear to be letters, numbers, and so on. Also, a type of printer.

DOUBLE DENSITY (DD): Distribution of data on disks in a manner which approximately doubles the amount of data that can be stored on a disk.

DOUBLE SIDED (DS): The use of both surfaces of a disk for data storage.

DOWNLOAD: To capture data or programs sent to your computer from another over telephone lines or by direct wire from another computer.

DSDD: Double sided, double density.

DSSD: Double sided, single density.

FIELD: The information unit—such as name, place, or date—kept in a file record.

FILE: Groups of data that comprise an overall entity, such as a family's data records.

FLOPPY: Nickname for a disk that is soft plastic based (minifloppy and microfloppy are variants for smaller and smallest of three common sizes: 8 inches, 5 inches, and 3 inches).

FRICTION FEED: A paper transport system in which two rollers move paper through a printer.

GRAPHICS: Pictorial displays of information on a screen or printer paper.

HARD COPY: The product of a computer created by a paper-based printer.

HARD DISK: Magnetic media in round platter form that is rigid (as opposed to floppy).

HARDWARE: The physical equipment used in a computer system.

HEAD: An electromagnetic device for reading, recording, or erasing data on magnetic media, such as disks or tape.

HIGH-LEVEL LANGUAGE: A programming language that uses near normal English words and abbreviations.

IMPACT PRINTER: A computer printer that transfers a ribbon's ink to paper by striking the ribbon with a pattern of pins or a type face.

INITIALIZE: To prepare a disk or computer file for usage in following operations.

INPUT/OUTPUT (I/O): The transfer of information to or from a computer device.

INTEGRATED CIRCUIT (IC): Combined electronic components residing on a single computer chip.

INTEGRATED SOFTWARE: Multiple applications programs packaged together, sharing common data files and commands.

INTERFACE: The connector between two components or "buss" for interfacing devices with cables or plug-in boards.

INTERPRETER: A program that translates another program written in high-level language, such as BASIC, to machine language, instruction by instruction, during operation.

KEYBOARD: The standard data-entry device on a computer which resembles a typewriter keyboard.

KILOBYTE (K): A group of 1024 bytes (characters).

LETTER-QUALITY: An adjective describing printer output approximately the same in quality as electric typewriter printing.

LCD: (Liquid Crystal Display): A screen display using reflected light and often found in digital watches and battery operated computers.

LISTING: A printout of a computer program's instructions.

LOAD: To transfer a file or program from external memory, such as a disk, to internal memory, or RAM, for processing.

MACHINE LANGUAGE: The low-level language directly usable by a computer and expressed in binary characters (0 and 1).

MAINFRAME COMPUTERS: Large computers.

MEGABYTE (M): Approximately one million bytes.

MEMBRANE KEYBOARD: An inexpensive, pressure sensitive, flat surfaced computer keyboard.

MEMORY: The storage place of binary information and computer programs.

MENU: A video screen display of optional functions from which the user can choose.

MICROCOMPUTER: A computer system based on microprocessor-chip technology.

MICROPROCESSOR: An alternative name for the CPU or central processing unit.

MNEMONIC: An easy to remember computer command abbreviation such as "P" for PRINT.

MODEM: (MOdulator-DEModulator): The computer-to-phone coupler.

MONITOR: The television-like display screen.

MOUSE: A handheld device linked to the computer that allows you to move the cursor and enter commands at a chosen point.

MS-DOS: (MicroSoft Disk Operating System): The DOS by Microsoft Corporation used on 16-bit computers.

OBJECT CODE: The translated program, resulting from the use of a compiler, which is in the computer's native or machine language.

ON-LINE: Connected to something, such as another computer or a program help-file, that is constantly available.

OPERATING SYSTEM: Same as DOS or disk operating system.

PARALLEL: Passing data eight bits at a time using parallel wires for each bit.

PC-DOS: (Personal Computer Disk Operating System): The IBM name for MS-DOS.

PERIPHERAL DEVICE: Accessories connected to a computer, such as a monitor, modem, disk drive, printer, keyboard, etc.

PORT: The interface or connection point that joins the computer to the peripherals.

PRINTER: A device that produces letter quality copy of the material stored in a computer.

PROGRAM: Instructions to a computer.

PROGRAMMING: Writing computer instructions.

PROMPT: A message on the screen that directs you to provide information to the computer in order to complete a task.

RAM (Random Access Memory): Read/write memory; temporary storage for holding data and programs being processed by the computer.

RECORD: A file, or piece of a file, containing the information fed into the computer about a given subject.

RESOLUTION: The sharpness of the characters displayed on a screen.

ROM (Read Only Memory): Factory-loaded programs residing in permanent memory.

RS-232-C: An electrical standard for the voltages used to pass data from a computer to the modems or printers.

SAVE: To transfer data or programs from internal memory (RAM) to disk or tape (external memory) by making a magnetic copy of the data.

SCROLL: To move the cursor up, down, left, or right on a video display in order to see data not on the screen at a given moment.

SECTOR: A section of the disk surface and a subdivision of a disk track.

SERIAL: One bit at a time input or output of data between the computer and some accessory device.

SINGLE DENSITY (SD): The original spacing between data bits on a disk.

SINGLE SIDED (SS): Only one side of a disk can contain data or programs.

SOFTWARE: Another name for programs; the nonphysical component of a computer which resides in memory.

SOURCE CODE: The program instructions as they have been written by a programmer.

STRING: A word or phrase or any continuous group of characters.

TELECOMMUNICATION: Passing data and programs from one computer to another over telephone lines.

TERMINAL: A keyboard, monitor, and modem without a central processing unit, that permits remote operation of a computer over a telephone line or wire.

TRACK: Invisible concentric circle on a disk surface where information is stored.

TRACTOR FEED: A device which transports paper through a printer by means of a sprocket engaged in holes along the edge of continuous-form paper.

UPLOAD: To send data over a telephone line or direct wire to another computer.

UTILITY: Special program that allows you to accomplish a special task.

WINCHESTER DISK: Another name for a hard disk, derived from an IBM project name.

WORD (byte): A unit of information that occupies one storage location.

WRITE: To record information on a disk.

About the Authors

ANDERECK

Paul Arthur Andereck is nationally recognized for his expertise in two areas: the use of microcomputers in education of the handicapped, and the use of microcomputers in genealogical research and records management. He works for the United States Education Department, designing and monitoring government contracts and grants that entail the use of new technologies in special education. Working with educators and innovators nationwide, he has gained a knowledge and appreciation for the capabilities of low-cost computers.

In the other area of his national prominence, he and his wife Saralou Schrock have been a convening force for people interested in the intersection of genealogy and computing. Together they publish and edit a bimonthly periodical, *Genealogical Computing*, which circulates throughout the United States as well as in many other parts of the world.

PENCE

Richard A. Pence holds a degree in journalism from South Dakota State Universtiy. He was technical publications editor at Iowa State and North Carolina State Universities. He has edited *Carolina Farmer*, a rural consumer publication with 180,000 circulation, for eight years, was editor of the *Rural Electric Newsletter*, a national legislative newsletter, for eight years, and was editor of *Rural Electrification*, a national trade magazine. He now handles special programs for the National Rural Electric Cooperative Association in Washington, D.C. He is editor of *The Next Greatest Thing*, a 256-page photographic history of rural electrification published in 1984.

Dick wrote *Tracing Your Family Tree*, a nationally syndicated guide for starting to trace your family tree. He has used his computer to publish two books on the Pence family and is nearing publication on a third.

Index

A

Acorn Software, 99, 160, 229
Acree, Chuck, 229
Ada, Augusta, 3
ahnentafel, 25, 161-62, 228
all-purpose file management programs, 75
all-purpose relational database managers, 75
Alpe, Paul, 261
alphabetic lists, 152-53
ALT, 51
Ancestor File Program, 100, 125, 163
=*Ancestors*=, 100, 161, 163
Ancestors, 100, 161, 163
Ancestral File, 230, 250-51
Ancestry I/III, 99, 161, 163
AND search, 117
Andereck, Paul, 235, 271
Anderson, Esther, 37
Apple Corps of Dallas, Apple Corps Genealogy SIG, 263
Apple DOS, 70-71, 92
Apple II, 11, 71
Apple IIe, 92
Apple MacIntosh, 84
Apple Tree III, 99
applications software, 69-73, 87 *passim*
Arbor-Aide, 59, 100, 125-26, 161, 163
Armstrong Genealogical Systems, 59, 98-99, 125-26, 162-63
Armstrong, John J., 22
Array Systems, Inc., 99, 126, 161, 163, 222
arrow keys, 82
ASCII, 225, 228
asymmetrical charts, 162
auto-hypenation, 81
automatic search, 95

B

backup copies, 48, 93, 98, 254
Barnes, Donald R., 28
basic input-output system (BIOS), 71

BASIC, 69, 77, 107, 225
batch processing, 252
Beginners All-Purpose Symbolic Instruction Code. *See* BASIC
BInary digIT, 41. *See also* bits
binary logic, 41
binary numbers, 9
BIOS, 71
bits, 41-42
BLANKS, 105
Boolean Logic, 97, 245
Branches, 101
bubble memory, 45, 49
by first name index, 125
by surname index, 125
byte, 42
Byteware, 59, 99, 161, 163

C

C. & M. Systems, 101
Calendar G/J, 101, 222
Capital Heath Users Group, Genealogy Special Interest Group, 263
cassette tape drives
    limitations, 45
    price, 45
cathode ray tubes, 52. *See also* CRT
Cavanaugh, Karen, INTRO, 223
central processing unit (CPU), 38, 44, 69, 76
Central Research of Utah, 99
Champ, Minnie, 263
character font, 52
characters per line, 52, 58
chart printing and preparation
    family group sheet, 35-36
    pedigree chart, 35-36
CHARTS, 104, 154, 159
    ascendant, 104
    descendant, 104
    free-form, 104
charts, types of
    asymmetrical, 162
    free-form, 160-162
chips, 38-39, 41-42
CHUG, 263